The
Wilding *of*
America

Money, Mayhem, and the New American Dream

Charles Derber
Boston College

Worth Publishers
A Macmillan Higher Education Company

Vice President, Editing, Design and Media Production: Catherine Woods
Publisher: Kevin Feyen
Associate Publisher: Jessica Bayne
Acquisitions Editor: Sarah Berger
Developmental Editor: Kate Super
Assistant Editor: Katie Garrett
Executive Marketing Manager: Katherine Nurre
Marketing Assistant: Tess Sanders
Director of Editing, Design, and Media Production: Tracey Kuehn
Cover and Text Designer: Kevin Kall
Managing Editor: Lisa Kinne
Project Editor: Kerry O'Shaughnessy
Production Manager: Barbara Seixas
Photo Editor: Robin Fadool
Photo Researcher: Robin Fadool
Composition: ElectraGraphics, Inc.
Printing and Binding: LSC Communications
Cover Photo: Richard Procopio Stock Connection Worldwide/Newscom

Library of Congress Control Number: 2014936266

ISBN-13: 978-1-4641-0543-2
ISBN-10: 1-4641-0543-X

Printed in the United States of America

First printing

Worth Publishers
41 Madison Avenue
New York, NY 10010
www.worthpublishers.com

To my students, past and present, who give me hope for our future.

About the Author

Charles Derber is professor of sociology at Boston College and former director of its graduate program in social economy and social justice. He is a prolific scholar in the fields of politics, economy, international relations, and U.S. culture. He has written 17 internationally acclaimed books and several major research grants, as well as hundreds of scholarly articles, magazine essays, and newspaper columns.

Derber's books include *Capitalism: Should You Buy It? An Invitation to Political Economy* (with Yale Magrass; Paradigm Publishers, 2014); *Sociopathic Society: A People's Sociology of the United States* (Paradigm Publishers, 2013); *Hidden Power* (Berrett-Koehler, 2005, translated into Korean), a bestseller in South Korea and nominated by the Independent Bookstores of the United States as one of the three best current affairs books in 2005; *People Before Profit* (Picador, 2003, translated into Chinese, German, and British English); *Corporation Nation* (St. Martin's Press, 2000, translated into Chinese); *The Pursuit of Attention* (Oxford, 2000, translated into Polish); *Power in the Highest Degree* (with William Schwartz and Yale Magrass, Oxford, 1990); *Greed to Green* (Paradigm Publishers, 2010; translated into Korean); and *Marx's Ghost*, (Paradigm Publishers, 2011, translated into Chinese, Korean, and Tamil).

Derber espouses a public sociology that brings sociological perspectives to a general audience. Derber lectures widely at universities, companies, and community groups, and he appears on numerous media outlets. His op-eds and essays appear in the *New York Times, Newsday*, the *Boston Globe*, the *International Herald Tribune*, China's *People's Daily, Truthout*, and *Tikkun*, as well as other newspapers and online media, and he has been interviewed by *Newsweek, Business Week, Time*, and other news magazines. He speaks frequently on National Public Radio, on talk radio, and on television. His work has been reviewed by the *New York Times*, the *Washington Post*, the *Boston Globe*, the *Boston Herald, Washington Monthly*, and numerous other magazines and newspapers.

Derber is also a life-long activist for social justice. In the spirit of the great sociologist C. Wright Mills, he believes in the responsibility of intellectuals to speak truth to power and to match words with action.

Derber is married and lives in Dedham, Massachusetts. He has a beautiful wheaten terrier named Mojo, who lives up to his name.

Contents

Available for instructor download at worthpublishers.com/
sociology:

Wilding in the Church: Unaccountable Brethren and Voices
of the Faithful

Katrina: The Perfect Wilding Storm

Preface

As we move further into the twenty-first century, the crises of greed and violence that motivated my desire to write this book have deepened. The most sensational news stories of the 1990s were about individual wilders such as O. J. Simpson. The most dramatic wilding stories in the first decade of the twenty-first century were about Wall Street, the Catholic Church sex scandal, the political "culture of corruption," and America's war in Iraq. Greed and violence remained an epidemic among individuals, but it was wilding by institutions in the economy, the government, and civil society that made headlines, chronicled in the 2009 fifth edition of this book.

Today, systemic wilding has taken hold, changing the stakes. Wilding is now written into the DNA of our corporate and militarized capitalist system and has infected the politics and culture of our entire society.

The systemic dangers led me to publish this new edition in 2014. In new and revised chapters, I focus on the wilding built into our corporate capitalist system, our environmental and climate crisis, and our hyperindividualistic culture now expressed in rampant sports doping, risky financial speculation, widespread corporate profiteering, extreme inequality, academic cheating, survivalist reality shows, imperial wars, and gun violence.

When wilding becomes systemic, it changes and debases the American Dream. Wilding becomes normalized, and the new generation is socialized to an ethos that accepts selfishness, greed, and violence as the path to success. Elites at the pinnacle of corporations, the military, and the state redefine success itself as simply money and power.

But Americans, though deluged with stories of crime and corruption, are not making the connections that would help explain the real nature of the wilding problem or what might solve it. Wilding, as viewed by a sociologist, involves multiple forms of socially prescribed immorality perpetrated in the corporate suites as well as on the streets. Few media analysts suggest that the criminals in the corporate boardrooms and street wilders share elements of the same greed and the same dream, built around sociopathic values and perfectly legal wilding behavior.

Individual wilding and institutional wilding are racing out of control at the same time, reflecting new contradictions between today's American Dream and American prospects for success in an age of economic crisis and decline. As the Dream beckons and recedes, the price of failure is frustration and rage; the price of success, too often, is inner emptiness and debilitating fear of those left behind. Deepening inequalities, rising tides of social frustration, environmental disasters, and corrosive moral decay threaten the bonds of community and the very survival of the social fabric.

For the citizen, this is frightening; but for the sociologist, that fear is tied to a burning intellectual mission. The impending sense of social breakdown raises the question of what makes community—and society itself—possible at all. This is the core problem of sociology, one with special urgency for our highly individualistic and competitive capitalist society, but it is not a problem for sociologists alone.

The metaphor of societal illness that the wilding epidemic evokes points to the need for all of us to become practitioners of the art of social healing. This book offers one diagnosis of our weakened but still resilient collective condition. My hope is that the illness cannot long resist an awakened community brave enough to look deeply at its shared pathologies and empowered with the insights of the sociological imagination.

Acknowledgments

I am grateful to many friends and colleagues whose excitement about this book helped it come to fruition. The enthusiasm of David Karp and John Williamson nourished my own belief in the project, and their close reading of the manuscript helped me improve the book at every stage and in every edition. Morrie Schwartz spurred me on in the original edition with his insights and always generous emotional support. I thank Michael Burawoy, Noam Chomsky, Jonathan Kozol, Howard Zinn, Robert Reich, Robert Coles, Philip Slater, Jack Beatty, and Alvin Poussaint for reading the manuscript in various editions and responding to it.

I am also grateful to my colleagues Mike Malec, Paul Gray, Eve Spangler, S. M. Miller, Ritchie Lowry, and Severyn Bruyn for helpful suggestions for various editions. I thank also many former and present students, including Jonathan White, Deb Piatelli, Colleen Nugent, Michelle Gawerc, Alexandra Singer, Ted Sasson, Bill Hoynes, David Croteau, and Bill Schwartz, as well as all the other teachers, students, and readers who have let me know how valuable this book has been to them.

George Ritzer encouraged me to publish this book in the current series. Sarah Berger, my editor at Worth Publishers, brought vision, generous support, and enthusiasm to the work, making the new edition possible. Kate Super, also an editor at Worth Publishers, played an essential role, working closely with me on the revision of every chapter and offering numerous insights and generosity of words and spirit. I am very grateful to Sarah, Kate, and to all of those at Worth Publishers who have supported this book.

I owe much to my parents, who nurtured the concern for society that animates this book. And also to Elena Kolesnikova, who heroically endured the obsessions of an author about his work. She contributed ideas, helped me overcome my doubts, and nourished me all along the way.

one

The Good Man Fills His Own Stomach: All-American Crimes and Misdemeanors

The readings of history and anthropology . . . give us no reason to believe that societies have built-in self-preservative systems.

—Margaret Mead

Wilding in Black and White

On April 19, 1989, a group of six teenagers, ages 14 to 16, went into Central Park. According to police at the time, the youths came upon a young woman jogging alone past a grove of sycamore trees. Allegedly using rocks, knives, and a metal pipe, they attacked her. Some pinned her down while others beat and raped her. Police reported that one defendant, 17-year-old Kharey Wise, held the jogger's legs while a friend repeatedly cut her with a knife. They then smashed her with a rock and punched her face.[1]

What most captured public attention about the story were the spirits of the assaulters during and after their crime. According to 15-year-old Kevin Richardson, one of the boys arrested, "Everyone laughed and was leaping around." One youth was quoted by police as saying, "It was fun . . . something to do." Asked if they felt pretty good about what they had done, Richardson said, "Yes." Police reported a sense of "smugness" and "no remorse" among the youths.[2]

From this event, a new word was born: *wilding*. According to press reports, it was the term the youths themselves used to describe their behavior—and it seemed appropriate. The savagery of the crime, which left the victim brain-damaged and in a coma for weeks, evoked the image of a predatory lion in the bush mangling its helpless prey. Equally shocking was the blasé attitude of the attackers. It had been no big deal, a source of temporary gratification and amusement. They were "mindless marauders seeking a thrill," said Judge Thomas B. Galligan of Manhattan, who sentenced three of the teenagers to a maximum term of 5 to 10 years, charging them with turning Central Park into a "torture chamber." These were youths who seemed stripped of the emotional veneer of civilized humans, creatures of a wilderness where anything goes.[3]

The case became so ingrained in the national consciousness that Oxford English Dictionary made it the basis of a new word, defining wilding as "the activity by a gang of youths of going on a protracted and violent rampage in a public place, attacking people at random."[4] In this book, I offer a broader sociological definition of wilding as any self-interested or self-indulgent behavior that harms others and weakens the social fabric. As explained shortly, there are many forms of wilding, which can be carried out by people of any age, race, class, or gender, and by institutions such as corporations and governments as well as individuals.

The story of wilding after the Central Park incident quickly became tied to the race and class of the predators and their prey. The convicted youths were black and Latino, and from the inner city, although from stable working families. The victim was white, with degrees from Wellesley and Yale, and a wealthy 28-year-old investment banker at Salomon Brothers, one of the great houses of Wall Street.

To white, middle-class Americans, wilding symbolized something real and terrifying about life in the United States. Things were falling apart, at least in the hearts of America's major cities. Most suburbanites did not feel their own neighborhoods had become wild, but they could not imagine walking into Central Park at night.

The fear of wilding became fear of the Other: in this case, those inner-city minorities and others "not like us" locked outside of the American Dream. They had not yet invaded the world most Americans felt part of, but they menaced it. The Central Park attack made the threat real, and it unleashed fear among the general population and a backlash of rage among politicians and other public figures. Mayor Ed Koch called for the death penalty. Donald Trump took out ads in four newspapers, writing, "I want to hate these murderers. . . . I want them to be afraid." Trump told Newsweek that he "had gotten hundreds and hundreds of letters of support."[5]

On December 19, 2002, in a sensational turn of events, Justice Charles J. Tejada of Manhattan's State Supreme Court took only 5 minutes to reverse the convictions of the five "wilders," who had already served their multiyear sentences. The judge acted after another man, Matias Reyes, in jail for murder and rape, confessed to committing the Central Park rape himself, and DNA evidence conclusively linked Reyes to the crime. It appeared that the earlier confessions may have been forced in a circus trial involving police misconduct and racism. Patricia Williams, a law professor who attended the 1991 trial, remembers a hysterical atmosphere in the courtroom, with tourists and celebrities "lined up around the block for admission, as though it were a Broadway show." Williams noted that the confessions, which the teenagers had retracted weeks after giving them, were full of inconsistencies elicited by "unorthodox" police tactics. These included 18 to 30 hours "of nonstop questioning," sometimes taking place "in the back of a police car" and "in the middle of the night."[6]

In 2012, the renowned filmmaker Ken Burns released his documentary, The Central Park Five, that told the story from the point of view of the teenagers, now adults, wrongly convicted. It is a powerful testament to the continuing strength of racial and class prejudices—especially toward minorities and the poor—and how they lead to gross official and public misconduct. Burns vividly documents that the real wilding was, in fact, perpetrated by police, media, the justice system, and the public against the falsely convicted African-American teenage boys, who had not "wilded" at all.

But while the term *wilding* may have come into the media based on a false conviction and racism, it is a surprisingly useful way to characterize an evolving and deeply disturbing feature not of African-Americans or the Other but of American society as a whole. Instead of focusing mainly on the "black wilding" that did not occur in the park, suppose we think of wilding as a way to characterize morally unsettling and antisocial behavior that is rampant throughout our culture. Suppose we think of it not as a description of the Other, but as one lens—admittedly a very uncomfortable one—for looking at ourselves.

As an extreme example, consider a second remarkably vicious crime that grabbed people's attention all over the country just a few months after the Central Park rape, an event whose juxtaposition so close in time with the Central Park incident helped catalyze my writing of this book. On October 23, 1989, Charles and Carol Stuart, a white, upper-middle class couple, left a birthing class at Boston's Brigham and Women's Hospital, walked to their car parked in the adjoining Mission Hill neighborhood, and got in. Within minutes, Carol Stuart—eight months pregnant—was dead, shot point-blank in the head. Her husband, a stunned nation would learn from police accounts two months later, had been her assassin. He had allegedly killed her to collect hundreds of thousands of dollars in life insurance money in order to open a restaurant. Opening a restaurant, Americans everywhere learned, had long been Charles Stuart's American Dream.

Many white, middle-class Americans seemed to believe Stuart's story when he told police that a black gunman had shot him and his wife, leaving Carol Stuart dead and Charles Stuart himself with a severe bullet wound in the abdomen. When Stuart's brother, Matthew, went to the police to tell them of Charles's involvement, and when Charles Stuart subsequently apparently committed suicide by jumping off the Tobin Bridge into the Mystic River, some of the threads connecting his crime to the horrible rape in the Central Park case began to emerge. Stuart had duped a whole nation by playing on the fear of the wild Other. Aware of the vivid images of gangs of black youths rampaging through dark city streets, Stuart had brilliantly concocted a story that would resonate with white Americans' deepest anxieties. Dr. Alvin Poussaint, Harvard professor and adviser to Bill Cosby, said, "Stuart had all the ingredients. . . . [H]e gave blacks a killer image and put himself in the role of a model, an ideal Camelot type that white people could identify with."[7]

Charles Stuart's crime became a national obsession. One reason may have been that white, middle-class Americans everywhere had an uncomfortable sense that, as the 1990s emerged, the Stuart case was, in fact, telling them something about themselves. Stuart, after all, was living the American Dream and reaping its benefits—he was a tall, athletic man with working-class roots, making more than $100,000 a year selling fur coats, and married to a lovely, adoring wife, living the good life in suburban Reading, complete with a swimming pool. Had the American Dream itself become the progenitor of a kind of wilding? Was it possible that not only the inner cities of America but also its comfortable suburbs were becoming wild places? Could "white wilding" be a more serious problem than the "black wilding" publicized in the mass media and so readily embraced by the public at large? Was America at the turn of the decade becoming a wilding society?

To answer these questions, we have to look far beyond such exceptional events as the Central Park rape and the Stuart murder. We shall see that there are many less extreme forms of wilding, including a wide range of antisocial acts that are neither criminal nor physically violent. Wilding includes the ordinary as well as the extraordinary, may be profit-oriented or pleasure-seeking, and can infect corporations and governments as well as individuals of each race, class, and gender.

American wilding is a story in large measure about capitalist individualism run amok. Wilding is found in many other nations, but we focus here on the U.S. variety, since wilding in noncapitalist and nonindividualistic societies requires different explanations. In many other countries, wilding grows out of excessive tribalism or communalism rather than excessive individualism. Noncapitalist wilding in tribal societies can be as sociopathic as the U.S. form, showing that the avoidance of wilding requires a balance between individualism and community. Tilting too far in either direction increases vulnerability to a wilding crisis. The U.S. wilding discussed in this book has relevance for other countries as globalization spreads U.S.-style capitalism and individualism around the world.

▫ The Mountain People: A Wilding Culture

Between 1964 and 1967, anthropologist Colin Turnbull lived among the people of Uganda known as the Ik, who were unfortunately expelled by an uncaring government from their traditional hunting lands—where they had long lived in tribal communities known to be cooperative and child-loving. They were forced to move to extremely barren mountainous areas, where they starved for two generations. In 1972, Turnbull published a haunting book about his experiences that left no doubt that a whole society can embrace wilding as a way of life, particularly when their economic or political circumstances change dramatically for the worse.[8]

When Turnbull first came to the Ik, he met Atum, a sprightly, barefoot old man with a sweet smile, who helped guide Turnbull to remote Ik villages. Atum warned Turnbull right away that everyone would ask for food. Although many would indeed be hungry, he said, most could fend for themselves, and their pleas should not be trusted. Turnbull, Atum stressed, should on no account give them anything. But before he left that day, Atum mentioned that his own wife was severely ill and desperately needed food and medicine. On reaching his village, Atum told Turnbull his wife was too sick to come out. Later, Turnbull heard exchanges between Atum and his sick wife, and her moans of suffering. The moans were wrenching, and when Atum pleaded for help, Turnbull gave him food and some aspirin.

Some weeks later, Atum had stepped up his requests for food and medicine, saying his wife was getting sicker. Turnbull was now seriously concerned, urging Atum to get her to a hospital. Atum refused, saying that "she wasn't that sick."

Shortly thereafter, Atum's brother-in-law came to Turnbull and told him that Atum was selling the medicine that Turnbull had been giving him for his wife. Turnbull, not terribly surprised, said that "that was too bad for his wife." The brother-in-law, enjoying the joke enormously, finally explained that Atum's wife "had been dead for weeks" and that Atum had "buried her inside the compound so you wouldn't know." No wonder Atum had not wanted his wife to go to the hospital. Turnbull thought, "She was worth far more to him dead than alive."[9]

Startling to Turnbull was not only the immense glee the brother-in-law seemed to take in the "joke" that had been inflicted upon his dying sister, but the utter lack of embarrassment that Atum showed when confronted with his lie. Atum shrugged it off, showing no remorse whatsoever, saying he had simply forgotten to tell Turnbull. This was one of the first of many events that made Turnbull wonder whether there was any limit to what an Ik would do to get food and money.

Some time later, Turnbull came across Lomeja, an Ik man he had met much earlier. Lomeja had been shot during an attack by neighboring tribesmen and was lying in a pool of his own blood, apparently dying from two bullet wounds in the stomach. Still alive and conscious, Lomeja looked up at Turnbull and asked for some tea. Shaken, Turnbull returned to his Land Rover and filled a big, new, yellow enamel mug. When he returned, Lomeja's wife was bending over her husband. She was trying to "fold him up" in the dead position although he was not yet dead, and she started shrieking at Turnbull to leave Lomeja alone, saying Lomeja was already dead. Lomeja found the strength to resist his wife's premature efforts to bury him and tried to push her aside. Turnbull managed to get the cup of tea to Lomeja, who was still strong enough to reach out for it and sip it. Suddenly, Turnbull heard a loud giggle and saw Lomeja's sister, Kimat. Attracted by all the yelling, she had "seen that lovely new, bright yellow enamel mug of hot, sweet tea, had snatched it from her brother's face and made off with it, proud and joyful. She not only had the tea, she also had the mug. She drank as she ran, laughing and delighted at herself."[10]

Turnbull came to describe the Ik as "the loveless people." Each Ik valued only his or her own survival and regarded everyone else as a competitor for food. Ik life had become a grim process of trying to find enough food to stay alive each day. The hunt consumed all of their resources, leaving virtually no reserve for feelings of any kind or for any moral scruples that might interfere with filling their stomachs. As Margaret Mead wrote, the Ik were "a people who have become monstrous beyond belief." Scientist Ashley Montagu wrote that the Ik are "a people who are dying because they have abandoned their own humanity."[11]

Ik families elevated wilding to a high art. Turnbull met Adupa, a young girl of perhaps six, who was so malnourished that her stomach was grossly distended and her legs and arms spindly. Her parents had decided she had become a liability and threw her out of their hut. Because she was too weak now to go out on long scavenging ventures, as did the other children, she would wander as far as her strength would allow, pick up scraps of bone or half-eaten berries, and then come back to her parents' place, waiting to be brought back in. Days later, her parents, tiring of her crying, finally brought her in and promised to feed her.

Adupa was happy and stopped crying. The parents went out and "closed the asak behind them, so tight that weak little Adupa could never have moved it if she had tried."[12] Adupa waited for them to come back with the food they had promised, but they did not return until a whole week had passed, when they knew Adupa would be dead. Adupa's parents took her rotting remains, Turnbull writes, and threw them out "as one does the riper garbage, a good distance away." There was no burial—and no tears.[13]

Both morality and personality among the Ik were dedicated to the single all-consuming passion for self-preservation. There was simply "not room in the life of these people," Turnbull observes dryly, "for such luxuries as family and sentiment and love." Nor for any morality beyond "marangik," the Ik concept of goodness, which means filling one's own stomach.

The Ik in Us

Long before the rape in Central Park or the Stuart murder, Ashley Montagu, commenting on Turnbull's work, wrote that "the parallel with our own society is deadly." In 1972, when Turnbull published his book, wilding had not yet become part of the American vocabulary, nor did most Americans face declining living standards, let alone the kind of starvation experienced by the Iks. Americans were obviously not killing their parents or children for money, but they dedicated themselves to self-interested pursuits with a passion not unlike that of the Ik.

In America, a land of plenty, there was the luxury of a rhetoric of morality and feelings of empathy and love. But was not the American Dream a paean to individualistic enterprise, and could not such an enterprise be conceived in some of the same unsentimental metaphors used by Turnbull about the Ik? The Ik community, he writes, "reveals itself for what it is, a conglomeration of individuals of all ages, each going his own way in search of food and water, like a plague of locusts spread over the land."[14]

America now faces a wilding epidemic that is eating at the country's social foundation and could rot it, reflecting partly a deterioration of the wages and security of ordinary Americans, a theme taken up in depth throughout this book. The American case is much less advanced than that of the Ik's, but the disease is deeply rooted and is spreading through the political leadership, the business community, and the general population. Strong medicine can turn the situation around, but if we fail to act now, the epidemic could prove irreversible.

Only a handful of Americans are "ultimate wilders" like Charles Stuart. Such killers are noteworthy mainly because they may help wake us up to the wilding plague spreading among thousands of less extreme wilders who are not killers. Wilding includes a vast spectrum of self-centered and self-aggrandizing behavior that harms others. A wilding epidemic tears at the social fabric and threatens to unravel society itself, ultimately reflecting the erosion of the moral order and the withdrawal of feelings and commitments from others to "number one."

The wilding virus comes in radically different strains. There is *expressive wilding*: wilding for the sheer satisfaction of indulging one's own destructive impulses, the kind found among the American youth who heave rocks off highway bridges in the hope of smashing the windshields of unknown drivers passing innocently below. The hockey and soccer parents who attack coaches and other parents are expressive wilders, as are drivers engaging in road rage.

Most *instrumental wilding* involves garden varieties of ambition, competitiveness, careerism, and greed that advance the self at the cost of others. The most serious forms include the greed and fraud perpetrated by Wall Street executives and their banks, described in Chapter 5, who drove the U.S. economy into a ditch in the 2008 Great Recession. Other U.S. forms include actions by presidents and other leading politicians who lead the nation into illegal or unjust wars, discussed in Chapter 9, that generate profits for U.S. companies but lead to the deaths of thousands of U.S. soldiers and many thousands of more deaths in the countries attacked.

Expressive and instrumental wilding are both antisocial and self-centered and are made possible by a stunning collapse of moral restraint and a chilling lack of empathy, driven by changes in our economic system, our politics, and our culture. I am mainly concerned in this book with instrumental wilding because it is the form most intimately connected with the American Dream and least understood in its poisonous effects on society.[15]

Although much wilding is criminal, there is a vast spectrum of perfectly legal wilding, exemplified by the careerist who indifferently betrays or steps on colleagues to advance up the ladder. Some forms of wilding, such as lying and cheating, are officially discouraged, but others, like the frantic and single-minded pursuit of wealth, are cultivated by some of the country's leading corporations and financial institutions. Likewise, there are important differences in the severity of wilding behaviors; killing a spouse for money is obviously far more brutal than stealing a wallet or cheating on an exam. But there are distinct types and degrees of infection in any affliction, ranging from terminal cases such as that of Stuart, to intermediate cases such as the savings and loan crooks of the 1980s, to those who either are petty wilders or who rarely exhibit symptoms at all. The latter categories include large numbers of Americans who may struggle internally with their wilding impulses but remain healthy enough to restrain them. The variation is similar to that in heart disease: Those with only partial clogging of their arteries and no symptoms are different from those with full-blown, advanced arteriosclerosis, and those least afflicted may never develop the terminal stage of the illness. But these differences are normally of degree rather than of kind; the same underlying pathology is at work among people with both mild and severe cases.

There are, nonetheless, real differences between white lies or misdemeanors (forms of petty wilding) and serious wilding of the Central Park or Charles Stuart variety. Petty wilding occurs in all cultures, will persist as long as most people are not saints, and, in limited doses, does not necessarily threaten civil order. When wilding is so limited that it does not constitute a grave social danger, it might better be described as *incipient wilding* and is not of concern here.

However, certain types of *petty wilding* exist in America at an alarming level, as I document in Chapter 3 in my discussion of minor lying, cheating, and ordinary competitiveness with an indifference to others. Such transgressions on an epidemic scale can reach a critical mass and become as serious a threat to society as violent crime or huge investment scams on Wall Street. Lying is an important example of petty wilding that now not only infects many friendships and marriages but also has become a pervasive problem in our political system, with leaders charged with lying to the nation about their reasons for going to war, about authorizing torture, and about misrepresenting scientific findings, such as whether such problems as global climate change are caused by human activity. It is not the degree of brutality or violence, but the consequences for society that ultimately matter, and I thus consider the full spectrum of wilding acts—from petty to outrageous—that together constitute a clear and present danger to America's social fabric.

Economic, Political, and Social Wilding

Wilding, in sociological terms that I noted at the outset, extends far beyond random violence by youth gangs to include three types of assault on society. *Economic wilding* is the morally uninhibited pursuit of money by individuals or businesses at the expense of others. *Political wilding* is the abuse of political office to benefit oneself or one's own social class, or the wielding of political authority to inflict morally unacceptable suffering on citizens at home or abroad. *Social wilding* ranges from personal or family acts of violence, such as child or spousal abuse, to collective forms of selfishness that weaken society, such as affluent suburbs turning their backs on bleeding inner cities.

Economic wilders include Bernie Madoff, the Wall Street financier who confessed to running a $60 billion Ponzi scheme and is now in prison under a 150-year sentence. He is an iconic symbol of the greed driving the 2008 Wall Street meltdown. Madoff is joined by a host of executives at AIG, Merrill Lynch, Lehman Brothers, and other Wall Street firms, whose economic wilding nearly brought down the entire system. Economic wilders are a different species from the rapist in Central Park, since they wild for money rather than for fun or sex. Partly because of differing opportunities and incentives, people wild in different ways and for exceedingly varied reasons and motives, ranging from greed and lust to the gaining of attention or respect. The different forms of wilding, however, are all manifestations of degraded American individualism.

The wilding epidemic is the face of America's individualistic culture in an advanced state of disrepair. An individualistic culture promotes the freedom of the individual and in its healthy form nurtures human development and individual rights. In its degraded form, it encourages unrestrained and sociopathic self-interest.

☐ Wilding and Not Wilding: Varieties of Individualism

Wilding—a degenerate form of individualism—encompasses a huge variety of antisocial behavior. It includes so many seemingly unrelated acts that it might appear to stand for everything—or nothing. But wilding includes only a small subset of the entire range of behaviors that sociologists describe as *individualistic*, a term that arguably can be applied to any self-interested behavior. In a society such as that of the United States, which is dominated by individualistic values and a market system that rewards self-interest, some might argue that virtually all socially prescribed behavior has an individualistic dimension.

I propose a far more restrictive definition of *wilding*. Not all individualistic behavior is wilding, nor is *wilding* an umbrella term for any form of self-interested or "bad" behavior. As noted earlier, wilding refers to self-oriented behavior that hurts others and damages the social fabric, which excludes many types of individualistic action. The Jewish sage Hillel wrote, "If I am not for others, what am I?" Yet he also said, "If I am not for myself, who will be for me?" His maxims suggest that many forms of self-interest are necessary and contribute to the well-being of others.

A doctor who works hard to perfect her medical skills may advance her own career, but she also saves lives. A superbly conditioned professional athlete may enrich himself by his competitiveness or ambition, but he also entertains and gives pleasure to his fans. If I strive to be the best writer I can be—an individualistic aspiration—I am educating others while fulfilling myself. In none of these cases is individualistic behavior itself necessarily wilding. Actions that advance one's own interests and either help or do not harm others are not forms of wilding, even when motivated by competitiveness or acquisitiveness.

Wilding includes only individualistic behavior that advances or indulges the self by hurting others. If the doctor advances her skills and career by cheating on tests, trampling on her colleagues, or using her patients as guinea pigs, her self-interest has degraded into wilding. The athlete who illicitly uses steroids to win competitions is wilding by cheating against his rivals and deceiving his fans.

Whereas all wilding behavior hurts others, not all hurtful behavior is wilding. If I get angry at a friend, I may hurt him, but that reaction does not necessarily make it wilding. Such anger may be justified because it was motivated by a wrong done to me, and it may ultimately serve to repair the relationship. Interpersonal relations inevitably involve misunderstanding, aggression, and hurt, which degrade into expressive wilding only when the hurt is intentional and purely self-indulgent, and when the perpetrator is indifferent to the pain inflicted on the other. Motivation, empathy, and the level of harm inflicted are key criteria in deciding whether wilding has occurred. Deliberate physical or emotional abuse is clearly wilding, whereas impulsive acts that cause less harm and lead to remorse and remediation are more ambiguous cases and may not constitute wilding at all.

Similarly complex considerations apply to institutional wilding enacted by corporations or governments. Instrumental wilding takes place whenever institutions pursue goals and strategies that inflict serious harm on individuals, communities, or entire societies. Some of the most important forms of economic wilding, both

legal and criminal, involve routine profiteering by rapacious businesses exploiting employees, consumers, and communities. As discussed in Chapter 4, the line
between corporate self-interest and economic wilding is blurred in today's global
economy, but not all profits arise out of exploitation, and many profitable businesses
are not engaged in economic wilding. Socially responsible or employee-owned
businesses that add to social well-being by creating jobs, raising the standard of
living of employees, improving the environment, and enhancing the quality of life
of their customers may be highly profitable but are hardly examples of wilding.
Systemic connections exist between American capitalism and wilding, but not all
forms of capitalism breed wilding.

Finally, not all crime, violence, or evil behavior is individualistic wilding. The
horrific ethnic cleansing in Bosnia and the genocidal warfare in Rwanda and the
Sudan constitute wilding by almost any definition, but such wilding is rooted in
fierce and pathological tribal or communal loyalties and is hardly an expression
of rampant individualism. Individualism and communitarianism can each generate their own forms of wilding; I focus on the individualistic variant in this book
because it is the type endemic in the United States. My indictment of individualistic wilding should not be viewed as a preference for the communitarian form,
because wilding in many of the world's cruelest societies has its roots in the
excesses of community. Wilding can be avoided only by respecting the rights of
individuals and the needs for community, a balancing act too many societies have
failed dismally to achieve.

Varieties of Wilding

Wilding: Self-interested or self-indulgent behavior that hurts others and weakens the social fabric

Motives for Wilding

Instrumental Wilding: Wilding for money or other calculable gain, such as robbery

Expressive Wilding: Wilding for emotional gratification, such as committing rape

Domains of Wilding

Economic Wilding: Wilding in the economy for money, career advancement, or other material gain

Political Wilding: Wilding in politics for political power or advancement

Social Wilding: Wilding in civil society for status, respect, or other social ends

Environmental Wilding: Wilding in the natural environment, such as reckless polluting that causes global warming

Degrees of Wilding

Petty Wilding: Minor wilding, involving small gain or harm, such as cheating on a test

Full-Blown Wilding: Major wilding, involving significant gain or serious harm, such as large-scale financial fraud

Ultimate Wilding: Extreme wilding, such as the murder of a spouse or child for money

Perpetrators of Wilding

Individual Wilding: Wilding by individuals

Institutional Wilding: Wilding by corporations, governments, churches, or other institutions

Systemic Wilding: Wilding perpetrated by economic systems such as capitalism or cultural systems such individualism

Legality of Wilding

Criminal Wilding: Wilding that involves breaking the law, such as armed robbery

Legal Wilding: Wilding that is within the law, such as lying to a friend

Physicality of Wilding

Violent Wilding: Wilding that involves physical violence, such as murder

Nonviolent Wilding: Wilding that is not physically violent, such as white-collar fraud

---

▣ The Two Americas: Are We All Wilders?

Although the wilding epidemic now infects almost every major American institution, cooperative behavior survives, and in every community one finds idealists, altruists, and a majority of citizens seeking to live lives guided by moral principles. About two-thirds of Americans give money to charity, and about half roll up their sleeves and do volunteer work or become social activists; these are among the many hopeful indications that America can still purge itself of this epidemic.

For an analyst of wilding, there are two Americas: the America already seriously infected, which is the main subject of this book, and the America that has not yet succumbed and remains a civil society. The majority of ordinary Americans, it should be stressed, are part of the second America, and they retain a moral compass and emotional sensibilities that inhibit severe wilding behavior. But as the epidemic continues to spread, individual interests will increasingly override common purposes, and the self—rather than family or community—will increasingly grab center stage in both Americas. Not everyone will become a wilder, but nobody will be untouched by wilding culture.[16]

Wilders who catch the fever profoundly infect their own vulnerable communities, families, and workplaces. One dangerous criminal on a block can make a community wild, inciting aggression, violence, and a fortress mentality among normally peaceable neighbors. A particularly competitive salesperson or account executive can transform an entire office into a jungle, because those who do not follow suit may be left behind. The new ethos rewards the wilder and penalizes those who cling to civil behavior.

The ravages of wilding may be most noticeable among the poor and downtrodden, but the virus afflicts the fortunate and the comfortable just as much; it exists in the genteel suburbs as well as in the inner cities. Indeed, American wilding is, to a surprising degree, an affliction of the successful, in that the rich and powerful have written the wilding rules. It is ever more difficult to climb the ladder without internalizing those rules.

The progress of the wilding epidemic is shaped less by the percentage of sociopaths than by the sociopathy of society's elites and the rules of the success game they have helped define. A wilding society is one in which wilding is a route to the top, and in which legitimate success becomes difficult to distinguish from the art of wilding within—or even outside—the law.

The wilding epidemic is now seeping into America, mainly from the top. Although the majority of business and political leaders remain honest, a large and influential minority—concentrated on Wall Street—not only are serving as egregious role models but also are rewriting the rules of the American success game in their own interests.

Our current wilding crisis is rooted politically in the "free market" revolution that began with President Ronald Reagan. The "Reagan Revolution" advanced the most ambitious class agenda of the rich in over a century, creating an innovative brew of market deregulation and individualistic ideology that helped fan the flames of wilding across the land. Former President George W. Bush, despite his rhetoric of compassionate conservatism, tried to complete the revolution of greed that Reagan began, while also taking the country to war on false pretenses (see Chapter 9), one of the worst forms of political wilding. Despite idealistic rhetoric and some innovative policy, as in his national health care law inclusive of all Americans, President Barack Obama has not been able to take America in a new direction.

☐ Wilding and the New American Dream: Individualism Today and Yesterday

Many signs point to a corruption of the American Dream in our time.[17] Most Americans do not become killers to make it up the ladder or to hold on to what they have, but the traditional restraints on naked self-aggrandizement seem weaker—and the insatiability greater.

The fantasy began in modern times with the Reagan Revolution in the go-go 1980s, mushroomed in the late 1990s with young dot-com entrepreneurs dreaming of becoming millionaires before turning 30 and reaching climactic heights in the housing bubble and stock market run-up leading to the 2008 Wall Street crash. A new version of the American Dream has now emerged, more individualistic, expansive, and morally perverted than most of its predecessors. Journalist Laurence Shames suggests that the name of the American game has become simply "more."[18] Unrestrained greed has certainly been the name of the game for America's richest people, including the "masters of the universe"—the elite money managers on Wall Street. In 2008, managers in the nine big banks receiving government bailouts took for themselves an astonishing $32.6 billion in bonuses, even as their banks lost money.[19] About 5,000 top managers received $5 billion in bonuses, with 200 in Goldman Sachs sharing $1 billion and 101 in Morgan Stanley sharing $577 million.[20]

The greed and wealth of the Wall Street elites, whose wilding behavior precipitated the 2008 Great Recession, became the focus of the Occupy Wall Street movement, which exploded on the scene in 2011. The occupiers introduced into popular vocabulary the "one percent." These are the richest one percent of Americans who embody the values and possess the drive to make money, whatever it takes. This attitude defines the new American Dream. In 2010, the one percent took for itself an astonishing 93 percent of all income growth in the United States.[21] In 2011, the one percent had accumulated more wealth than the bottom 95 percent of all Americans.[22] Between 1983 and 2009, 40 percent of all wealth gains in the country went to the top one percent, who also took 60 percent of the nation's income gains.[23] If that were not enough, in 2009, the Wall Street banks that received federal bailout money awarded themselves $140 billion in bonus money.[24]

In 2011, to become part of the Forbes 400 list of the richest Americans, one had to make at least $1.05 billion.[25] The total wealth of the Fortune 400 in 2011 was an astonishing $1.53 trillion, compared to $500 billion total wealth in 1995.[26] The richest Americans in 2013 were among the richest ever in the world, with Bill Gates topping the list at $66 billion, a figure larger than the entire wealth of several countries.[27]

The picture for the 99 percent—the overwhelming majority of Americans—is radically different. In the decade between 2002 and 2012, 70 percent of Americans saw their wages stagnate or decline, and "from 1979 to 2012, typical workers saw wage increases of just five percent, despite productivity growth of nearly 75 percent, while wage gains for low-wage workers were flat or declined."[28] Inequality increased in the United States in 2011 to a level higher than it had been in the past four decades,[29] a level parallel to that of the 1920s just before the Great Crash and the 1890s robber baron Gilded Age. In the decade between 2001 and 2011, average family incomes fell for the first time since World War II and the Great Depression,[30] and declining pay led workers' wages in 2013 to the lowest percentage of gross domestic product (GDP) since 1929.[31]

For the 99 percent, the new Gilded Dream became a recipe for wilding based on collapsed possibilities. A dream of having more had been sustainable when real income for ordinary Americans kept growing, as it had through most of American history. But when real income begins to stagnate and decline for the vast majority, an unprecedented development in the last decades of the twentieth century, an outsized Dream becomes an illusion, inconsistent with the reality of most Americans' lives.

After the Great Recession hit, unemployment skyrocketed to about ten percent, and wages and household income plunged further among middle and lower income workers, while the top tier of managers took home their million-dollar bonuses. The ratio between the average CEO's pay and the average worker's wage went from 41 to 1 in 1975 to 354 to 1 in 2013.[32] As wages declined, millions more Americans went into debt in order to try to achieve an American Dream receding out of their reach, helping catalyze the economic collapse of 2008. Outsized Dream, downsized lives. To weave grandiose materialist dreams in an era of restricted opportunities is the ultimate recipe for social wilding.

A new age of limits and polarization in the early twenty-first century sets the stage for an advanced wilding crisis. In an America deeply divided by class, the American Dream, and especially the new Gilded Dream, cannot be a common enterprise and is transformed into multiple wilding agendas, unleashing wilding among people at every station, but in different ways. Among those at the bottom, the Dream becomes pure illusion; wilding, whether dealing drugs or robbing banks, beckons as a fast track out of the ghetto and into the high life. Among the insecure and slipping great American middle class, wilding becomes a growth area for those who are unwilling to go down with their closing factories and downsized offices, priming themselves to do anything it takes to survive. For the professional and business classes at the top, wilding passes as professional ambition and proliferates as one or another variant of dedicated and untrammeled careerism. Ensconced inside heavily fortified suburban or gentrified enclaves, these elites also pioneer new forms of social wilding in what former labor secretary Robert Reich calls "a politics of secession," abandoning society itself as part of a panicky defense against the threat from the huge, covetous majority left behind.[33] The wilding crisis, as we see later, arises partly out of a virulent new class politics.

The seeds of America's wilding plague were planted long before the current era. Over a century ago, Alexis de Tocqueville observed that conditions in America led every "member of the community to be wrapped up in himself" and worried that "personal interest will become more than ever the principal, if not the sole spring" of American behavior.[34] Selfish and mean-spirited people can be found in every culture and every phase of history, and wilding, as I show in the next chapter, is certainly not a new phenomenon in American life. As one of the world's most individualistic societies, America has long struggled to cope with high levels of violence, greed, political corruption, and other outcroppings of wilding.

Over the last 100 years, American history can be read as a succession of wilding periods alternating with eras of civility. The robber baron era of the 1880s and 1890s, an age of spectacular economic and political wilding, was followed by the Progressive Era of the early twentieth century, in which moral forces reasserted themselves. The individualistic license of the 1920s, another era of economic and political wilding, this time epitomized by the Teapot Dome scandal, yielded to the New Deal era of the 1930s and 1940s, when America responded to the Great Depression with remarkable moral and community spirit. The moral idealism of a new generation of youth in the 1960s was followed by the explosion of political, economic, and social wilding in the current era.

American wilding is a timeless and enduring threat, linked to our national heritage and our most basic values and institutions. Although this book focuses on wilding today, the wilding problem riddles our history, for it is embedded in the origins of free market capitalism and the individualistic culture that has helped shape the American Dream and our own national character. What distinguishes the current epidemic is the subtle legitimation of wilding as it breeds a new culture of corruption and overwhelming corporate influence in Washington; the severity of the wilding crisis in U.S. militarist foreign policy that endangers our most precious civil liberties; the wilding epidemic, symbolized by Bernie Madoff and top Wall Street executives in banking and commerce, whose companies' wilding crashed the entire U.S. economy; the spread of wilding into universities, films, TV, popular music, and other vital cultural centers; and the subsequent penetration of wilding culture so deeply into the lives of the general population that society itself is now at risk.

Roots of Wilding: Durkheim, Marx, and the Sociological Eye

More than a century ago, the founders of sociology had their own intimations of a wilding crisis that could consume society. The great French thinker Émile Durkheim recognized that individualism was the rising culture of the modern age. While Durkheim believed that individualism could ultimately be a healing force, he also feared that it could poison the bonds that make social life possible. Karl Marx, who gave birth to a different school of sociology, believed that the economic individualism of capitalism might erode all forms of community and reduce human relations to a new lowest common denominator: the "cash nexus."

Sociology arose as an inquiry into the dangers of modern individualism, which could potentially destroy society itself. The prospect of the death of society gave birth to the question epitomized by the Ik: What makes society possible and prevents it from disintegrating into a mass of sociopathic and self-interested isolates? This core question of sociology has become the vital issue of our times.

Although sociology does not provide all the answers, it does offer a compelling framework for understanding and potentially solving the wilding epidemic. Durkheim never heard of wilding or the Ik, but he focused like a laser on the coming crisis of community. He saw that the great transformation of the modern age was the breakdown of traditional social solidarity and the rise of an individual less enmeshed in community. In Durkheim's view, egoism posed a grave danger, arising where "the individual is isolated because the bonds uniting him to other beings are slackened or broken" and the "bond which attaches him to society is itself slack." Such an individual, who finds no "meaning in genuinely collective activity," is primed for wilding, the pursuit of gain or pleasure at the expense of others with whom there is no sense of shared destiny.[35]

The other great danger is *anomie*, which Durkheim defined as a condition of societal normlessness that breeds crime and suicide. Anomie arises when social rules are absent or confusing and individuals are insufficiently integrated into families, neighborhoods, or churches to be regulated by their moral codes. Durkheim believed that modern individualistic societies were especially vulnerable to this kind of failure of socialization. As community declines, it leaves the individual without a moral compass, buffeted by disturbing and increasingly limitless "passions, without a curb to regulate them."[36] Anomie fuels instrumental wilding, making the individual more vulnerable to fantasies of limitless money and power. It also feeds expressive wilding, such as spouse abuse, weakening the personal and community controls that sustain civilized values.[37]

Although Durkheim captured the kind of breakdown of community that is currently contributing to the American wilding epidemic, he lacked the economic and political analysis that would help explain why wilding is startlingly pervasive among America's ruling elites and trickling down to the population at large. As I will argue in chapters to come, American wilding is a form of socially prescribed, antisocial behavior, modeled by leaders and reinforced by the rules of our "free market" game. As such, it reflects less the insufficient presence of society in individuals than overconformity to a society whose norms and values are socially dangerous.

Marx wrote that the market system "drowns the most heavenly ecstasies of religious fervor, of chivalrous enthusiasm, of philistine sentimentalism, in the icy water of egotistical calculation." In capitalism, from a Marxist perspective, wilding is less a failure of socialization than an expression of society's central norms. To turn a profit, even the most humane capitalist employer commodifies and exploits employees, playing by the market rules of competition and profit maximization to buy and sell their labor power as cheaply as possible.[38]

From a Marxist perspective, the American Dream is capitalism's master script. It dictates that each of us look out for "number one." If we fail to play our egoistic, competitive role in this capitalist script, profits are threatened and capitalism itself would unravel.[39] For Marx, values themselves are the most carefully crafted "products" of the economic system. The capitalist elites script the individualistic American Dream because their wealth and power depend on the population believing fervently in the script's economic rationality and moral legitimacy.

While this script might seem pure greed or selfishness, it comes wrapped in high morality.[40] One of the founders of classical economics, the eighteenth-century political philosopher, Adam Smith, developed the principle of the "invisible hand," which says that the best way to ensure the common good is for each individual to pursue his or her own self-interest. The invisible hand of the market transforms this self-oriented behavior by millions of producers and consumers into a miraculous common good.[41] Self-interest, paradoxically, protects the "commons," the shared resources and prosperity that ensure the well-being of society as a whole.[42]

In 1981, when Ronald Reagan became president of the United States, he proclaimed in his inaugural speech that his goal was for every American to become rich. The Reagan Revolution helped turn the American Dream into one of fevered and extreme individualism that became a form of socially approved wilding. By dismantling regulations that had helped to rein in financial speculation, debt, and monopolies, this economic wilding, based in greed, helped make the wealthy even wealthier. The new motto: Get rich fast!

Americans looked up to the business leaders and politicians who got rich the fastest, symbolized by Gordon Gekko, the movie character played by Michael Douglas in the film *Wall Street*. Gekko's memorable line, "Greed is good," is a philosophy that permeated the greedy AIG, Bank of America, Goldman Sachs, and Bear Stearns executives on Wall Street and trickled down to millions of workers and consumers out to make a fast buck and spend it even faster. If we didn't have enough, and nothing seemed enough, Wall Street made available easy credit and debt, leading most of us to live beyond our means.

Marx would see extreme deregulation as one reason for the evolution of the American Dream into a wilding script. But, more important, Marx would explain the new extreme individualism as a reflection of growing systemic capitalist crises.[43] As capitalism matures or "ages," it tends toward stagnation.[44] One reason is the "wage paradox": Each corporation tries to force down wages to make more money. But when all corporations do this, they create a crisis of aggregate consumer demand, because the low wages mean workers can't buy what the companies produce.[45] In the age of globalization, this becomes an extreme crisis in the United States, since corporations have access to billions of impoverished global workers and can force wages of U.S. workers way down, leaving them with little income to spend at the mall.

American capitalists tried to solve this dilemma by making available super-easy credit and debt to the beleaguered U.S. worker, so he or she could keep buying.[46] "Use that plastic card in your wallet to keep shopping. If you couldn't afford a house, we'll give you a subprime mortgage and let you worry about the debt later. Do whatever it takes to survive and make it!" This logic, of course, led to the great economic meltdown of 2008. The actions of both the lenders and the borrowers, but especially the lenders, were one of the great forms of economic wilding in modern history, a sign of how capitalism can script a wilding culture that undermines capitalism itself.

The champions of Western capitalism—from Adam Smith to Milton Friedman—agree that self-interest is the engine of the system and individualism, its official religion; but they reject Marx's equation of a regime built around economic self-interest with exploitation and wilding. Marx was wrong, in fact, to assume that capitalism inevitably destroyed community and social values. In some national contexts, including Confucian Japan and social-democratic Sweden, the individualizing forces of the market are cushioned by cultures and governments that limit exploitation and help sustain community.

In the United States, however, rugged individualism has merged with raw capitalism, creating a fertile brew for wilding. A Marxist view of institutionalized wilding—and of political and business elites as carriers of the wilding virus—helps correct the Durkheimian hint of wilding as deviance. Durkheim, in a major oversight, never recognized that egoism and anomie can themselves be seen as norms, culturally prescribed and accepted.[47]

This point is a theoretical key to understanding wilding in America. Wilding partly reflects a weakened community less able to regulate its increasingly individualistic members. In this sense, the American wilder is the product of a declining society that is losing its authority to instill respect for social values and obligations, particularly in a population whose jobs and very survival seem at risk.

But Marx's view of institutionalized wilding suggests that wilders can simultaneously be oversocialized, imbibing too deeply the core values of competition and profit seeking in American capitalism. The idea of oversocialization, which I elaborate on in the next chapter, suggests not the failure of social authority but the wholesale indoctrination of societal values that can ultimately poison both the individual and also the society itself. As local communities weaken, giant corporations, including the media, advertising, and communications industries, shape the appetites, morality, and behavior of Americans ever more powerfully. For the rich and powerful, the dream of unlimited wealth and glamour, combined with the Reagan and Bush II revolution of corporate deregulation and corporate welfare, opens up endless fantasies and opportunities. As Durkheim himself noted, when the ceiling on ordinary expectations is removed, the conventional restraints on pursuing them will also rapidly disappear. This situation produces socially prescribed anomie and wilding among elites that is based on unlimited possibilities.

As suggested above, a different version of socially prescribed wilding trickles down to everyone else. For those exposed to the same inflated dream of wealth, glamour, and power, but denied the means of achieving it, illegitimate means provide the only strategy to achieve socially approved goals. Whether involving petty or serious wilding, such behavior gradually permeates the population, with millions increasingly operating on a "survivalist" mentality as they struggle to find work in a downsizing economy. Sociologist Robert Merton wrote that crime is a product of a disparity between goals and means. If that disparity becomes institutionalized, crime and other forms of deviance are normalized, and antisocial behavior becomes common practice. Wilding itself becomes a societal way of life.

New economic realities, including the fact that the coming generation faces the prospect of living less well than its parents, could trigger a healthy national reexamination of our values, and the pursuit of a less materialistic and individualistic life. The polarization of wealth and opportunity could also prompt, before it is too late, a rethinking of our class divisions and economic system. But without such a rescripting of the American Dream and our ruthless corporate capitalism, the new circumstances could create the specter of an American nightmare reminiscent of the Ik.

Discussion Questions

1. What is the definition of wilding?
2. What are the most common and destructive forms of wilding in the United States?
3. Is all crime wilding? Is all wilding criminal?
4. Do the causes of wilding lie in nature or society?
5. How would social theorists, such as Karl Marx and Émile Durkheim, explain wilding?
6. Are you a wilder?
7. What is the relation between the American Dream and wilding? Are all Americans wilders? Are wilders engaged in deviant behavior in the United States?

two

The Ultimate Wilders: Prisoners of the American Dream

Why should we be in such desperate haste to succeed? And in such desperate enterprises?
—Henry David Thoreau

In December 2004, a jury convicted 31-year-old Scott Peterson of killing his pregnant wife. In a case capturing the attention of the nation, prosecutors accused Peterson, from Modesto, California, of weighting Laci Peterson's body with concrete anchors and dumping her into the San Francisco Bay on Christmas Eve 2002. Prosecutor Rick Distaso argued that Peterson was unhappy in his marriage and that his motive was to free himself from the unwanted burden of paying child support and alimony if he were to divorce.[1]

Like Charles Stuart, the Boston killer discussed in Chapter 1, Peterson, a business manager and salesman, blamed a robber for the murder. After the murder, also like Stuart, he lived a high lifestyle with his mistress, Amber Frey, an attractive masseuse. (Frey was not aware that Peterson was married.) He faced growing financial problems before murdering Laci, with 70 percent of the couple's take-home income going toward credit card debt and Peterson badly failing to meet his sales quotas at his company. Moreover, the Petersons had recently taken out $250,000 life insurance policies on each other. After his murder conviction, Peterson sued from jail to collect the money, apparently as eager as Stuart had been to reap the spoils of his wife's death.[2]

Peterson is just one in a long list of people who have been convicted in recent years for killing their spouse for money. On August 21, 2013, a jury convicted Kathryn Ellis, 49, of murdering her husband, Robert, for money in Kingsburg, California, in September 2012.[3] She had wanted to cash in on his life insurance policy. Prosecutor Stephanie Savrnoch said, "She was waiting for him to doze off while he was laying on his side watching *The Big Bang Theory* in the living room. And as he laid there, she walked around the couch and she shot him, bang."[4]

The couple married in 1989 and had a teenage son. Robert was a purchasing manager but didn't make enough to cover the family bills. He had $200,000 in life insurance, and Kathryn had gone twice to the insurance agency, asking them to increase the amount and not tell her husband. She had mismanaged family money, driving the family into bankruptcy with overdue loans and maxed-out credit cards. This case did not get the national attention of the Peterson case, since Kathryn didn't have flamboyant sociopathic personality tendencies. But this makes her, arguably, more significant because her case hints at how survival pressures in a tough economy with stagnant wages can lead even relatively "normal" people such as Kathryn to commit extreme wilding acts.[5]

On April 27, 2008, in a nationally publicized case that became the subject of an August 2012 episode of the ABC program *Final Witness*, as well as the subject of an earlier Dominick Dunne television film in 2009, a jury convicted Hans Thomas Reiser, 45, of the first-degree murder of his wife, Nina Reiser, who had disappeared in 2006.[6] On July 28, 2008, while serving his sentence in California's San Quentin prison, Reiser led police to the location where he had buried Nina, delivering the body in exchange for a reduction to a second-degree murder sentence. Reiser, who was a prominent computer software developer and had founded his own software company, Namesys, had both financial and personal reasons to kill Nina. Reiser's company was failing and he had to pay substantial alimony and child support to Nina that he claimed he could not afford, returning repeatedly to family court to report his financial problems (which would have been alleviated by her murder). Moreover, he believed Nina had embezzled hundreds of thousands of dollars from his firm. In addition, Hans and Nina had been involved in a bitter divorce and child custody case, and Nina had had an affair with Sean Sturgeon, Hans's best friend.[7]

Prosecutor Paul Hora described Reiser as "narcissistic," a common characteristic of men who coldly kill their wives.[8] Reading from a clinical diagnostic manual, Hora said these men typically are marked by "an inflated feeling of self, a belief that one is special and unique, arrogance and lack of sympathy toward others."[9] Hora said that Reiser was described by professional colleagues and acquaintances as arrogant, cold, self-centered, and grandiose.[10]

As the Kathryn Ellis case shows, it is not only men who engage in such extreme wilding. On April 17, 2008, in a case that was dubbed the "Black Widow" murders and also the "Grannies Murders," a Los Angeles jury convicted Helen Golay, 77, of murdering two homeless men, Kenneth McDonald, 50, in 2005, and Paul Vados, 73, in 1999. Golay had a collaborator, Olga Rutterschmidt, 75, who was also convicted of murdering McDonald, although the jury was deadlocked about her guilt in the murder of Vados. Police said that the women had befriended the two homeless men, taken out insurance policies on both of them, and then staged hit-and-run accidents, killing them. The grannies could collect $2.8 million from the insurance policies. Golay was convicted of conspiracy to commit murder for financial gain on both counts.[11]

Prosecutors said the women had recruited the men from Los Angeles's large homeless population, put them up in apartments, took out the insurance policies, then drugged the men and ran over them in secluded alleys. The grannies eventually made the case for prosecutors easier, conceding that McDonald had been murdered, but each accusing the other. Prosecutors called them both the "worst of the worst."[12]

But the grannies had competition for this label from a much younger woman. Years earlier, Pamela Smart, an ambitious, pretty New Hampshire high school media services director, seduced an adolescent student and persuaded him to help her kill Gregory Smart, her 24-year-old husband. After the murder, her teenage lover went to jail, and Smart got thousands in insurance money. But she wasn't able to enjoy it for long because the real story finally leaked out from the boy and his friends. Smart was convicted of first-degree murder and sent to jail in Bedford Hills, New York, where she is incarcerated to this day. Still, Smart realized one of her ambitions—to become famous. Hollywood made a movie, *To Die For* (1995), about her venomous crime, with Nicole Kidman playing the "black widow," as women who kill their husbands for money are called.

All of these killers are "ultimate wilders," Charles Stuart "look-alikes" prepared to do anything for money. Smart is most reminiscent of Stuart because she was ambitious, competitive, successful, and an "all-American" cheerleader and honor roll student. She aspired to be the next Barbara Walters, and many believed she'd make it. Smart, like Stuart, seemed the embodiment of the American Dream.

In this chapter, I describe people who have murdered their own spouses or children. Crimes of this horrible nature have many causes and happen in many cultures. Personal psychopathology, idiosyncratic family dynamics, and other personal or temperamental factors help explain these crimes. But I discuss them here because there are also wilding themes in American culture and today's American Dream that help unleash these crimes. Some individuals are more vulnerable to these cultural influences than others, with the people described here being obviously a small minority of Americans, different from their neighbors because of personal and psychological factors. The role of culture does not exonerate these individuals from personal responsibility, but it does show that we are looking at sociological patterns rather than just individual cases of psychopathology. For example, the startling fact that the most common source of death among pregnant women in the United States is murder by their husbands suggests that social as well as psychological forces help explain the behavior of people such as Charles Stuart and Scott Peterson. As you reflect on these grim case studies, keep in mind also that one-third of all female murder victims are killed by their husbands or boyfriends. These trends make clear that we are dealing in this chapter not just with deviance or psychopathology but disturbing social and cultural patterns.

Sociologist C. Wright Mills argued that the sociological imagination connects personal biography to the social structure and culture of the times. In Chapter 1, I argued that our current wilding wave began around 1980, as a new American Dream and a new economy began to take form. Consider below one of the most infamous wilders who committed his crimes in the early years of this latest epidemic, but perfectly illustrates the personality characteristics as well as the U.S. cultural and economic sociopathic forces that mold extreme wilders.

Robert Oakley Marshall: "Speed Demon on the Boulevard of Dreams"

After the prosecutor had summed up the case against their father, and there could be no doubt in anyone's mind, not even their own, about the horrific fact that he really had killed their mother, Roby and Chris, ages 20 and 19, respectively, were thinking the same thing: Their lives were a lie. They had always been envied, admired, and privileged. They had had money and a perfect family. "How much in love with each other they'd all seemed. . . . The all-American family. The American Dream that came true."[13]

The sons now knew the truth—that their father, Rob, a spectacularly successful New Jersey life insurance salesman, had indeed arranged for professional assassins from Louisiana to come up on the night of September 7, 1984, to Atlantic City; that he had arranged the same night to drive his wife, Maria, to dinner at Harrah's in his Cadillac Eldorado. After dinner and wine and some late gambling in the casino, Rob had driven his sleepy wife back toward Toms River, pulled off the parkway at the Oyster Creek picnic area to check out what he told Maria seemed to be a problem in the tire. Going out to examine the tire, he had waited for the paid executioners to steal up to the car, shoot Maria point-blank in the back, and swat Rob on the head to draw a little blood and make it look like a genuine robbery.

Rob had returned home looking strangely buoyant after his trauma, striking one detective as behaving more like a man ready to go out sailing on his yacht than someone who had just lost his wife. Marshall had reason to feel a large burden had been lifted from his shoulders: He now stood to collect approximately $1.5 million from the insurance policy he had taken out on Maria, more than enough to clear $200,000 in gambling debts that he owed in Atlantic City and to set himself up handsomely for his next steps on the ladder of the American Dream. He could pay off the mortgage, buy new cars for himself and each of his boys, and indulge in a whirlwind romance with his sexy mistress.

Rob Marshall had good cause to feel that the police would not come after him. When Gene, his brother-in-law and a lawyer, pointed out that it did not look especially good that Rob was deep in debt and stood to gain such a huge insurance payment, Rob responded that the police could not possibly suspect him: "I'm much too high up the civic ladder. My reputation in the community, in fact, places me beyond reproach."[14]

He was right about one thing: The police themselves called Rob, a very successful businessman in an affluent neighborhood, a "pillar" of the community. Back in the early 1970s, Rob had quickly proved himself a sensational salesman, selling more than $2 million in life insurance in his first year; in his second, he was again among the top fifty Provident Mutual Life salespeople in the country. Rob and his family had moved into a big house, and he had driven around town in a flashy red Cadillac. Rob had also scored big in his private life, capturing Maria, a Philadelphia Main Line doctor's daughter who was exquisitely beautiful.[15]

There was not much doubt about how Rob had gotten so far so fast. The man was driven, being the most aggressive salesperson Toms River had ever seen. Kevin Kelly, the prosecutor who had once bought insurance from Rob, said Rob pushed through the deal while half his hamburger was still on his plate and his car engine was still hot in the parking lot. "The guy could fit in three or four lunches a day, the way he hustled."

Over the course of his nationally publicized trial, later celebrated in the TV miniseries *Blind Faith* (1990), Rob's shameless behavior confirmed the nefarious picture of a sociopathic, greed–soaked personality painted by the prosecutor. In the first few weeks after the murder, Rob could barely conceal his excitement about his new freedom, not only making quick moves to get his hands on the insurance money but also charming at least three different women into his wife's bed, even before he had figured out how to dispose of her remains.

Prosecutor Kevin Kelly summed up Rob's personality: He's "self-centered, he's greedy, he's desperate, he's materialistic, and he's a liar. . . . [H]e will use anybody, he will say anything, and he will do anything—including use his own family—to get out from under." Rob "loves no one but himself."[16] Kelly was not greatly exaggerating, but what he knew and did not say was that many of the same epithets could be applied to many other Toms River residents. The fact is, as one native observed, Rob was in many ways not very different from his neighbors. Rob's case, one resident wrote, was compelling precisely because there was an intimate connection between "the town's collective values and the story of Rob and Maria Marshall." Indeed, the spotlight on Rob—and the community's obsession with the trial—stemmed from the fact that it helped to bring into sharp definition what the community, and increasingly the entire country, was really about.[17]

Toms River in the 1970s was a preview of the mad rush to make money in the go-go culture of the Reagan 1980s, the high-tech and stock boom of the 1990s, and the high-rolling Wall Street culture in the 2000s. The town was full of people in a hurry, many of them like the Marshalls, recent immigrants to the town who were scurrying to cash in on one of the biggest housing booms on the New Jersey shore. Ocean County was the second-fastest-growing county in the country, which caused real estate values to soar and triggered big business opportunities. The mostly blue-collar and lower-middle-class migrants who flocked to Toms River caught the fantastic entrepreneurial fever. Everyone in Toms River was suddenly making deals, and limits on the money to be made evaporated.

Rob, a number of commentators observed, was remarkably tuned in to the spirit of his times. The commercials about getting yours and getting it now were ringing in his ears. "See, all around Rob," one old friend said, "everybody was scoring everything: sex, dope, big-money deals. At least, he thought so."[18] If those young kids out of business school could be making their first million on Wall Street before they were 30, Rob was missing something he deserved. As his success grew, so did his aspirations, his sense of deprivation, and his gambling debts. Like the nation as a whole, Rob planned to leverage himself into a real fortune.

Yet if the resonance between Rob and the collective values of his time was electric, most people in Toms River and Atlantic City were not murdering their wives to cover their debts and advance one more step up the ladder. Rob was different, but mainly because he personified so purely and acted out so unrestrainedly the hungers driving his neighbors. Others were dreaming the same big American Dream. But Rob was completely engulfed by it, his personality a machine perfectly dedicated to "making it." Rob was abnormal because the American Dream that was becoming the new standard had penetrated every fiber of his being, purging all traces of the emotional or moral sensibilities that restrained his neighbors. Rob's aggressiveness was startling even in an age of hustlers, his narcissism more extreme than that of most of his fellow travelers in the "Me Generation," and in an age of moral decline, his conscience was exceptionally elastic.

Undoubtedly, Rob's "abnormality" had roots in his past—perhaps in the Depression, which had ruined his family and turned his father into an alcoholic; perhaps in his chronic sense of being an outsider, having moved at least 10 times before he was 16. But if Rob had not murdered his wife, he would never have come under the psychiatric microscope, because his extreme traits were exactly those that people on the way up were supposed to exhibit—to propel them to the top. For 15 years, Rob's "abnormality" had helped make him the biggest success in his community.

Rob got into trouble only because his dreams finally outstripped his own formidable capacities. He probably would not have killed Maria if he had not fallen so deeply into debt, and he might not have gotten into such debt if he had not been lured by the bigger dreams and looser moral sensibilities that his friends said had gotten under his skin and then possessed him. The reckless and grandiose entrepreneurial culture of Toms River that had swept across America released the extremes in Rob's personality, nurturing his sense of himself as a legend in his own time, free to make his own rules and look after number one first. When he got into deep financial trouble, values and a culture that might have restrained him were not in place, and his deep-seated potential for wilding was unleashed.

Them and Us: Violence and the Oversocialized American Character

Utter shock that anyone could indifferently wipe out a wife, husband, mother, or child for money is linked with a sliver of recognition that there is something familiar about these killers. "The first thing people want to know," Alison Bass wrote in the *Boston Globe*, is "how could anyone so carefully and coolly plan the murder of a wife, a child, anyone?"[19] But the second, usually subliminal, question is, "Could my spouse do it?" or, even more subliminally, "Could I?"

Do ultimate wilders tell us something important about ourselves and our society, or are they just bizarre sideshows? Reassuring responses come from many commentators, such as psychiatrist Dr. Charles Ford, who believes that although people such as Rob Marshall, Scott Peterson, Hans Reiser, Charles Stuart, and Pamela Smart "on the surface look very normal," they are suffering from either mental illness or deep-seated "character disorders" such as narcissism or sociopathy, that radically differentiate "them" from "us."[20] Criminologists James Alan Fox and Jack Levin describe sociopaths such as Scott Peterson, Hans Reiser, and Charles Stuart as people who "blend in well and function appropriately" but are "far from normal." Criminologists explain that sociopaths "know the right thing to do" in order to emulate the rest of us; they are consummate actors: "Sociopaths lie, manipulate, and deceive. They are good at it. Like actors, they play a role on the stage of life."[21]

When they murder, ultimate wilders clearly act differently from the majority of the population, but the clinical accounts of their character disorders do not provide a persuasive argument for the difference between "them" and "us," and make reassurances by psychological professionals ring hollow. The bible of psychiatry, the *Diagnostic and Statistical Manual of Mental Disorders*, describes *narcissistic personality disorder* as "[t]he tendency to exploit others to achieve one's own ends, to exaggerate achievements and talents, to feel entitled to and to crave constant attention and adulation."[22] Criminologists Fox and Levin define sociopaths as "self-centered, manipulative, possessive, envious, reckless, and unreliable. They demand special treatment and inordinate attention, often exaggerating their own importance. . . . On their way to the top, sociopaths ruthlessly step over their competitors without shame or guilt." These are common human faults, and Fox and Levin acknowledge that they are widespread among Americans. In trying to predict when the difference between "them" and "us" emerges, Fox and Levin end up in another conundrum, for they acknowledge that most sociopaths rarely reach the point "at which they feel it necessary to kill. Most of them live ordinary lives." [23]

It is time for sociologists to adopt the idea of a "sociopathic society," a concept as useful for understanding wilding as a sick psyche.[24] A sociopathic society is one, like that of the Ik, marked by a collapse of moral order that is the result of the breakdown of community and the failure of institutions responsible for inspiring moral vision and creating and enforcing robust moral codes. In such a society, the national character-type tends toward sociopathy, and idealized behavior, although veiled in a rhetoric of morality, becomes blurred with antisocial egoism. The founders of modern sociology, especially Émile Durkheim, as noted in Chapter 1, worried that modernity threatened to turn the most developed industrial cultures into sociopathic cauldrons of raw egoism and anomie, and they conceived of the sociological enterprise as an effort to understand how societies could find their moral compass and preserve themselves in the face of the sociopathic threat.

The concept of a sociopathic society is explained differently by Marx's analysis of capitalism. In contrast to Durkheim's idea of anomie and the breakdown of institutions and social rules, Marx argues that it is the increasingly powerful institutions and rules of capitalism themselves that tend to become more sociopathic over time. As competition and financial markets force corporations to squeeze worker wages and replace jobs with robots, as discussed in Chapter 6, survival for much of the population becomes a daily struggle, breeding an Ik-like propensity for extreme wilding. At the same time, extreme wealth at the top incites greed and envy, leading many to embrace the norms of doing whatever is necessary to get rich, a reflection of corporate and Wall Street values and behavior.[25]

In sociopathic societies, a clinical effort to dissect the sociopathic personality cannot be separated from an analysis of national character and ideology, as well as the economic and political regime. Rob Marshall, Scott Peterson, Hans Reiser, Charles Stuart, and Pamela Smart may be deranged, but their derangement mirrors a national disorder. The official religion of the free market sanctifies sociopathy in the guise of individual initiative, entrepreneurship, and "making it." As the American Dream becomes a recipe for wilding, clinicians and criminologists need to deepen their sociological understanding, or they will continue to misread Marshall, Peterson, Reiser, Stuart, and Smart as a failure of socialization rather than a pathology of oversocialization. Marshall internalized too deeply the core American values of competitiveness and material success, discarding any other values that might interfere with personal ambitions. Marshall, Peterson, Reiser, Stuart, Smart, and other ultimate wilders are most interesting as prisoners of the same American Dream that compels the rest of us, but which does not consume us with quite the same intensity.

☐ Then and Now: An American Tragedy

In 1925, *An American Tragedy*, by Theodore Dreiser, was published. One of the country's great works of literature, it is about a young man, Clyde Griffiths, who plots to kill his pregnant girlfriend, Roberta, so that he can take up with a woman who is rich and well connected. The story is based on a real murder committed in 1906 by Chester Gillette, a New Yorker who drowned his pregnant girlfriend in order to be free to pursue a woman in high society. The striking resemblance of Dreiser's protagonist to contemporary men in a hurry such as Charles Stuart and Rob Marshall, suggests that wilding, even ultimate wilding, is not new. But if the parallels tell us something important about the deep historical roots of American wilding, there are also noteworthy contrasts that hint at how the virus has mutated for the worse.

Like Rob Marshall, Clyde was an authentic prisoner of the American Dream (as, presumably, was the real Chester Gillette, for as H. L. Mencken notes, Dreiser stayed "close to the facts and came close to a literal reporting"). When Dreiser described Clyde as "bewitched" by wealth, as a personification of desire for all the glitter and beauty that money can buy, he could also have been describing Marshall. Indeed, Dreiser saw young Clyde as so vulnerable to the seductive temptations that surrounded him, so helpless in the face of the material pleasures just beyond his reach, that Dreiser asked whether the real guilt for the crime lay not with Clyde but with the culture that had debased him. Perhaps future novelists or historians will instructively engage the same question about Rob Marshall, whose vulnerability to modern capitalist seduction is one of the most poignant aspects of his story.

Dreiser selected the Gillette case, as critic Lawrence Hussman informs us, because he considered it "typical enough to warrant treatment as particularly American." Dreiser recognized that whatever psychological pathology was involved could be understood only in the context of a diagnosis of the health of American society and an inquiry into the moral ambiguity of the American Dream. *An American Tragedy* was compelling to millions of Americans in the 1920s because it held up a mirror in which they could see their collective reflection. The novel's success suggests that there was something of Clyde in many Americans of his era, which tells us how deeply the wilding virus had already insinuated itself into American life. Indeed, as early as the robber baron era of the late 1800s, the wilding streak in American culture had become too obvious to ignore, a matter of preoccupation for satirist Mark Twain, philosopher Henry David Thoreau, and critic Lincoln Steffens.[26]

Yet if Dreiser's work suggests that wilding defines a continuity, not a break, in American life, it also hints at how things have changed. Unlike Rob Marshall, Clyde could not actually go through with his diabolical scheme. After becoming obsessed with plans to kill his girlfriend, he lures her into a canoe with the intent of drowning her, but, whether out of weakness or moral compunction, he cannot do it. His problem is solved only because she accidentally falls into the water, along with Clyde himself. Clyde does not try to save her, partly because he is afraid that her thrashing about will drown him, too, but that is quite different from deliberate murder. Perhaps in the America of 1925 it was still not credible to Dreiser or his audience that anyone could actually carry out such a crime, although the real Chester Gillette was only one of a number of such accused killers in the first quarter of the twentieth century. While such murders still shock the public, Americans today, according to pollsters, not only believe that such crimes can be committed but, as noted earlier, worry whether their spouses, or they themselves, could succumb to the impulse.

That the constraints on wilding may have weakened over the last 75 years is suggested further by the centrality of the theme of guilt and moral responsibility in Dreiser's work. Clyde is a morally weak character, but he is not entirely devoid of conscience. After Roberta's death, Clyde is not able to absolve himself of responsibility because he is plagued by the question of whether he was guilty of not trying to save her. In contrast, the most extraordinary aspect of Rob Marshall is his apparent lack of remorse. Friends of Rob Marshall, Pamela Smart, and Charles Stuart commented on how well they looked after the killings; it was widely reported that they all seemed happier and better adjusted after their violent deeds and never appeared to suffer even twinges of conscience.

Dreiser's *An America Tragedy* is ultimately an indictment of the American Dream. The "primary message of the book," Lawrence Hussman reminds us, concerns the "destructive materialistic goals" that obsess Clyde and drive him to his murderous plot. Dreiser refused to accept that the evil could be explained away by Clyde's moral weakness or some presumed individual psychopathology; it was only the inability to question "some of the basic assumptions on which American society is based" that could lead anyone to that line of thinking. Dreiser himself concluded that Clyde had to be held morally accountable but that society was the ultimate perpetrator of the crime. He implicitly instructed his readers that such American tragedies would recur until the country finally triumphed over its obsessions with materialism and ego and rediscovered its moral compass.

Dreiser's musings on the American Dream remain stunningly relevant today, and the book is an eerie prophecy of current cases of wilding. But if Dreiser saw how the American Dream of his era could beget extreme individual wilding, he could not have foreseen the historical developments that have made the dream a recipe for a wilding epidemic. In Dreiser's day, the "American Century" was dawning on a glorious future; the prosperity of the 1920s was a harbinger of a new era of plenty in which all Americans could reasonably look forward to their share of an apparently endlessly expanding pie. Despite the dark side of the materialistic preoccupation, which divided people as they competed for the biggest slices, the Dream also brought Americans together, for as long as the pie was growing, everybody could win.

It took a new age of limits and decline, during which growing numbers of Americans would see their share of the pie shrinking and others see it permanently removed from the table, to set the stage for a full-blown wilding epidemic. Dreiser saw a foreshadowing of this in the Great Depression, which turned him toward socialism. But America pulled together in the 1930s, and the wilding virus was kept largely in check, as crime rates declined and neighbors, fellow workers, and communities cooperated to support one another, drawing on the help of a sympathetic federal government. It would take a very different set of economic and political reversals, half a century later, to fuel the kind of wilding epidemic that Dreiser vaguely anticipated but never experienced.

It is apt testimony to Dreiser, as well as to the ferocious spread of the epidemic he could only dimly envisage, to mention in conclusion the rapidly growing crowd of modern-day Chester Gillettes. Charles Stuart is one of the most remarkable Gillette "look-alikes," not only because he killed his pregnant wife but because, like Chester, he was from a working-class background and had disposed of his wife because she had become an impediment to his upward mobility. Stuart, of course, trumped Gillette's achievement by collecting several hundred thousand dollars in insurance money.

[ ] Susan Smith: Infanticide and the Honor Student

Susan Smith, now serving a life sentence in prison, hauntingly evokes *An American Tragedy*'s main character and theme. Smith is the young mother from Union, South Carolina, who confessed to strapping her two young sons—Michael, age 3, and Alex, age 14 months—into their car seats in her Mazda and driving the car onto a boat ramp leading into John D. Long Lake. She watched as the vehicle rolled into the water, carrying her two trusting infants to a grave at the bottom of the lake. The car sank slowly, still floating as the infants cried plaintively for their mother, who had run off to give her alibi to police. Because Smith initially told police that the children had been kidnapped by a gun-toting black man, reporters compared her to Charles Stuart, who had concocted a similar racist story to throw off Boston police. Like Stuart, Smith triggered a national firestorm of self-examination. Americans everywhere wondered how a hardworking, church-going, honor society graduate in South Carolina's "City of Hospitality" could commit such a horrifying double murder.

Pundits and politicians offered their own explanations, including former Speaker of the U.S. House of Representatives Newt Gingrich, who at the time of the killings on October 25, 1994, was one of the most powerful politicians in America. Gingrich said the Smith murders showed "the sickness of our society" and were a "reason to vote Republican." But Gingrich, once a history professor, should have noticed the resemblance of Smith to Chester Gillette and realized that both Smith and Gillette had deeply imbibed the intensely individualistic version of the American Dream that Gingrich was selling.[27]

The relevance of Dreiser's novel and the American Dream to the Smith saga began with Smith's mother, Linda Sue, who in 1977 divorced her first husband, a blue-collar worker named Harry Ray Vaughan, to marry a stockbroker. Vaughan, Susan Smith's father, committed suicide a year after Linda Sue had left him to "marry up."

Susan Smith's romantic ambitions resembled her mother's and are intimately tied to the murders. Shortly before the killings, Smith had separated from her own blue-collar husband and had started to date Tom Findlay, the wealthy son of a corporate raider. Tom's father owned the textile factory where Susan worked as a secretary. Smith was struggling financially, living on $125 a week of child support and a $325 weekly salary; she found it hard to meet the $344 monthly payments on her red brick house. Susan dreamed of marrying Tom, who lived in a plush mansion called "the Castle." Tom, who was known to secretaries in the office as "the Catch," was feverishly pursued by many local women, and he complained to one friend not long before the killing, "Why can't I meet a nice single woman? Everyone at work wants to go out with me because of my money. But I don't want a woman with children—there are so many complications."[28]

Police regard the triggering event as the letter Tom sent to Susan on October 18, in which he broke off their relationship, explaining that he "did not want the responsibility of children." Susan got painful evidence of Tom's seriousness about leaving and enjoying a less encumbered life when, only hours before she killed the children who had become the obstruction to her dreams, she found Tom in a bar flirting with three pretty single women.

After her confession, speculation in Union was rife that she did it for the money. In her confession, she wrote that she was depressed because of her financial problems and that Findlay's rejection meant the loss not only of love but also of the wealthiest man in the county. Police believed that Smith's desperation "to jump from the listing boat of the working class" appeared to be "a major motive" for her crime.[29]

There are haunting similarities with the Dreiser story, down to the detail of drowning as the way to free oneself for marrying up. Like Gillette, Susan and her mother both saw marriage as their path to the American Dream. Known in high school as the most "all-American," Susan found it too painful to see her dream slip away. Wealthy Tom Findlay was the ticket, and Susan saw no way to keep him other than killing her own children.

Susan Smith and the whole rogues' gallery of modern-day Dreiser characters are just the tip of the iceberg, not only of the larger wilding epidemic but also of the roster of ultimate wilders, male and female, rich and poor. What is striking is not just the numbers, but the percentage of these ultimate wilders who were frequently described by friends, associates, and the police as all-American types. They defied the suspicion of many because they so purely embodied the qualities and the success that Americans idealize. Most Americans, of course, do not become killers, but as we see in the next chapter, an epidemic of lesser wilding has consumed much of popular culture and marks the lives of millions of ordinary Americans.

Discussion Questions

1. Can an extreme wilder, one who kills a spouse for money, be sane?

2. Can an extreme wilder, one who kills a spouse for money, be carrying out some aspect of the American Dream?

3. What is the difference between seeing wilding as "undersocialization" and "oversocialization?" Why does Derber focus on oversocialization?

4. How common is extreme wilding in the United States?

5. Could you ever engage in an act of extreme wilding?

[three]

Cheaters, Liars, and Survivors
Wilding Culture in the Media, Sports, and on College Campuses

This whole world is wild at heart and weird on top.

—"Lula" in *Wild at Heart*, 1990

Bizarre cases of everyday wilding have become commonplace. On February 4, 2009, a white masked man wielding a Klingon bat'leth steel sword, familiar from the *Star Trek* series, robbed two 7-11 stores in Colorado Springs, Colorado.[1] In January 2009, police in Lenexa, Kansas, reported a string of "early morning drop-off day care robberies," where robbers stole purses left in the car for a couple of minutes as mothers said goodbye to their kids. Police said the trend of perfectly timed drop-off robberies had spread to nearby cities.[2]

The cases over the last decade have often been uglier and more violent. In September 2000, five teenagers in Queens, New York, were arrested for ordering take-out food from a Chinese restaurant and allegedly bludgeoning the owner to death when he personally delivered the order. They had no grudge against the owner; they had killed, police said, for a free meal of shrimp egg foo yung and chicken with broccoli.[3] A few months later in Reading, Massachusetts, near Boston, one hockey dad assaulted and killed another, the latest in a string of attacks across the country by fathers against coaches, players, and other parents. On December 4, 2000, Shirley Henson, 41, from a suburb of Birmingham, Alabama, was sentenced to a 13-year jail sentence after shooting to death another driver, Gina Foster, a 34-year-old mother of three, in an infamous incident of road rage.[4] On June 24, 2003, Anna Gitlin, 25, who was angry about being held up in traffic after a fatal accident in Weymouth, Massachusetts, yelled at a police officer, "I don't care who [expletive] died. I'm more important." She was later charged with attempted murder of the officer when her car struck him, putting him in the hospital.[5]

As discussed in Chapter 1, the majority of Americans have been touched but not consumed by such extreme wilding and continue to struggle honorably to maintain their integrity. But powerful cultural forces, discussed in this chapter, coming in the context of a declining economy, are a toxic brew poisoning everyday life and threatening to worsen the wilding epidemic. The pushers of dreams, the creators of "Americana," are feverishly selling the high-roller version of the American Dream in movies, magazines, and videos, and American universities are selling their own version of careerism and material success. While Americans are being willingly seduced, swimming in exquisitely alluring images of the pleasures only money can buy, money itself is getting harder to come by for a large percentage of the population. This contradiction between the glamorous life on the screen and the contrasting opportunities of real life has the potential to spread the epidemic deeply into the "second America" that, until now, has kept it at bay.

☐ Survival: Reality TV and the Ik-ing of America

If the ratings are to be believed, millions of us are addicted to reality TV. *Survivor* was the pioneer and iconic reality show featuring wilding as a way of life. It attracted 50 million viewers in the final episode of its first season,[6] and copycat shows like *Big Brother*, and Donald Trump's *The Apprentice*, followed by his sequel, *Celebrity Apprentice*, have also been very popular.

Richard Hatch, the first winner of *Survivor*, symbolizes the fundamentals of reality TV. *Survivor* itself is an enduring template for a reality television approach, mirroring the national culture of ruthless competition and survival. Hatch never concealed his intention to win the million-dollar prize by remaining completely emotionally detached from everyone else. While others might have found it difficult to repress real feelings for other players, Hatch was the consummate strategist and schemer. Drawing on his skills as a management consultant, he seemed to build alliances effortlessly with other participants while plotting to dispense with each of them. But on January 6, 2005, Hatch was convicted of tax evasion for not reporting the $1 million he won on the show, and on May 16, 2006, he was sentenced to 51 months in jail. Hatch served over 3 years in prison and was released to home confinement on May 14, 2009.[7] Hatch's alleged wilding in the real world seems like a criminal extension of his reality show wilding.[8]

The subtext of *Survivor* is that if you want to survive and make large amounts of money, you have to learn how to manipulate people even as you partner with them. The manipulation is ruthless, since it requires throwing people off of the island—a kind of mirroring on TV of the culture of downsizing that prevails in U.S. business. Robert Allen, the CEO of AT&T who laid off 70,000 workers while raising his own salary by millions, said that he "felt good about himself" because he was just looking after business—and succeeding.[9] All *Survivor* participants have to buy into a similar premise: that it is necessary to cultivate strategies for eliminating others on the team while plotting a path of success. Inflicting harm on your own teammates becomes not only essential but also virtuous.

On September 18, 2013, a new series, *Survivor: Blood and Water*, premiered, offering new wilding twists and representing the 27th season of the still popular CBS show. Further, a variety of other shows contain the same elements of *Survivor*, including *Fear Factor*, NBC's effort to compete, which features degrading competitive acts, masquerading as sports stunts, that threaten the lives of the competitors. Meanwhile, *Shark Tank* features venture capital investors, dubbed "sharks" because they are vicious as they consider entrepreneurial business ideas from contestants. The show is said to vividly depict "the desperation and pain experienced by victims of a broken-down economy."[10] The scene of desperate people up against other desperate or ruthless people who will do anything to survive and make money seems the formula for success, with such wilding on television mirroring the real world. TV creates a virtual culture that imitates the wilding culture of the Ik. The only way to survive on *Survivor* is to act like an Ik—that is, to find a way to cheat and ultimately dispose of everyone around you. Among the Ik, this is necessary because everyone is a competitor for the food one needs to stay alive—and, therefore, it's kill or be killed. On *Survivor*, the survival strategy is essentially the same because the producers wrote the rules that way. Why does this scenario get such high ratings in the richest country in history? Suffice it to say, *Survivor* sells because it mirrors a survival strategy that millions of Americans have embraced.

Lost, House, The Shield, Breaking Bad, and *House of Cards*: TV Wilding and Ruthless Men

"Three people on that island have been killed in cold blood, and they're 'good people' who you're rooting for every week," says Paul Scheer, a 29-year-old fan of the popular ABC series *Lost*. The show includes some rough men who end up on an island after a plane crash, battling for survival. But it is even rougher than the reality show version. One of *Lost's* main protagonists, Sawyer, is an alcoholic narcissist who has no sympathy for Michael, another character who is trying to find his kidnapped son. Sawyer offers the show's moral code: "It's every man for hisself."[11]

Networks like Spike TV, owned by Viacom, interviewed thousands of American males to see what they want to watch on television. The answer is characters like Vic McKay in *The Shield*, who shoots a corrupt fellow officer directly in the face. The actor playing McKay, Michael Chiklis, won an Emmy for his performance in that episode, which received the highest audience rating in the history of the FX network.[12]

Spike TV producers have responded quickly to the demand for sociopathic male heroes. There is Michael Scofield in *Prison Break*, who plots to help his brother escape from jail. Dr. Gregory House, in the show bearing his name, revels in popping drugs like Vicodin. Vic McKay, in *The Shield*, is happy to brutalize suspects in his custody. The code of the actors in all of these programs, according to Brent Hoff, 36, another fan of *Lost*, is, "Life is hard. Men gotta do what men gotta do, and if some people have to die in the process, so be it."[13] Such characters are becoming staples on the TV landscape. Denis Leary, in *Rescue Me*, plays Tommy Gavin, a firefighter who helps plan the revenge murder of a man who had run over and killed Gavin's son. Gary Randall, a producer who helped create *Melrose Place*, is currently developing a show for Spike TV called *Paradise Salvage*, also starring antiheroes with wilding sensibilities. Randall says that the networks are creating these antisocial stars to get men in touch "with our Neanderthal, animalistic, macho side," in an era when men are supposed to be both more sensitive and more aggressive. The antiheroes help men deal with their internal conflicts and feel better: "You think, 'It's O.K. to go to a strip club and have a couple of beers with your buddies and still go home to your wife and baby and live with yourself.'"[14]

Scheer, the *Lost* fan, who is an actor himself, says that realistic portrayals on television today do not make traditional moral judgments, even about extreme violence. "You don't have to be defined by one act," he says, even if it is murder. Referring to the three people killed on the island in *Lost*, he concludes, "You can say 'I'm messed up and I left my wife, but I'm still a good guy.'"[15] Journalist Warren St. John, whose writing I have drawn upon extensively in this section, notes that the new male heroes are obviously different from earlier good guys like Magnum or Barnaby Jones. "They are also not simply flawed in the classic sense: men who have the occasional affair or who tip the bottle a little too much. Instead," notes St. John, "they are unapologetic about killing, stealing, hoarding and beating their way to achieve personal goals."[16]

Many other shows, such as *Breaking Bad* and *Dexter*, have succeeded with a similar grim view of male survivalism and sociopathy. *Breaking Bad*, which received much critical acclaim and ended its final season in September 2013, featured a high school chemistry teacher, Walter White, diagnosed with terminal cancer, who turns to a life of crime selling meth as a way of making a lot of money before he dies, initially to protect his family. But his persona becomes increasingly dark and sociopathic over time, with the show's creator, Vince Gilligan, saying his protagonist was becoming so morally questionable that "it was going to be a relief not to have Walt in my head anymore."[17] Bryan Cranston, the actor who played White, echoes the sentiment, saying, "I think Walt's figured out it's better to be the pursuer than the pursued. He's well on his way to badass."[18]

Over ten million people watched the final episode of *Breaking Bad*, desperate to know what Walt would do and what he was really all about. From the beginning he had told his family that, "no matter how it may look, I only had you in my heart." All his evil deeds were altruistic, for love of wife and kids. But at the end, in that iconic last episode, Walt told the truth: "I did it for me. I liked it . . . I was good at it. I was really . . . I was alive."[19]

Breaking Bad won the 2013 Emmys biggest prize for Outstanding Drama and was acclaimed as one of the greatest televisions shows ever. But what were Americans celebrating? Was it the show's willingness to show the culture for what it was: a wilding culture disguised in the myth of family values? Was *Breaking Bad* telling Americans what they needed to hear? That despite all the rhetoric about American exceptionalism, Americans were becoming exceptional mainly in their ability to carry out sociopathic acts as the way to feel alive and live out a newly dark American Dream?

Frank Underwood, the ruthless politician at the center of the blockbuster Netflix original series *House of Cards*, may be the ultimate male television symbol of this frightening American Dream. Underwood, played by Kevin Spacey, takes extreme wilding into the White House, turning the vice president into a schemer even more ruthless than Walt White in *Breaking Bad*.

House of Cards is one of the most widely watched and discussed television series of all time, with some of its most avid fans being Bill Clinton and Barack Obama, who confessed to admiring the ruthless pragmatism of Spacey's sociopathic character. "I wish things were that ruthlessly efficient," Obama said in December 2013. "I was looking at Kevin Spacey, I was thinking, 'Man, this guy is getting a lot of stuff done.'" Spacey, who said that his character was not that far from the reality of Washington, joked that Obama had "Frank Underwood envy."[20]

There's nothing funny, though, about Underwood's wilding in Washington. In the first season of the show, Underwood is the Majority Whip in the House of Representatives, who takes down anyone in his way as he lusts for power. He is an expert at manipulating and intimidating, the ultimate political bully with no remorse. He even murders Peter Russo, a congressman who becomes a threat to his ambitions, whispering to the semi-conscious Russo as he asphyxiates him, "There is no solace above or below. Only us—small, solitary, striving, battling one another. I pray to myself, for myself."[21]

Underwood later murders Zoe Barnes, an ambitious young journalist who agrees to a Faustian bargain of sex for information. Zoe learns too much about the Russo murder. Pushing her to her death onto the tracks of an oncoming subway train that crushes her, Underwood says, in an epigram reflecting his wilding philosophy of life: "For those of us climbing to the top of the food chain, there can be no mercy. There is but one rule: Hunt or be hunted."[22]

House of Cards focuses on the personal rather than the policy wilding of politicians, petty but brutal recriminations against individuals rather than policy decisions—such as decisions to go to war in places like Iraq—that cause far more death and societal harm. In this sense, the program is itself a form of wilding since it distracts the audience from the major ways in which the government is committing economic and political wilding as discussed in later chapters. Nonetheless, it highlights the sociopathic personal amorality that passes for the ticket to power and fortune in Washington and the rest of the nation.

The embrace of *House of Cards* by presidents, as well as millions of Americans, suggests the subtle ways that extreme wilding has seeped into American culture. The nation's leaders can be credibly constructed as ultimate wilders. We can fantasize our own personal wilding by connecting with Underwood, even if we won't engage in Underwood-style homicide. We see leaders such as Underwood as mirrors of ourselves, antiheroes as heroes.

Young and Wild: Drinking, Cheating, and Other Campus Sports

The young, including millions of students, are among the more flamboyant wilders in America. They are the most vulnerable to the slings and arrows of economic fortune, and some are an ominous harbinger of America's future.

My impression as a teacher is that a large percentage of today's college students remain generous and decent, although increasingly confused and torn between "making it" and remaining faithful to their moral ideals. Unfortunately, many sacrifice their intellectual loves to make big money, such as the student with a profound passion for the study of history who decided to give it up and become a corporate lawyer so that he could live the high life.

Growing student cynicism, as the cost of college goes scarily up and the job market sinks, is helping create a rising tide of wilding on campuses across the country, a phenomenon that started nearly 20 years ago. A report by the Carnegie Foundation for the Advancement of Teaching released in 1990, but still relevant today, found that "a breakdown of civility and other disruptive forces" is leaving campus life "in tatters." Of special concern was an epidemic of cheating, as well as a mushrooming number of racial attacks, rapes, and other hate crimes. Words, the currency of the university, have increasingly been "used not as the key to understanding, but as weapons of assault."[23]

Campuses are no longer ivy-walled sanctuaries but are increasingly becoming sites of shootings, theft, sexual assault, property damage, and other crimes. Some incidents are infamous massacres, such as the one at Virginia Tech discussed below. Most campus crimes are not massacres, but they include thousands of shootings or rapes and many more property crimes. In 2011, the FBI reported 2,696 violent crimes and 87,160 property crimes on U.S. campuses. A study of campuses with over 10,000 students showed that the most violent schools were, surprisingly, among the most highly academically rated. The five most violent were UCLA (first), followed respectively by University of California, Berkeley; Duke; Florida A & M; and Vanderbilt. In 2011, despite a decline from the previous year, UCLA suffered about 70 violent crimes and almost 1,000 property crimes, including "12 forcible rapes; 11 robberies; 17 aggravated assaults; 195 burglaries; 625 larcenies; 18 motor vehicle thefts; and three incidents of arson."[24]

The epidemic of alcoholism among students—70 percent qualify as binge drinkers at some colleges—has contributed to these rising crime rates. A study of 104 campuses conducted by the Harvard School of Public Health identified 44 colleges in which a majority of the students were binge drinkers. On these campuses, nine out of ten students said that they had suffered assaults, thefts, or other forms of violent intrusion, often by drunk students.[25]

Much campus crime, however, is committed soberly by cold, calculating student wilders, a trend evident over the last two decades. A Harvard University student pleaded guilty in 1995 to stealing $6,838 raised at Harvard for the Jimmy Fund, a charity to help kids with cancer. Joann Plachy, a law student at Florida State University, was charged in 1995 with hiring a professional killer to murder a secretary who accused Plachy of having stolen a copy of an exam. She pleaded no contest and was convicted.[26]

On April 16, 2007, Cho Seung-Hui, 23, fatally shot 32 people in a dorm and classroom at Virginia Tech, the most lethal mass killing on a campus in U.S. history.[27] On February 8, 2008, Latina Williams, 23, opened fire in a class at Louisiana Technical College and killed two fellow students.[28] On December 8, 2011, Ross

Truett Ashley, 22, a business student at Radford University in Blacksburg, Virginia, shot and killed a police officer on the campus of Virginia Tech, later returning to the campus and committing suicide.[29] On April 7, 2012, in Oakland, California, One Goh was accused of killing seven fellow students and wounding three others at Oikos University, a small Christian college.[30] On October 31, 2012, at a Halloween party on the University of Southern California campus, an argument escalated and a student, Geno Hall, was shot seven times and critically wounded; Brandon Spencer, 20, was arrested for the crime.[31]

This murderous violence—part of a horrifying wave of school violence since 2000—was driven most often by rage among students, some mentally disturbed, who took out grudges against fellow students, professors, or administrators with the most horrific acts of expressive wilding. There are also growing numbers of reported rapes, other sexual assaults, and armed robberies on campus. On one Facebook site concerned about campus violence, Terrence C. Kemp, a student at Savannah State University, wrote: "It's already hard enough to get through college having to worry about classes and how I'm going to pay for this fee and that fee. . . . Now as students we gotta worry about not getting killed."[32]

The view of the campus as a haven from violent crime or other societal wilding is now as obsolete as the notion of the family itself being a safe haven. Ernest L. Boyer, the former Carnegie Foundation president, said that college promotional material "masks disturbing realities of student life" that mirror the "hard-edged competitive world" of the larger society.[33] Desperate for good grades, huge numbers of students routinely plagiarize papers and cheat on exams. National studies show that about 75 percent of students admit to cheating at least once during their college careers, a figure that probably underestimates the actual volume of cheating but has remained relatively steady for 20 years, although many colleges report an increasing problem.[34] Studies on many campuses, including Indiana University and the University of Tennessee, show that a majority of students admit to submitting papers written by others or copying large sections of friends' papers. A majority also confess to looking at other students' answers during in-class exams. "You could check for cheating in any class and you'd certainly find a significant portion of the people cheating," one M.I.T. student said, adding casually, "It's one way of getting through M.I.T."[35]

One of the most widely publicized cheating cases happened at Harvard in 2012. Of the 279 Harvard undergraduate students who were signed up for a course called "Introduction to Congress," 125 were investigated for cheating by "collaborating" on the take-home final exam. In 2013, Harvard announced that more than half of those investigated were found guilty or admitted to cheating and were forced to withdraw. A Harvard dean called the case "unprecedented in its scope and magnitude."[36]

Cheating begins early in academic careers. Mothers, fathers, and other relatives often ghostwrite their children's essays, and professional entrepreneurs are making entire careers off of the new trend. Michele Hernandez, who used to work for admissions at Dartmouth, opened a dot-com that caters to applicants who need somebody to craft a college admissions essay for them. For $1,500, she will help write and polish the essay; you can pay her $4,500 to complete your entire application.[37]

Technology, especially computers, has also made life easier for the new generation of student cheaters. Students routinely ask their friends for online copies of
old course papers. It doesn't take much effort to rework a paper on a computer for
a new class. One student at elite Boston University said that nobody on campus
thinks twice about the morality of such high-tech cheating. Students can buy term
papers online about popular texts, including *The Wilding of America*.

Wilding and the Corporatization of the University

While it is easy to blame students as irresponsible slackers or cheaters, structural
and institutional forces are at work that help explain why so many act in self-
interested or predatory ways. Students are part of society. When students cheat,
trample on others to get ahead, or steal, they are responding to new built-in
incentives and brutal survival constraints in a drastically changing academic environment. Universities are increasingly focused on money, and we are witnessing
the "corporatization of the university," as institutions of higher education become
large corporations themselves and engage in institutional wilding not unlike that
of big Wall Street banks, giant global nonfinancial companies, and the government.
Such institutional and corporate wilding is the main subject of the next several
chapters, but it deserves an introduction here because it is so intimately related to
the wilding of students, and it is a major driving force of moral decline among
youth and of the broader corruption in the schools, college sports, and popular
culture discussed in this chapter.

One tell-tale sign of universities going corporate is the astronomical salaries
they are doling out to their presidents, even as they raise tuition and complain
of rapidly escalating costs and declining revenues. Looking only at public university salaries from 2011 to 2012, *ABC News* reported that the highest paid
president was Graham Spanier, president of Penn State University, who received
total compensation of $2.9 million in the year that he had to finally resign due
to the crisis surrounding Coach Jerry Sandusky's sexual abuse scandal. Many faculty and staff believed that Spanier, while getting paid this fortune, had helped
cover up Sandusky's abuses. E. Gordon Gee, president of Ohio State University,
received more than $2 million in total compensation the same year, even as the
Ohio legislature was cutting back on university funding. Among private colleges,
where the *Chronicle of Higher Education* reported on controversial rises in university presidents' pay and perks, Bob Kerrey of the New School in New York City,
received total compensation of $3,047,000.[38] These multimillion-dollar packages
are comparable to those of many corporate CEOs of large firms, with a huge gap
between presidential pay and the wages of faculty and staff, who are often paid
poorly. A majority of college teachers are now adjuncts or other off–tenure-track
faculty, who have no job security, low wages, and little autonomy—another way
in which the corporatization of the university is unfolding and showing strong
parallels with treatment of workers in other corporate sectors.

As the pay of university presidents goes up by about five percent a year, even during budget cuts and severe public sector funding cuts, students are being squeezed by large tuition increases to help pay for their university leaders' fat salaries. Data from 2010 and 2011 showed that tuition and fees rose annually by 4.5 percent in private colleges and over eight percent at public universities. This increase was far greater than inflation. Remarkably, tuition cost has grown about 500% since 1986.[39]

The sources and consequences of these high tuition increases, in a period of declining student job opportunities, point to serious institutional wilding, much of it by the universities targeting their own students. Higher tuitions are the way universities get students to pay for the presidents' salaries and other inflated administrative pay as well as increased research and instructional costs, at the same time that state legislatures cut university budgets. To cover increasing costs and shrinking revenues, universities have decided to squeeze their students rather than take more out of ample endowments or alumni or corporate contributions, or reduce salaries of top administrators and coaches. Part of the university calculations, some scholars say, is the lack of consumer protection for students and the loans they take out, with universities exploiting opportunities—often in tandem with government or private loan companies—to take advantage of students who see the college degree as the essential credential needed for better jobs, even when those jobs may not be forthcoming and the loans may not be affordable.[40]

Rapidly rising student loans are creating a crisis in survival for millions of students, and contribute to much student wilding. Muckraking journalist Matt Taibbi wrote a piece for *Rolling Stone* in 2013 titled "Ripping Off Young America: The College Loan Scandal" that every student needs to read.[41] Taibbi offers plenty of testimonials by students, who average $27,000 in loans when they graduate and face a tough job market, about the financial disaster that student loans have created for them:

"I was 19 years old," says 24-year-old Lyndsay Green, a graduate of the University of Alabama, in a typical story. "I didn't understand what was going on, but my mother was there. She had signed, and now it was my turn. So I did." Six years later, she says, "I am nearly $45,000 in debt. . . . If I had known what I was doing, I would never have gone to college."[42]

"Nobody sits down and explains to you what it all means," says 24-year-old Andrew Geliebter, who took out loans to get what he calls "a degree in bullshit"; he entered a public-relations program at Temple University. His loan payments are now 50 percent of his gross income, leaving only about $100 a week for groceries for his family of four.[43]

Taibbi argues that students often blame themselves, something that I have also found in talking with my students about their student loans. But while students may bear some personal responsibility, Taibbi makes clear that institutional wilding by the universities and government is a major contributing cause. As he argues vividly, the students "all take responsibility for their own mistakes. They know they didn't arrive at gorgeous campuses for four golden years of boozing, balling, and bong hits by way of anybody's cattle car. But they're angry, too, and they should be. Because the underlying cause of all that later-life distress and heartache—the reason they carry such crushing, life-alteringly huge college debt—is that our university-tuition system really is exploitative and unfair, designed primarily to benefit two major actors."[44]

The first actor, or institutional wilder, Taibbi argues, are the universities them-selves and "the contractors who build their extravagant athletic complexes, hotel-like dormitories, and God knows what other campus embellishments. For these little regional economic empires, the federal student-loan system is essentially a massive and ongoing government subsidy, once funded mostly by emotionally vulnerable parents, but now increasingly paid for in the form of federally backed loans to a political constituency—low- and middle-income students—that has virtually no lobby in Washington."[45]

A particularly ruthless subset of university wilders are the for-profit universities, such as the University of Phoenix and Trump University, recently renamed the Trump Entrepreneurial Institute after challenges were made about the authenticity of Trump's seminars as certifiable university courses. For-profit universities tend to charge their students high loans, often requiring payment for 2 or 4 years of college upfront before entering the first class. Students cannot default later in life on many of these loans, even by declaring personal bankruptcy. These universities know that high majorities of their students will drop out after their first year of study, but may be saddled for life with their expensive loans. In February 2013, the University of Phoenix, the nation's largest for-profit university with about 320,000 students and scores of campuses, faced several lawsuits for improperly obtaining millions of dollars in student aid to attract students and make money for their corporate owner, the Apollo Group. Phoenix, like many for-profit schools, relies on federal support for student financial aid of—in Phoenix's case—$3.2 billion in 2012, constituting 84 percent of Phoenix's annual revenue. Accreditors—whose job is to certify that universities are in good legal and academic standing—put Phoenix on a 2-year "notice," reflecting concern about exorbitant student loans and high student dropout rates. The loan default rate on federally financed loans at Phoenix was 26 percent, more than twice that at public nonprofit universities.[46] Phoenix's graduation rate is a rock bottom 16 percent, one of the lowest in the country, leaving many students unable to get jobs despite their crippling loans.

On August 24, 2013, New York's Attorney General, Eric Schneiderman, sued Donald Trump, claiming that his Trump University, started in 2005, was a "fraud." Trump allegedly promised to make the 5000 students who signed up rich by sell-ing them the art of the business deal, but Schneiderman said: "Trump University engaged in deception at every stage of consumers' advancement through costly programs and caused real financial harm. . . .Trump University, with Donald Trump's knowledge and participation, relied on Trump's name recognition and celebrity status to take advantage of consumers who believed in the Trump brand.[47] Schneiderman claimed students got worthless certificates, with a photo of them standing next to a cutout of Donald Trump, while ending up with mountains of student debt and often no jobs.

Beyond universities, the government is the second actor and institutional wilder, contributing to the student loan crisis and student wilding. Taibbi writes that while "it's not commonly discussed on the Hill, the government actually stands to make an enormous profit on the president's new federal student-loan system, an estimated $184 billion over ten years, a boondoggle paid for by hyper-inflated tuition costs and fueled by a government-sponsored predatory-lending program that makes even the most ruthless private credit card company seem like a "Save the Panda" charity. Why is this happening? The answer lies in a sociopathic marriage of private-sector greed and government forces that will make you shake your head in wonder at the way modern America sucks blood out of its young."[48]

While the government's funding of a huge sum of student loans might seem a generous social program, a close look reveals the opposite: an institutionalized wilding scheme to generate massive government funds by indebting for life a new generation of students. Congress has made their relation with their loans as "unbreakable as herpes," preventing them from disgorging their loans even through bankruptcy, as noted above, while also restricting their ability to refinance the loans. Only a small percentage of students are even told their loan rate, according to a leading analyst, and a lot "were told lies."[49] Meanwhile, more than 38 million students owe a total of more than $1 trillion in loans, greater than the total credit card debt in the United States. The government does little to enforce strict lending standards even on fly-by-night schools because it has given itself the right to recover loans even if most students drop out long before graduation.[50]

The wilding here is a hint of the Wall Street institutionalized wilding that crashed the U.S. economy, discussed in Chapter 5. The parallels are rarely mentioned, but they are not surprising, since the "corporatization" of the university leads to money-making greed and abuse inherent in the DNA of current U.S. corporate culture and structure, whether in higher education or financial services. In university settings, though, the cultural and personal dimensions of the wilding are especially important, since institutions of higher education are expected to cultivate the values and moral sensibilities of young people. When leaders of universities enrich themselves at the expense of their students, they are setting a role model that will deform the moral character of the youth generation.

Dopey Sports: Wilding as the Great American Pastime

On May 7, 2009, the commissioner of baseball suspended famed Los Angeles Dodger slugger Manny Ramirez for 50 games after Ramirez tested positive for a drug associated with steroid use. Just a few months earlier, in February 2009, the New York Yankees' superstar Alex Rodriguez ("A-Rod") acknowledged using performance-enhancing drugs between 2001 and 2003. As names of these and other stars linked to drugs kept leaking out in 2009, it was a sad and shocking time for baseball fans everywhere. Two of the best players in the game were joining the long list of wilders who cheated to get ahead, badly staining the reputation and moral integrity of American baseball.

Worse news for baseball fans came in 2013, with the "Biogenesis scandal," that exposed more doping among top players and led to major suspensions of some of the biggest stars in baseball. In March 2013, Major League Baseball sued the Biogenesis Health Clinic, in Coral Gables, Florida, to obtain information alleging that the clinic had been soliciting or accommodating player requests for human growth hormone, a banned performance-enhancing drug.[51] Five of the game's top stars—A-Rod, Ryan Braun, Nelson Cruz, Everth Cabrera, and Jhonny Peralta—were charged with doping in association with the clinic, which closed in 2012. A-Rod and Braun were among baseball's greatest superstars and the other three were all 2013 All-Stars.

After the League's investigation, all five players, many of whom had been investigated repeatedly in earlier years for doping, were hit with suspensions, as were eight other players. All accepted their suspensions except A-Rod, who had received the most severe punishment, 211 suspended games, followed by Braun, who cannot play for 65 games. A-Rod appealed, and finally won a modest reduction of his suspension to 162 games plus no play in any 2014 post-season games. All the others were suspended for 50 games, the largest simultaneous suspension of players since 1913.[52] Baseball's disgrace, as we show later in this section, explains much about how wilding has taken root in America.[53]

Consider first that the wilding virus has also tarnished football, basketball, boxing, wrestling, track and field, ice skating, hockey, cycling, and even the Olympics. It has spread to professionals and amateurs, and to athletes of every age, from seniors to college athletes to Little Leaguers. Moreover, the wilders include not just storied players, but coaches, owners, and even umpires and referees.

The wilding behavior involves not just doping but betting on games, engineering point-shaving schemes, spying on other teams, breaking recruiting rules, faking eligibility, and engaging in violence to hurt competitors. While the players get the most attention and bear personal responsibility, the problem is systemic. It reflects the transformation of sports into big business, where big profits trump the traditional role of sports as a way to build character and fair play among the young.

The sheer variety of athletes and wilding acts is stunning. In the National Football League, the world-champion New England Patriots were caught in a 2007 "spygate" affair. The NFL fined Patriots' head coach Bill Belichick $500,000 for videotaping defensive signals of the New York Jets during a game.[54] The Patriots' wilding tarnished the performance of champions who young people and sports fans saw as heroes.

More recently, things have gotten worse in the NFL—a multibillion-dollar business. One of the dreadful examples of sports wilding is the NFL's role in denying the growing crisis of concussions in football. In October 2013, PBS's *Frontline* released "League of Denial," a searing indictment of the National Football League's role in discrediting research and concealing information about the growing epidemic of brain injuries caused by high-impact contact in the sport. The image that emerged was of the NFL as a clone of the tobacco industry, denying for decades the information that they knew about how the sport was putting players at high risk for concussions that caused neurological damage and illnesses like Parkinson's, Alzheimer's, and other dementias at an early age. The NFL worried it would lose revenue if it told players and the public about the risks and it created safety rules that would diminish the high-impact violence of football, a part of its attraction for fans. In 2013, the NFL agreed to a settlement of about $750 million to compensate some retired players who developed brain disease before age 45, but this was chump change for a league taking in $10 billion each year.[55]

Perhaps the most publicized case of doping, an act of sustained wilding, involves that of the most famous world cyclist, Lance Armstrong, who won seven fabled Tour de France competitions. After years of denying, sometimes under oath, that he doped, Armstrong finally came clean. In a January 16, 2013, televised interview with Oprah Winfrey, Armstrong finally admitted that he had used performance-enhancing drugs for years, including in all his seven Tour de France victories, and had helped create a culture where his team and the entire sport were suffused with banned drugs. The legend of him as a mythical hero was "one big lie . . . I am a flawed character."[56]

Oprah probed him about his reported attitude that he would do anything to win. He acknowledged this, but attributed some of it to his struggle to overcome his testicular cancer: "It was truly win at all costs. When I was diagnosed and I was being treated I said, 'I will do anything I have to do to survive.' And that's good. And I took that attitude—that ruthless and relentless and win-at-all-costs attitude—and I took it right into cycling, because quite frankly it followed it up almost immediately. And that's bad."[57]

In a particularly revealing segment, Armstrong said it seemed sort of scary to him now but that he had not really viewed what he was doing as cheating, because it was necessary to win, everyone was doing it, and cheating actually made the game more fair:

OW: Was it a big deal to you, did it feel wrong?
  LA: At the time? No.
OW: It did not even feel wrong?
  LA: No. Scary.
OW: Did you feel bad about it?
  LA: No. Even scarier.
OW: Did you feel in any way that you were cheating?
  LA: No. The scariest.
OW: You did not feel that you were cheating taking banned drugs?
  LA: At the time, no. And I look up—I have this exercise where, you know, because I kept hearing . . .
OW: That you're a cheat.
  LA: That I'm a drug cheat, I'm a cheat, I'm a cheater. And I went and just looked up the definition of cheat.
OW: Yes?
  LA: And the definition of cheat is to gain an advantage on a rival or foe—you know—that they don't have. I didn't view it that way. I viewed it as a level playing field."[58]

In other words, cheating was part of the implicit rules of the game, necessary to make it "a level playing field." This is highly significant, since it points to hard realities about wilding in our larger society. People see cheating as normal, even virtuous as a way of playing the game as it's supposed to be played. True, it is legally banned or discouraged in sports and much of business, but what Armstrong is telling us is that it's actually the rules of the game—the rules of our way of life subtly incentivized by the prize money and fame, and often enforced by the officials and league, even when they claim to be offended. This is crystal-clear insight into the meaning of sociopathic or wilding society, where the dominant values and unstated rules and norms are to cheat, or do whatever is necessary to win.

To understand further the root causes of today's wilding throughout the sports world, we return to professional baseball. In 2007, at the request of Major League Baseball, former Maine senator George Mitchell carried out the most comprehensive investigation of drug use in any sport. Mitchell's report shows not only how deeply wilding penetrated the sport but hints that the love of money is, indeed, the root of all evil.[59]

The drug use by A-Rod and Manny Ramirez was just the tip of the iceberg among star baseball players. Five of the 15 greatest home run hitters of all time, including Barry Bonds, Mark McGwire, Rafael Palmeiro, Rodriguez, and Ramirez, had been linked to drugs by 2008.[60] These names were detailed in the Mitchell Report, as was that of Roger Clemens, the seven-time Cy Young award winner and one of the greatest pitchers of the modern era. Mitchell lists by name scores of other tainted players, but most observers believe that many hundreds more took banned substances. Mitchell himself observes that in 2002, Ken Caminiti, the 1996 National League Most Valuable Player (MVP), estimated that "at least half" of all players in baseball used steroids.[61] In 2009, the 1988 MVP José Canseco said, "It's very simple, if you're going to get rid of all the players that are using steroids, there will be no game left."[62]

The wilding by superstars such as Bonds, Ramirez, Ortiz, and A-Rod involves a willingness to trash all of baseball for their own greed. Fred McGriff, a Hall of Famer himself who now coaches the Tampa Bay Rays, says about the doping superstars, "Even if your name gets dragged through the mud, these guys are walking away with $200 million. You deal with it, and you're still hanging out on your yacht when you're done playing." All the other players, says McGriff, are hurt through guilt by association, and even if you're a player who's played by the rules, "you can't defend yourself."[63]

Even though hundreds of more ordinary players were involved, many really had little choice. The Mitchell Report didn't exonerate the players but made clear their dilemma. "They—the players who follow the law and the rules—are faced with the painful choice of either being placed at a competitive disadvantage or becoming illegal users themselves."[64] Mitchell is pointing out the obvious: If you didn't take steroids, it was very hard to compete with those who did. The "dopers" made it extremely difficult for honest players to survive in the game. Mitchell also points out that the superstar dopers—who know they are role models to American youth—are helping fuel a steroid craze among hundreds of thousands of young Americans playing in Little League and in sandlots. If Barry Bonds or A-Rod or Manny or Ortiz take drugs, millions of kids who see them as heroes are certain to imitate them.

The Mitchell Report indicts the owners and top executives of Major League Baseball. "Obviously, the players who illegally used performance-enhancing substances are responsible for their actions. But they did not act in a vacuum. Everyone involved in baseball over the past two decades—[c]ommissioners, club officials, the Players Association, and players—shares to some extent in the responsibility for the steroids era. There was a collective failure to recognize the problem as it emerged and to deal with it early on. As a result, an environment developed in which illegal use became widespread."[65]

The steroids explosion began after a 1994 players' strike that led to a fall in attendance—and a fall in profits. Major League Baseball feared the sport could go into decline and were looking for a way back into the limelight. The rise of superstars such as Barry Bonds and Roger Clemens was a big part of the solution. When you have a hitter shattering Hank Aaron's home run lifetime tally and a pitcher topping the performance of the greatest in the game's history, fans start jamming the stadium again, wanting to be part of the action. Big profits poured in and none of the owners wanted to see them disappear.[66]

The 1990s was a go-go era of the "corporatization" of America, with virtually all institutions, from universities to churches to media to sports teams, restructuring themselves as large corporate franchises. With the superstars as irresistible magnets, and super-profitable television deals to be fashioned around star players and team brands, the teams and leagues remade themselves as giant corporations at the center of a multibillion-dollar sports entertainment empire. Even at the "amateur" level, which includes college basketball, the teams became essentially professionalized to attract money and advertising to the university and corporate sponsors. Money washed over the sports world and transformed it.

This is not to suggest that the owners colluded to give steroids to people like Bonds and Clemens. Rather, they turned a blind eye while it was becoming obvious to everyone in the sport that the use of drugs was spreading. Too much was at stake, especially for the bottom line of the corporate owners and the superstars themselves. For big money, they were willing to risk bringing down their own sport in the long term, while also sacrificing the moral authority of their players and the moral character of all the young fans. In business, the bottom line is the bottom line, reminding us of the blurry line between capitalism and wilding.

Grand Theft Auto and Doom: Video Wilding for Fun and Profit

In the wildly popular video game series *Grand Theft Auto*, players can carjack a vehicle and then run over and kill pedestrians.[67] Players can also work for a crime boss and kill rival gang members. They can even pick up a prostitute, have sex, and then murder her in order to get back their money.[68]

Grand Theft Auto III, created in 2001, was a blockbuster wilding creation. In *Grand Theft Auto: Vice City*, players join up with a Haitian or Cuban gang, then secretly team up with the other side, and use racial hate language as they enjoy murderous shoot-outs.[69] In the next sequel, *Grand Theft Auto: San Andreas*, one of the requirements to advance in the game is to murder a police officer. *Grand Theft Auto IV*, released in 2008, is filled with pimps, drug peddlers, low-life hucksters and criminals, organized crime hit men, and other violent wilders on the streets of New York. *Grand Theft Auto V*, set in LA, premiered in 2013, and, like previous series, made hundreds of millions of dollars.

Grand Theft Auto is just one of a huge number of computer and video games that are among the most popular ways to have fun in America. They are especially popular among young people, including college students.

Violence is the common denominator of the video games. Among the most violent games: *Doom*; *Grand Theft Auto: San Andreas*; *Gunslinger Girls 2*; *Half-Life 2*; *Halo 2*; *Hitman: Blood Money*; *Manhunt*; *Mortal Kombat: Deception*; *Postal 2*; and *Shadow Heart*. *Doom* is the ultimate monster murder series, based on Mars, where the player goes through hell while perfecting his strategies to kill off bloodthirsty demons.[70] *Mortal Kombat* is a martial arts series drenched with blood that rewards players with a "Fatality" move, where you get to kill a defeated opponent in a particularly savage way.

In 2009, *MadWorld* appeared, described this way by one video game blogger: "What's black and white and red all over? Your victims as they're splattered against the wall after being skewered on a lamppost. Or perhaps the answer could include disposing of your enemies in a meat grinder, or playing darts using only your opponents and a baseball bat."[71] Another video game that made this blogger's recent list of the top ten most violent video games is *Gears of War 2*, which portrays "slicing a foe with a chainsaw from the groin upward," and "us[ing] a corpse as a human shield," all with a profuse spewing of blood.[72]

The remarkable popularity of the games suggests a widespread appetite among Americans for a kind of violence that can only be characterized as full-blown wilding. The main reward in these games is the sheer thrill of brutal killing and sexual violence, forms of expressive wilding. Of course, violent themes have played out in cowboys and Indians films and other movies for a long time. What is new is the incredible savagery of the violence and the direct personal engagement that the technology makes possible. Computers and video sticks turn the spectator into the active protagonist in games like *Grand Theft Auto* or *MadWorld* so that the player becomes the perpetrator of multiple murders. The earlier spectator of cowboys and Indians films is now the actor, with virtual violence blurring the distinction between game and life.

Controversy rages whether games like *Grand Theft Auto* or *Doom*—and many more recent video game creations in 2013 featuring extreme violence and rape, such as *Tomb Raider* and *Hotline Miami*—actually incite violence or simply reflect its legitimacy and prevalence in social institutions. Either way, they can be seen as part and parcel of a wilding culture. Some studies suggest that players of the most violent games become more aggressive and violent, a matter of widespread concern after so many school shootings but also a matter of considerable debate among researchers.[73] The U.S. military has used games like *Grand Theft Auto* as a recruiting tool.[74] This approach may suggest that the military sees the games as good measures of who is likely to want to become a soldier or a good killer in real combat.

Institutions, including the military, are developing their own video games to teach recruits both skills and a worldview, according to Professor James Gee, a video game expert and professor of education at the University of Wisconsin. In the game *America's Army*, soldiers learn how to carry out combat operations. Other violent organizations, including neo-Nazi groups like National Alliance, have developed their own recruiting and training games. In the National Alliance's game, *Ethnic Cleansing*, "a player runs through a rotted city killing blacks, Latinos, and Jews." To promote critical reflection on contemporary U.S. culture, Gee says, "People ought to use *Grand Theft Auto* in the classroom to think about values and ideology."[75]

While the players are mostly engaged in expressive wilding, it's a different matter for the companies who make huge profits off the sales. Gee points out that the gaming industry makes more money than Hollywood.[76] Corporations such as Rockstar Games, which produces *Grand Theft Auto*, are less concerned with the thrills than the bottom line and financial killing, the core of instrumental wilding. Companies that sell murder and rape, particularly for the enjoyment of young people, are certainly good candidates for what I call "corporate wilding."

In the 2004 film *The Corporation*, based on a book of the same name, the creators ask how a psychiatrist would diagnose a corporation if it were a person.[77] The answer: a psychopath. Psychopaths have no moral qualms about doing harm to others to make money or get power. This would seem a fair characterization of the corporations, such as Rockstar Games, that make the most violent and vicious video games. Whether it is also a fair characterization of the giant firms at the heart of the global and American economy is the subject of our next two chapters.

[four]

U.S. Business vs. Us

Global Capitalism and Corporate Wilding

*What do you mean **we**, kemo sabe?*

—Tonto to the Lone Ranger

▢ A Fish Rots from the Head First

On Wednesday, April 24, 2013, at 9 AM, an 8-story factory building called Rana Plaza, housing five sweatshops and over 3,500 Bangladeshi garment workers, collapsed. The workers, mostly young women, produced clothes for giant Western retailers, such as Benetton, Joe Fresh, Cato Corp, The Children's Place, Primark, and other major U.S., Canadian, and European brands. Eleven hundred twenty-nine workers died, and about 2,500 others became amputees, losing hands, feet, and arms, or suffered head traumas. It was the worst garment labor tragedy in history and the deadliest industrial accident ever.[1]

It was a preventable disaster. The day before, on Tuesday, April 23, the workers had noticed huge cracks appearing in walls and floors of the building. But they were told by management they had to come to work the next day, or else lose a month's pay.[2]

A survivor, Jannat, who worked for New Wave Style in Rana Plaza, told a harrowing story, evoking memories of the Twin Towers collapse on 9/11. "Suddenly we saw our floor was collapsing, going down, and falling apart very fast. In a minute, I was knocked down in a dark place . . . I was suffocating. There was no air and we were trapped in darkness."[3]

Reports quickly emerged about the conditions of work before the accident in Rana Plaza. The workers averaged 13- to 14-hour workdays. They were paid wages ranging between 14 and 26 cents an hour. Despite the conditions, they came back to work on Wednesday. They couldn't survive without the money.[4]

The working conditions—and the catastrophe at Rana Plaza—were no surprise to people who knew anything about the global garment industry. Over 3 million workers toil in the export-oriented garment factories of Bangladesh, the third-largest apparel producer in the world. The minimum monthly wage is $37, one of the lowest in the world. These laws, like all labor laws in Bangladesh, are weakly enforced. Government ministers are often relatives of local plant owners. It is hardly surprising that such low wages—along with long hours and horribly unhealthy and unsafe working conditions—attract the world's largest clothing producers like moths to a flame. As we will soon show, they constitute extreme corporate and political wilding built into the DNA of our current system of globalization.

After the Rana Plaza catastrophe, mainstream media began digging into the conditions of Bangladeshi workers. CBS sent an undercover team in May 2013, to the Monde Apparels Factory outside of Dhaka, where 1,400 mostly female young workers produced over a million boxer shorts for Walmart as well as shirts for Wrangler. CBS summarizes their findings:

- The CBS crew filmed **emergency fire exits blocked** by cartons of garments stacked to the ceiling.

- Thirteen of 15 fire extinguishers were missing.

- The highest wage earned by senior sewing operators was just **24 cents an hour.** Workers did not receive pay slips and were routinely cheated of their legal wages.

- Workers sewing garments for **Walmart, Wrangler,** and **ASICS** are paid so little they are forced to live in miserable, crowded slums, with entire families living in one tiny room made of thatch and scraps of sheet metal.

Workers are routinely threatened and coached to lie to naive corporate monitors visiting the Monde Apparels factory.[5] The CBS report about the factory as a "fire trap" makes clear that Rana Plaza was a disaster waiting to happen. In fact, less than a year before Rana Plaza collapsed, another apparel factory, Tazreen Fashions, burned down and collapsed. One of the workers inside was Sumi Abedin, 24, who sewed pockets onto pants. She was making $55 a month, just enough to help support herself, her father, a rickshaw puller, and her mother at a survival level. When her factory burned to the ground in November 2012, Sumi jumped out a third floor window and broke her left hand and wrist. Her co-worker, who also jumped, died. Sumi is desperately looking for another job since her family cannot survive without her meager earnings.[6]

We have focused thus far on wilding by individuals, but wilding by corporations and governments plays a huge role in our growing crisis. Such wilding, as discussed in Chapter 1, involves behavior by institutions that enhance their own wealth and power by harming workers, citizens, and communities. Our new wilding crisis—in the United States and increasingly in the world at large—is fueled by the predatory behavior of global Wall Street banks and other multinational firms that seek fast profits at any price. Such corporations collude with governments and are driven both by the financial markets and by unfettered greed.

This chapter's focus on global corporate wilding helps make clear that wilding starts from the top. The leaders of the global economy's giant corporations and their political and intellectual allies are at the heart of the wilding crisis. They create the institutional conditions and reigning ideologies that catalyze wilding at all levels of society.

A thin line has always divided the capitalist quest for profit from economic wilding. John D. Rockefeller, Andrew Carnegie, and the other robber barons of the late nineteenth century who built American capitalism were spectacular economic wilders, famous for their brutal treatment of workers and corrupt, monopolistic practices. In the famous 1893 Homestead Steel strike, Carnegie ordered his workers shot. Since then, we have suffered repeated cycles of wilding—the Roaring Twenties, with its huge speculative binges and political scandals, for example—that have chipped away at the nation's moral fabric.

The tenuous line between business success and wilding is being even more dangerously blurred by two fundamental changes. The first is the institutionalization of the radically individualistic political economy ushered in during the 1980s. The Reagan Revolution enshrined a new privatization and deregulation, worshiping business and profits and demonizing labor unions and government. It has become the dominant ideology of our times and is fanning the flames of wilding from Wall Street to Main Street.

The second change is the rise of global capitalism, the most fundamental economic shift of our times. The new global system threatens to destroy the social dikes against corporate wilding that national governments, labor organizations, and communities have struggled to build throughout the last two centuries.

Capitalism vs. Community: Sociological Prophets and Global Profits

Globalization is being created by a new "corpocracy"—a worldwide nexus of financial markets and corporations that now dominates the world. The 200 largest companies rule, with sales comprising more than 25 percent of the world's total gross domestic product (GDP). Financial institutions are especially important, with the 100 largest banks controlling $21 trillion in assets, about three-fourths of the world's wealth. The biggest companies, such as Walmart, ExxonMobil, and Chevron, are global empires with no national loyalty. They are larger and more powerful than most countries; Walmart's annual sales are greater than the GDP of Israel or Denmark.[7]

Globalization creates the most revolutionary development of our times, with the potential to bring big and seductive benefits, including a more robust world economy and even the development of a new world community. But in its current form, it pits the interests of businesses against those of their host societies, creating a new predatory capitalism based on worldwide economic wilding.

Concepts developed a century ago by the founders of sociology are powerful tools for understanding this new wilding threat. As we saw in Chapter 1, the great French sociologist Émile Durkheim argued that early industrial capitalism, by destroying traditional communities and encouraging individual ambition and mobility, endangered social solidarity and the survival of society itself.[8] The burgeoning industrial era bred a culture of egoism and anomie—egoism reflecting the loss of community and anomie, the rise of socially unregulated greed and violence. Egoism and anomie are fertile breeding grounds for wilding, spawning self-interest, greed, and violence that can spiral out of control and subvert society.

Globalism promises to further weaken the social ties and values that civilize both individuals and business. Unencumbered by national loyalties, corporations now roam the world searching for the cheapest labor in desperately poor countries. As corporations move overseas, U.S. communities themselves become more vulnerable, with shuttered plants and industrial ghost towns becoming fixtures of the American landscape. Thrown into competition with workers in developing countries, millions of U.S. workers, even before the 2008 Great Recession, faced an uncertain future, and many became "temps," involuntary part-timers or other insecure workers, unable to find steady, full-time employment. These trends intensified after the 2008 meltdown, which also significantly increased the number of long-term unemployed people. In 2013, only 58% of U.S. working-age adults were part of the labor force, with a large number being "surplus people" unable to find any work.[9] In the words of some observers, the multinational corporation is itself becoming a virtual, or hollow, community, with robots or transient "contractors" replacing permanent employees. This erosion of community intensifies both egoism and anomie, transforming growing numbers of employees into rootless, atomized consultants, freelancers, or "entrepreneurs," many of whom are constantly seeking reemployment. At the same time, the multinationals and their top managers are increasingly liberated from governmental regulation, free to pursue unbounded appetites for global power and vast worldwide profits.

Although the twentieth century proved Karl Marx's predictions about capitalism's imminent death to be folly, globalism eerily vindicates Marx's view of the potential for capitalist wilding. The market's function of reducing all behavior to the cash nexus and naked self-interest becomes increasingly relevant in a global economy. Employees who must act as entrepreneurs find no shelter from the market and survive only by embracing relentless self-promotion. Major American corporations, seeking bonanza profits, pursue child labor in India and prison labor in China.

Marx recognized that the great moral problem of capitalism is the incentive of business to make money by exploiting its employees. In a global economy, this problem assumes a new scale, threatening workers, their communities, and the natural environment on which human civilization depends. The core of the current wilding threat arises from the intensification of appetites whetted by the new fantastic global possibilities and from the ingenious new multinational corporate strategies for realizing them.

The Musical Chairs of Global Business: The New Corporate Wilding

Corporate globalization is a game of global musical chairs—a master strategy for maximizing profits by pitting national workforces against one another. Corporations able to hire cheap labor around the world can threaten to leave a community unless workers submit to lower pay or local governments agree to various incentives to keep companies from pulling up stakes. Such intimidation, a vicious form of corporate bullying, has long been one of business's trump cards, played 75 years ago by Massachusetts and New Hampshire textile mill owners, for example, who relocated from New England to the South after northern workers unionized. But musical chairs becomes a game plan for unparalleled wilding when the theater shifts from the nation-state to the world—and the mill owners can relocate to South Korea or Mexico.

Here, the analyses of Durkheim and Marx converge. Musical chairs in the national arena has been a regulated game, with national governments playing the role of arbiter and community protector of last resort. Such national regulation restricts the degree of egoism and anomie that can arise from the capitalist system and limits exploitation by prohibiting child labor, enforcing minimum wages, and protecting the environment. Within U.S. national capitalism, labor agreements and government programs created during and after the 1930s New Deal era helped ensure that higher profits for companies translated into higher wages for the companies' workers and more resources for their host communities. This linking of corporate and community interests lent some credibility to the corporate manifesto expressed in the 1950s by the president of General Motors: "What's good for G.M. is good for America."

Under global capitalism today, however, there is no effective regulatory watchdog protecting the world's workers, communities, and environment. As an unregulated game, global musical chairs opens societies all over the world to a purely egoistic and anomic world economy. The danger is that such a game evolves, as we shall see in the rest of this chapter, toward new rules that allow businesses to maximize profit by undermining the health of their host societies.

Global economic wilding is the fruit of active collaboration between multinational companies and national governments. Markets, whether national or global, are always shaped by those with power, and while it may seem strange that national governments would collaborate in their own demise, they have, during the last two decades, played a major role in subverting their own authority as they help write the rules of the new global game. This collaboration reflects incestuous entanglements among multinationals and political elites in both developed and developing countries who have struck deals that too often subvert their own societies. These deals have triggered a downward competitive spiral—a "race to the bottom," as some global observers have dubbed it—among economies around the world, pushing much of America toward third-world wages and working conditions while intensifying the misery of already-impoverished masses in poor countries; simultaneously globilization is wrecking the environment through unfettered pollution and the massive increase of greenhouse gases inherent in global production.[10]

Wilding around the World: The Third World as Global Sweatshop

On the campus where I teach, a Vietnam-style revolt mushroomed in the years prior to the Great Recession. Students were outraged about Boston College (BC) caps and sweatshirts allegedly being made in sweatshops in Indonesia, Mexico, and El Salvador. As my students have pushed the university, with considerable success, to stop using sweatshop products (the BC bookstore now sells only BC sweatshirts and caps produced by plants certified to be "sweat-free"), similar protests spread like wildfire across many other campuses throughout the country.

Some students may have read about the famous Gilded Age journalist Upton Sinclair who ventured into the terrifying meat factories of Chicago. In his classic book *The Jungle*, published in 1906, he described a world of 16-hour workdays, in which laborers were paid pennies per hour to work in slaughterhouses that produced poisoned meat rotting with blood and hair. A century later, Sinclair's graphic sketch of the sweatshop economy still scorches the brain and shapes our understanding of economic wilding of an earlier age.

The Upton Sinclair of today's global economy is Charles Kernaghan, the muck-raker most famous for his exposure of sweatshops in Mexico, Honduras, Bangladesh, and China. Ground zero of the global workshop is China, with more than one billion workers.

On February 5, 2009, Kernaghan released a report called "High Tech Misery in China."[11] Based on interviews with workers, photographs of factory conditions, and other company documents smuggled out of the company, Kernaghan documents the story of the Metai factory in southern China. It employs 2,000 workers, mostly young women, who make keyboards and other hardware for name-brand companies such as Microsoft, IBM, Dell, and Hewlett-Packard. Kernaghan reports sickening facts in graphic detail:

- "Workers sit on hard wooden stools as 500 computer keyboards an hour move down the assembly line, 12 hours a day, seven days a week, with just two days off a month. The workers have 1.1 seconds to snap on each key, an operation repeated 3,250 times an hour, 35,750 a day, 250,250 a week and over one million times a month.

- "Workers are paid 1/50th of a cent for each operation they complete.

- "Workers cannot talk, listen to music or even lift their heads to look around.

- "All overtime is mandatory and workers are at the factory up to 87 hours a week, while earning a take-home wage of just 41 cents an hour.

- "Ten to twelve workers share each overcrowded dorm room, sleeping on metal bunk beds and draping old sheets over their cubicles for privacy.

- "Workers are locked in the factory compound four days a week and prohibited from even taking a walk.

- "For breakfast the workers receive a thin rice gruel. On Fridays they receive a small chicken leg and foot to symbolize "their improving life."

■ "Workers are instructed to 'love the company like your home'... 'continuously striving for perfection'... and to spy on and 'actively monitor each other.'"[12]

One worker summed it up: "I feel like I am serving a prison sentence.... The factory is forever pressing down on our heads and will not tolerate even the tiniest mistake.... The security guards are like policemen watching over prisoners. We're really livestock and shouldn't be called workers."[13]

Kernaghan describes an equally grim picture at another Chinese factory, where workers reported producing toys for Walmart:

> At the Huangwu No. 2 Toy factory, workers are forced to work 15 to 19 hours a day, from 7:30 A.M. to 10:30 P.M., or even until 3:00 A.M., seven days a week. Workers must complete one operation every three seconds, repeating the same furious motion 10,000 times a day. The constant repetition wears off their skin, leaving them with sore, blistered and bleeding hands and fingers. It is not a pretty sight, but Walmart says it has a code of conduct and everything is fine in its suppliers' factories in China, which is why, we imagine, Walmart continues to hide its fine factories.

Kernaghan concludes, "Workers are kept in a state of terror, knowing that if they were to say a single truthful word about abusive factory conditions, they would be immediately fired. Walmart's monitoring is a sham. Walmart's bargains are based on misery."[14] Walmart has responded that in recent years it has expanded its in-house global monitoring program to address such abusive practices.

China is not the only offender. Most developing countries have established special "export processing zones" or "free trade zones" that offer "tax holidays" to multinationals and exempt them from environmental codes and labor laws. Sometimes walled off behind barbed-wire fences, these zones—where corporations locate their sweatshops and get state protection for every manner of economic wilding—have been described as "huge labor camps," often controlled by special police forces. The most famous of these zones, and among the most important to American companies, is along the U.S.-Mexican border, which is the site of the *maquiladora* plants that now reach well into the Mexican interior.[15]

In 2008, the Mexican *maquiladoras* employed 2.4 million workers, mostly young women.[16] One such woman is Carmen Duran, who works in a Tijuana plant that produces television components. In the noted 2006 documentary, *Maquilapolis*, Carmen is featured as a brave Mexican female worker who endures shocking factory conditions while trying to raise her kids and organize the workers.[17] She is profiled below in a promotion for a 2009 showing of the film at the University of Houston:

> Carmen works the graveyard shift in one of Tijuana's maquiladoras, the multinationally owned factories that came to Mexico for its cheap labor. After making television components all night, Carmen comes home to a shack she built out of recycled garage doors, in a neighborhood with no sewage lines or electricity. She suffers from kidney damage and lead poisoning from her years of exposure to toxic chemicals. She earns six dollars a day.[18]

Very low wages and horrible working conditions have earned the maquiladora sector the name "little China." In 2008, the *maquiladoras* on the border had already been hit hard by the developing recession in the United States and the shuttering of plants in recent years that went to Vietnam, Honduras, and China, as well as

Southern Mexico, for even cheaper wages. Nonetheless, in 2008 the *maquiladora* sector still accounted for 84 percent of Mexican manufacturing exports, and remains a major part of the Mexican economy, which itself has become "increasingly an extension of foreign, mainly U.S., companies."[19] As Tom Barry, a long-time scholar of the area writes, "Over the last couple of decades, it has become the embodiment of Mexico's dependent, heartless, and ruthless economic policy."[20]

Growing out of the Border Industrialization Program of 1965, the *maquiladoras* are a classic instance of collaboration between multinationals and government. The Mexican government offered corporations favorable land deals, waived custom clearance and import duties, and agreed to low taxes and, tacitly, the right to run their businesses with a free hand, exempt from environmental and labor laws. The U.S. government did its share by running political interference for U.S. companies and giving them technical assistance and tax breaks for going south of the border. The passage of NAFTA in 1993 facilitated the huge American corporate exodus to south of the border.[21]

A very serious form of global economic wilding, long visible in the *maquiladoras*, is the sexual abuse of young female workers. Young women between the ages of 14 and 26 make up more than two-thirds of the workforce in most free trade zones. Labor lawyers and social workers in the *maquiladoras* report that young women are often propositioned by their male supervisors and can lose their jobs if they don't sleep with them.[22]

Corporate wilding also includes massive environmental abuse—which globalization threatens to turn into a worldwide ecological catastrophe. *Maquiladoras* have dumped millions of tons of raw sewage into rivers, many flowing up into the United States. A study by the AFL-CIO found the water supply on the border to be massively polluted; indiscriminate dumping of toxic waste in unsafe, often clandestine, sites threatens fish and wildlife with extinction and endangers the ecosystem as a whole.[23]

In addition, workers are subjected to toxic conditions inside the plants. Anthropologist Maria Fernandez-Kelly, who worked in the plants in Ciudad Juarez, reports that workers' health tends to deteriorate rapidly because of the brutal work pace, unsafe machinery, and hazardous fumes, with the most frequent complaints being "eyesight deterioration, and nervous and respiratory ailments." A survey conducted by the University of Massachusetts at Lowell found widespread musculoskeletal disorders related to the pace of work and poor workplace engineering. Many studies have found serious health problems caused by toxic chemicals and other unregulated pollution.[24]

The prevailing subhuman conditions in the plants and the surrounding communities are a product of coordinated repression by multinational corporations and the Mexican government, which has intervened repeatedly, using the police and the army to suppress labor protests and permitting multinational companies to evade environmental and labor laws. Wages and working conditions have declined as the multinationals have expanded because the huge firms have worked so effectively with the U.S. and Mexican governments and with company-sponsored unions to erode workers' rights and community social protections. These are neither free nor fair markets but rather the predictable outcome of a global game of musical chairs gone wild.

▣ Globalization without Wilding: The Future of Globalization after the Battle of Seattle

In December 1999, the streets of Seattle became a fiery battleground with U.S. tanks on the streets, Nike windows shattered, and tear gas shots heard around the world. Fifty thousand protesters—many of them college students teaming up with workers and environmentalists ("Teamsters and Turtles")—rallied to shut down the meeting of the WTO. Their goal was not to end globalization entirely but to challenge the WTO—which helps make the rules of the global economy—to make new regulations protecting human rights and the environment as well as protecting money.[25]

The Battle of Seattle was a *constitutional moment*, a period when financial elites from the richest nations made basic rules to determine how the world is run for decades to come. The protesters, who want a more limited globalization without social or environmental wilding, have shown their determination; they have mounted electrifying protests since Seattle at nearly every meeting of the financial elites who make the rules.

As noted at the beginning of this chapter, globalization could be reined in and organized in a different way to avoid inflicting harm on millions of the world's workers and communities and to prevent destruction of the environment. Why then, have our political leaders allowed globalization to proceed in its current form? And how might the global economy be restructured and regulated to balance the enormous power of multinational corporations and contain their greed?

The United States will retain significant influence in the web of global institutions, from the International Monetary Fund (IMF) and the World Bank to the WTO. But the players gaining the most power in the new world economy are not governments but the multinationals themselves. The reason both Republican and Democratic presidents acquiesce to the multinationals' agenda is simple: Both political parties are dependent on business funding to win elections and are not prepared to risk opposing huge global corporations on issues of central importance to them. Five hundred of the largest U.S. corporations have offices in Washington and employ thousands of lobbyists, as do 400 of the largest foreign multinationals. Together, these corporations constitute by far the largest and most influential special-interest group in Washington. Ultimately, business sets the parameters for economic policymaking in America because of its lobbying efforts and because members of the U.S. corporate elite themselves occupy the highest governmental economic posts, thereby controlling the money and investment decisions essential to the survival of both the population and the government.[26]

Students and other post-Seattle protesters have already shown that their actions can force change. Their protests, along with the 2008–2009 great global recession, have triggered a major crisis of legitimacy and credibility in global banks, in the WTO, IMF, and World Bank, and in neoliberal "free trade." The U.S. government has pulled back some of its support for institutions such as the IMF, and President Obama has supported inserting labor and environmental rights in trade agreements.

The aim of the protesters is to turn globalization into a means of empowering people and dignifying their lives, as well as protect the environment and prevent the ultimate catastrophe of climate change. One approach is to promote global labor movements that will represent the interests of the new global workforce and the global environment to balance the power of the multinationals. Both American workers and employees in developing nations need strong unions and other worker and human rights organizations to prevent the horrendous exploitation of global sweatshops and of the environment.

American unions now realize that when corporations are allowed to operate sweatshops abroad, workers will begin to encounter sweatshop conditions at home. After years of hostility to foreign workers and foreign labor movements, the AFL-CIO labor chiefs have begun to speak about international labor solidarity. John Sweeney, former president of the AFL-CIO, has provided vocal support and funding for organizing efforts in the *maquiladoras* and other trade zones. As early as 1994, workers in a Ford truck-assembly plant in St. Paul, Minnesota, voted to send funds to Ford workers in Mexico to support a union drive in the *maquiladoras*. The American workers, who recognized that wretched Mexican wages and working conditions affected their own jobs and security, wore patches on their jackets saying "Cross-Border Solidarity Organizers." A growing number of labor unions—such as the U.S. United Electrical Workers, with help from the Teamsters—have begun to contribute to independent labor organizing in the *maquiladoras*.[27]

The rise of new international labor confederations—in coalition with student groups, environmentalists, and other human rights groups—could help prevent multinationals from playing one country's workers against another's in a race to the bottom. It could also help create new controls over the unchecked lightning-fast movement of speculative capital around the planet. As the 2008 Wall Street meltdown showed, such fast money can easily destabilize the economies of entire continents and erode the ability of nations to protect their own people. We need foreign investment and trade, but only when there are regulations that allow nations and communities to control their own destinies.[28]

Ultimately, a new democratic coalition must become a major player at the tables where the new constitution of the global economy is being written. The finance ministers of the rich nations and the corporate advisory teams who meet regularly at the WTO, IMF, and World Bank will have to make room for a whole new set of worker and citizen representatives. Global rules will have to shift from their exclusive focus on protecting property rights and free trade. The new mission must be to create a democratic model of globalization, centered on respect for human rights, environmental protection, and a fair distribution of wealth between rich and poor nations, as well as between corporate CEOs and their global workforce.[29]

Multinational companies in the United States and elsewhere have used globalism to escape their social responsibilities and weaken the accountability that the workers and governments of their own nations historically have imposed on them. This approach of the multinational companies will lead to a permanent regime of corporate wilding unless a new social covenant is negotiated between multinationals and the workers and citizens of the world. Building a new world community through the struggle for global employee rights and democratic and accountable global businesses may prove to be the most important new social movement of the coming era.

Discussion Questions

1. Is globalization a form of corporate wilding?

2. Would either Karl Marx or Émile Durkheim see globalization today as wilding?

3. Is outsourcing jobs from the United States to poor countries paying cheap wages a form of corporate wilding?

4. If corporations go abroad to avoid taxes and regulations, is this corporate wilding?

5. Can there be a form of globalization that is not wilding?

6. What can ordinary citizens, such as students, do to end the wilding in the global economy?

[five]

Subprime Capitalism
The Great Recession and Systemic Wilding from Wall Street to Washington

On March 12, 2009, Bernard (Bernie) Madoff, former chair of the Nasdaq stock exchange and a pillar of Wall Street, confessed in a Manhattan federal district court to running a giant Ponzi scheme. He admitted defrauding financial clients of at least $50 billion. He ruined 13,500 private investors, charities, foundations, colleges, and pension funds who had invested with him.[1]

After pleading guilty to 11 counts of fraud, perjury, and money laundering, Madoff, then 70, was convicted and sentenced to 150 years in prison.[2] He will go down in history as a symbol of spectacular Wall Street wilding that caused a worldwide economic meltdown.

Madoff had been operating his scam for decades, and his basic business model didn't require a Harvard MBA. He accepted funds from his rich friends and promised them high, secure returns, while diverting most of the money to his own private bank accounts. When investors wanted to redeem their money, Bernie paid them with money he collected from new investors waiting for their own golden chance to become rich by investing in the Madoff enterprise.

Madoff's Ponzi scheme had financed a high life. He owned a $7.5 million penthouse in Manhattan. He owned a chateau in southern France and maintained a suite at the exclusive Hotel du Cap-Eden-Roc in Antibes. He owned a $7.5 million Palm Beach mansion that had seven bathrooms, and he had a dock for his $800,000 yacht named "Bull." He also had a $3 million mansion in Montauk, New York. He owned two private planes.[3]

In court, Madoff told the judge he was sorry for his crimes. But Madoff seems the perfect model of a remorseless economic wilder. Madoff betrayed and wiped out friends and clients alike. When men whom Madoff knew well died in Palm Beach or Boca Raton, the children would come to Bernie to plead with him to accept the estate and manage it for their mothers. Bernie would hug them and, if they were wealthy, would promise to help. He would then take the entire estate and plunge it into his Ponzi scheme. The trusting families would lose everything when Madoff's scheme crashed.[4]

Bernie seemed to feel no remorse for ruining so many people. In contrast, consider one of his major clients, René-Thierry Magon de la Villehuchet, a rich French money manager who invested most of his clients' money with Madoff.

After learning of Madoff's collapsed scheme, de la Villehuchet, 65, locked himself in his office, took a bottle of sleeping pills, slashed open his left arm with a box cutter, and bled to death. De la Villehuchet's brother, Bertrand, said that René-Thierry sent him a note saying, "If you ruin your friends, your clients, you have to face the consequences." Bertrand says his brother "felt responsible and he felt guilty. Today, in the financial world, there is no responsibility; no one wants to shoulder the blame."[5]

That is a precise description of Bernard Madoff. Bernie is the quintessential sociopathic broker, the perfect economic wilder who appeared to feel nothing while destroying the people closest to him.

☐ Marx, Madoff, and Capitalism Gone Wild

The importance of Madoff is less his sensational individual wilding than his role as a symbol of the economy's moral collapse. In this chapter, I show that the 2008 Wall Street implosion is *systemic wilding* at the heart of American capitalism. Nobel Prize–winning economist and *New York Times* columnist Paul Krugman wrote that the American economy "is looking like the Bernie Madoff of economies; for many years it was held in respect, even awe, but it turns out to have been a fraud all along."[6]

MIT economist Simon Johnson, the former chief economist at the International Monetary Fund (IMF) writes about the entire system of U.S. financiers as wild gamblers and cheaters resembling Madoff.[7] Greedy financiers "played a central role in creating the crisis, making ever-larger gambles with the implicit backing of the government, until the inevitable crisis. . . . More alarming, they are now using their influence to prevent precisely the sorts of reforms that are needed."[8]

We have already seen that there is a blurry line between capitalism and wilding, for capitalism is built on the script that dictates each individual should focus on his or her own gains. Karl Marx would not be surprised by extreme individual wilders like Bernie Madoff, but he would have been far more interested in the institutional wilding by mortgage giant Countrywide Financial Corporation, the huge Wall Street broker and banker Merrill Lynch, and the insurance titan AIG, all working hand in glove with each other and with Congress and the White House. Wall Street and Washington colluded in wilding that melted down the global capitalist system itself, destroying the lives of millions of workers.

Over the last few decades, as unregulated global firms pushed wages down in the global economy's race to the bottom, the U.S. "real economy" stagnated.[9] Since workers lacked money to buy "real" products like refrigerators, cars, or clothing in quantities that would ensure high profits, capitalists turned to "financialization"—investing in financial trades and speculation to make money.[10] Wall Street became the center of action, with a remarkable 41 percent of American gross domestic product (GDP) coming from financial trading and speculation by 2008.[11] The real economy that made tangible products shrank as Wall Street grew. Financialization was a form of wilding because Wall Street allocated financial resources to itself—making high-risk bets—and sucked away resources from other more productive sectors of the economy. Wall Street's gambles came at the cost of Americans' jobs and communities.

As they were dishing up their new risky mortgages and other exotic loans, the banks were sucking in endless new customers by creating super-easy credit and debt. Many hard-pressed workers were seduced into the new fast world of the debt-driven American dream.[12]

Thus did capitalism turn into a version of a full-blown Ponzi scheme. Like Madoff, the banks didn't have to worry because there were always new "suckers"—us! This was the Madoff script writ large, a dream too good to be true. Ultimately, millions of workers lost their jobs and millions of other Americans lost their homes in the most massive foreclosure crisis since the Great Depression. The greed of bankers produced a long-term crisis in the basic life prospects of the poor, blue-collar workers, and even many in the middle classes.

In the rest of this chapter, we show how wilding evolved as a systemic cancer. Since the housing bubble pushed a perversely financialized capitalism over the edge, we follow a mortgage from the initial borrower (you or me) down the wilding chain of institutions from Wall Street to Washington. The systemic wilding we describe is economic, political, and cultural.

Countrywide: Our Financial Jurassic Park

Over recent decades, owning your own home has become the symbol of making it in the American Dream. When the 2008 economy meltdown happened, the tipping point was wilding in the housing market by the country's biggest mortgage firms.

On October 14, 2008, Illinois Attorney General Lisa Madigan, in conjunction with California Attorney General Jerry Brown, announced an $8.7 billion settlement against Countrywide Financial Corporation, the largest mortgage corporation in America. Madigan said that "this settlement holds the number-one mortgage lender in the country accountable for deceptively putting borrowers into loans they didn't understand, couldn't afford and couldn't get out of. These are the very practices that have created the economic crisis we're currently experiencing."[13]

Madigan's lawsuit against Countrywide was only one of hundreds targeting the nation's biggest issuer of subprime mortgages. The subprime loans are a special category that required no down payment and virtually no documentation of income or assets. They were usually associated with "teaser" rates that started out low but ballooned into unaffordable interest charges and principal payments. High fees were concealed in the fine print and never revealed or explained to the homeowners. There were so many lawsuits charging Countrywide with fraud and deception, lying and falsifying statements, predatory lending, racism, cheating, insider trading, secret stock dumping by top management, and other crimes that entire Web sites emerged to keep track of them. Yet many of the most harmful wilding actions by Countrywide—and by many similar gigantic mortgage companies such as Washington Mutual and Wells Fargo—were perfectly legal. Call it "subprime wilding" within the law, a sign of how far off from an ethical path the housing market and larger financial system had bolted.

Countrywide continued to defend its massive subprime operation as a way to fulfill the American Dream for millions of low-income Americans. Countrywide executive Rick Simon said, "Countrywide is proud of its role in making homeownership affordable to lower-income households and, as the largest lender to African-Americans, Hispanics, and Asians, closing the gap in homeownership between whites and minorities."[14]

Countrywide had, in fact, extended subprime mortgages to millions of low-income Americans, selling these mortgages disproportionately to African-Americans and Hispanics. But subprime mortgages were so toxic that members of Congress had unsuccessfully tried to make them illegal as far back as 2003 and 2004, realizing that they were a superprofitable form of predatory lending that could create an explosion of foreclosures, destroying people in the name of giving them a chance to realize their American Dream.

The director of a low-income community organization in Boston told me how it worked in her neighborhood, where most people were African-American or Hispanic. Countrywide and other predatory lenders would hire a few people such as "Manny," who lived there and had large numbers of relatives in the neighborhood. Countrywide would pay Manny $5,000 for each subprime mortgage he sold to a member of his family or one of his friends. Countrywide didn't train Manny much, but just told him to sign people up fast. Manny would get paid if he got his family and friends to sign up. He didn't show them the fine print about how the rates would skyrocket a few years down the road. Countrywide turned the American Dream into the American Nightmare for Manny's brothers and sisters, most of whom would face foreclosure as their rates spiked, but the company made a fantastic fortune in the process.

Angelo R. Mozilo, Countrywide's founder, had built the company into a $200 billion mortgage giant—the largest in the country—by 2007. Mozilo plunged Countrywide into a housing supermarket—offering appraisal, brokerage, accounting, tax services, and banking services across the country. Mozilo himself took home a cool $410 million from the Countrywide empire in the years after he was elevated to CEO in 1999. Not bad for the son of a Brooklyn butcher.[15]

Mozilo was the ultimate salesman. A flashy dresser, he drove Rolls Royces tinted gold.[16] But Mozilo, according to friends, was not just flaunting his wealth for its own sake—he was using it to push sales and build up market share. Mozilo was ready to do whatever it took to become number one in sales. In 2005, he plunged forward into the subprime world, despite his initial concerns about excessive risk. He wanted the money and had to be number one. There was no way he would back down; as one friend said, "Angelo doesn't do reverse."[17]

Mozilo was also lured in by huge profits being generated by rivals such as Washington Mutual (WaMu), the second biggest mortgage company in the subprime business. WaMu was well known for pressuring sales reps to pump out loans without worrying about documentation or risk, giving $10,000 a pop to real estate agents for bringing in customers. WaMu also pushed appraisers to inflate property values to make loans seem safe so they could be bundled and sold more easily on Wall Street. Steven Knobel, an appraiser working with WaMu, said, "If you were alive, they would give you a loan. Actually, I think if you were dead, they would still give you a loan."[18]

Not to be outdone by WaMu, Mozilo created a wilding culture at Countrywide modeled on his own personality. One former executive said, "People used to say that Countrywide was like Jurassic Park. It is filled with dinosaurs, powerful guys living in a different era."[19] These guys running Countrywide were like the junk bond salesmen of the 1980s, the Michael Milkens and Gordon Gekkos who assumed that greed was good.

Assessing Countrywide's legal liability, *Fortune*'s editor, Roger Parloff, notes that Mozilo and other top executives were talking up Countrywide stocks while it appeared they were selling off their own stock, with Mozilo saving his skin by selling his stock back to the company. This is where risky and unethical lending (a form of often-legal wilding across the entire subprime mortgage world) may turn into criminal wilding.[20] In 2009, the SEC charged Mozilo with insider trading and security fraud. In 2010, Mozilo settled with the SEC, paying $67.5 million in fines and agreeing to a lifetime ban on serving as a director of a public company. It is the largest settlement ever reached against a mortgage company executive, but it saved Mozilo from going through a trial and having to acknowledge guilt or be convicted.[21]

Merrill Lynch, Bank of America, JP Morgan Chase, and Goldman Sachs: Banks Gone Wild

Merrill Lynch, the venerable massive investment bank on Wall Street, was one of the biggest wilders among banks themselves, playing a central role in buying up subprime mortgages, "securitizing" them, and then passing them along to "suckers" down the financial food chain while often secretly betting against or insuring themselves against the failure of their own toxic products, a form of wilding later taken up with a passion by Goldman Sachs, Bank of America (BOA), and other famous Wall Street giants. Merrill Lynch was among the first famous Wall Street firms to collapse, a victim of its own extravagant wilding.

Shortly after 9/11, Merrill scooped up superprofitable subprime mortgages issued by Countrywide, WaMu, and the other mortgage giants as fast as it could. By 2006, it had made billions of dollars by buying the risky mortgages, slicing and dicing them with other risky loans, and then "bundling" them with other loans to sell as exotic securities or "collateralized debt obligations" (CDOs). In December 2006, Merrill Lynch decided it could make even more money by originating subprime mortgages itself, buying First Franklin, a company that specialized in the riskiest subprime loans. Merrill Lynch wanted all ends of the subprime pipeline so that it could originate the mortgage, repackage the subprime mortgages into toxic CDOs without anybody asking questions, and sell them off fast to investors who could not possibly understand the true value or risks of the CDOs they were buying.[22]

Whether Merrill Lynch and other big Wall Street banks profiting from high-risk mortgage securitization were involved in criminal or simply unethical behavior will be resolved in litigation. On May 12, 2009, Massachusetts Attorney General Martha Coakley reached a settlement with Goldman Sachs for its role in securitizing subprime mortgages and selling them off, with the profits used to originate new subprime mortgages. Without acknowledging wrongdoing, Goldman Sachs agreed to reduce subprime loans for some Massachusetts homeowners, helping keep borrowers in their homes.[23] Five years after the crash, through July 2013, there had been only a few federal lawsuits, mainly against smaller mortgage firms, seeking to establish legal wrongdoing by the banks and create accountability. But while in August 2013 Attorney General Eric Holder said that there will be some new prosecutions to hold the big banks criminally accountable, there is great skepticism in the legal community that any criminal convictions of the big banks and their top executives will be realized.[24] One of the reasons is the striking reality that much of the big banks' wilding role in the crisis was perfectly legal. This is a measure of the wilding built into the system, a financial order in which deceptive and risky behavior became the legally sanctioned norm.

As for Merrill Lynch, its wilding led to its own self-destruction. In 2008, it bought Countrywide, a disastrous move that forced it to write down more than $5 billion in Countrywide's bad mortgages. This was followed by BOA's acquisition of Merrill Lynch itself, finalized on January 1, 2009. BOA had plenty of its own problems even before these economically and morally questionable purchases. After its purchase of Merrill Lynch and Countrywide, BOA became the largest wealth management company in the world and the number one originator of subprime mortgage loans, deeply involved in "securitizing" and selling CDOs whose worth was questionable.

All the biggest banks have been implicated in serious corporate wilding that helped cause the crisis. JP Morgan Chase, the largest and most prestigious Wall Street bank, agreed in November 2013, to a civil settlement of $13 billion, the largest in U.S. history, for marketing its own huge trove of bundled bad mortgages that bank executives and traders allegedly knew were toxic.[25] These were precisely the instruments of "mass financial destruction," as Warren Buffet called them, at the heart of the crash. Like BOA and Goldman Sachs, JP Morgan Chase sold its bad mortgage loans to both Fannie Mae and Freddie Mac, the institutions on which the national mortgage markets depend. Some of the toxic mortgages originated in Bear Stearns and Washington Mutual, which JP Morgan Chase bought up after the 2008 meltdown. JP Morgan Chase paid a large fine, but it was a cost of doing business that did not seriously dent the bank's bottom line.

The Justice Department indicated it was also looking into criminal charges against the bank for turning a blind eye to Bernie Madoff's pyramid scheme while doing business with him. Nonetheless, JP Morgan Chase CEO, Jamie Dimon, maintained during settlement talks and the Madoff investigation that he was "very proud" of his company, suggesting arrogance and a lack of remorse characteristic of the most serious wilders.[26]

We cannot conclude any discussion of the giant Wall Street banks without a focus on Goldman Sachs, perhaps the most famous, politically connected, and diabolical concocter of economic wilding on The Street, helping to bring down the whole financial system and jeopardize the entire society, while immunizing itself economically and politically and bringing home the bacon to its top executives. As the *New York Times* summarized, the famous bank has now become "synonymous with exploiting its customers for its own interests. Its good name has collapsed. Among its peers, it has posted the largest decline since 2007, according to Reputation Institute."[27]

The case against Goldman Sachs was laid out in agonizing detail in a 650-page report, titled "Wall Street and the Financial Crisis," released in May 2011, by the Senate Permanent Subcommittee on Investigations, chaired by veteran Democratic Michigan Senator Carl Levin. As journalist Matt Taibbi summarized it, "America has been waiting for a case to bring against Wall Street. Here it is, and the evidence has been gift-wrapped and left at the doorstep of federal prosecutors, evidence that doesn't leave much doubt: Goldman Sachs should stand trial."[28]

In an influential *Rolling Stone* essay, analyzing the Senate report, Taibbi brilliantly explained the extraordinary economic and political wilding carried out by Goldman and its top executives. In 2006, Goldman executives realized they were sitting on top of $6 billion of home loans and were dangerously exposed, leading to the conclusion that it had to securitize and sell them as fast as possible. "Distribute as much as possible on bonds created from new loan securitizations," a top Goldman mortgage executive wrote in a key memo, "and clean previous positions." Taibbi's translation: "In other words, the bank needed to find suckers to buy as much of its risky inventory as possible. Goldman was like a car dealership that realized it had a whole lot full of cars with faulty brakes. Instead of announcing a recall, it surged ahead with a two-fold plan to make a fortune: first, by dumping the dangerous products on other people, and second, by taking out life insurance against the fools who bought the deadly cars."[29] The bank "cleaned" its books by creating new securities that it aggressively sold to its clients, in infamous deals known as Hudson and Timberwolf, while it was simultaneously dumping its own holdings of these same toxic securities, keeping only a tiny sliver to appear to value the products that it was offloading and betting billions against them. In total, half of the giant bank's total risk was involved in a $13 billion bet against the mortgage market that its own securities were helping to create.[30]

When Goldman executives were called to testify to the Senate about these sordid dealings, Senator Levin said they lied, a criminal form of wilding since witnesses are sworn to tell the truth to Congressional committees."[31] (Taibbi is more colorful in his account: "The Levin report reveals a bank gone way beyond such pathetic little boundaries; the collective picture resembles a financial version of *The Jungle*, a portrait of corporate sociopathy that makes you never want to go near a sausage again."[32])

Taibbi concludes that, "If the Justice Department fails to give the American people a chance to judge this case—if Goldman skates without so much as a trial—it will confirm once and for all the embarrassing truth: that the law in America is subjective, and crime is defined not by what you did, but by who you are." And given the fact that Goldman top executives over the last two decades, such as Hank Paulson and Robert Rubin, have been Secretaries of the Treasury, in both Democratic and Republican administrations, it is hardly a surprise that no criminal cases have been filed at this writing.[33]

AIG: Wall Street's Heart of Darkness

"It's almost like these guys should have gotten the Nobel Prize for evil."[34] So said Austan Goolsbee, one of President Obama's top advisors, referring to high-level executives at the Wall Street insurance giant, American International Group (AIG). AIG executives were dishing out to themselves millions of dollars in bonuses, even as they were raking in an astonishing *$170 billion* in public bailout money. AIG suddenly became the new symbol of capitalist greed, a wilding supermarket at the heart of Wall Street's crisis.

AIG created the "insurance" that allowed banks such as Merrill Lynch to buy and bundle extremely risky mortgages from the mortgage companies, repackage them as securitized assets, and sell them at a big profit to hedge funds, pension funds, rich private investors, and other banks. The bonuses were ultimately far less important than the role AIG played in fueling the Wall Street wilding system of superleveraged debt and risk that brought down the whole economy.

But the public focused on the bonuses themselves, which were putting an extra $477 million into the pockets of the very executives who had driven the U.S. economy into the ditch. Edward Liddy, AIG's CEO, said he was legally obliged to pay the bonuses, and that they were retention payments required to keep the experts needed to understand and unwind the complex deals they had created.[35]

Rage at the bonuses exploded across the country. The AIG executives took off their pin-striped suits, removed the AIG logo from tote bags, and paid private security guards with bomb-sniffing dogs to protect them and their homes as they received death threats and threatening e-mails. The bailout and bonuses symbolized Wall Street's power and the people's powerlessness—a historic recipe for the unleashing of populist pitchforks.

But populist rage should focus more on the systemic wilding role played by AIG. AIG was the great dispenser of "credit default swaps," exotic financial instruments seen as insurance that allowed banks and investors to bet on the risk of default of a company or portfolio without having any financial stake in that firm or portfolio. As the *New York Times* editorialized, "That is definitely not insurance, it is gambling. The reason is that it is not illegal gambling is that, in 2000, Congress specifically exempted credit default swaps from gaming laws." The *Times* goes on to point out that "Eric Dinallo, the insurance superintendent for New York State, has said that some 80 percent of the estimated $62 trillion in credit defaults outstanding in 2008 were speculative."[36]

The systemic problem was that AIG's gambles freed its "counterparties"—all the big Wall Street banks that bought AIG's credit default swaps—to go wild with their own risky bundled mortgage trading schemes. The banks were correct in guessing that AIG "insurance" would rescue them, even if it took a huge U.S. bailout of AIG to do so. The taxpayers' $170 billion that went to AIG was then passed through AIG to its counterparties, the big banks who were having fun double-dipping into huge pots of public money. Merrill Lynch, Bank of America, and other big banks that got billions in direct bailout money in 2008 received billions more in 2009, funneled through the gigantic AIG bailout.[37]

Former New York Attorney General Eliot Spitzer, who had earlier investigated AIG, got it right when he said that AIG was at the "center of the web" of the Wall Street implosion. The "tentacles of this company," said Spitzer, "stretched to every major investment bank." AIG linked the mortgage companies and big banks into one vast wilding web, anchored in deceptive insurance that converted the U.S. financial system into a spectacular Ponzi scheme, bringing down the U.S. and world economies.[38]

Moody's and Standard and Poor's: "Rated F for Failure"

In September 2008, Moody's gave Lehman Brothers' debt a high A2 rating just weeks before Lehman collapsed. Moody's gave the unsecured debt of AIG an even higher Aa3 rating. Along with Standard and Poor's (S&P), the other leading U.S. credit rating agency, Moody's also gave high ratings to 11 of the 12 largest distressed financial firms just before they began to collapse.[39]

Moody's and S&P, along with Fitch, the third major rating agency, offer the closest thing to a Good Housekeeping Seal of Approval to investors, who depend on their credibility and judgment. Yet the rating agencies greased the wheels of Wall Street as it went off the tracks, putting their approval seal on thousands of the toxic subprime mortgage and other super-risky securities that Wall Street was pumping out.

It doesn't take a rocket scientist to figure out what went wrong. According to Jerome Fons, a former Moody's managing director, "The system is rife with conflicts of interest. The rating agencies get a fortune from corporations to evaluate their bonds and naturally don't want to bite the hand that feeds them."[40] Moody's and other rating agencies are paid by the companies they are rating. This is an obvious recipe for wilding.

Famous investor Warren Buffet, the world's second-richest person, is enmeshed in one of these conflicts of interest. Buffet owns 20 percent of Moody's.[41] But Moody's rates Berkshire Hathaway, Buffet's own company. As Buffet made bad bets that ensured Hathaway would lose money in 2009, Moody's continued to give it an AAA rating.[42]

Moody's and the other credit rating agencies are corporations themselves, whose mission is making a profit. Raymond McDaniel, Moody's CEO, received $7.6 million in total pay in 2008. Meanwhile, his company was failing at its job of warning investors in securitized debt that the debt was not worth the paper it was printed on.

Fons argues that the solution is simple, given the obvious and deep conflicts of interest. "The only way out of the trap is to reduce reliance on ratings." Investors, he says, need a better and more independent system of regulation. And they "should return to the tool they used" before the credit agencies were created. "That tool," he notes, "is called judgment."[43]

☐ CNBC and Media Wilding: Jim Cramer versus Jon Stewart

Jim Cramer is the wildly popular host of CNBC's show *Mad Money*. Cramer, a bombastic former hedge fund manager, interviews CEOs and makes recommendations about stock picks to the public. Presuming to inform and safeguard the public, the promo to his show says, "In Cramer We Trust." But after Cramer's March 2009 appearance on Jon Stewart's *The Daily Show* on Comedy Central, public trust in Cramer and the CNBC network—and perhaps all business reporting—would never be quite the same.

Stewart started out by telling Cramer that, "If I had only taken CNBC's advice, I would have a million dollars today—provided I started with $100 million." Stewart was mocking Cramer, since Cramer and CNBC had been bullish on financial and other stocks all through 2008—right up until Wall Street imploded in September. Stewart showed that CNBC, the country's premier financial news network, was anything but a public watchdog. Instead of serving as a "tool of illumination," Stewart said it was covering up a con game going on: "It is a game that you know is going on, but you go on television as a financial network and pretend it isn't happening. Isn't there a problem selling snake oil as vitamin tonic?"[44]

The con game was using the small investor's money—usually packaged into pension or mutual funds—to finance Wall Street's subprime racket. As a former hedge fund manager, Cramer knew the game from the inside; so did other CNBC experts. Cramer said on Stewart's show, "You walk away from talking to a CEO and you know he's lying." But Cramer and his colleagues never told the public about the lies or about the huge risks involved. CNBC became a 24/7 infomercial for Wall Street under the guise of informed public journalism.[45]

Cramer and CNBC made a lot of money by shielding the truth. Ratings went up, advertisers spent lavishly on the network, and Cramer and his colleagues became rich celebrities. CEOs on Wall Street favored Cramer and CNBC with interviews. Stewart showed that CNBC, America's most important financial media network, was a corporate wilder protecting its own. CNBC disgraced itself by failing to disclose the impending disaster it knew was coming, and it symbolized the media wilding throughout business journalism and the wider media.

Over recent decades, the rate of consolidation of independent media into a small number of huge corporate-owned media supermarkets has been as dramatic as the growth of giant monopolistic financial supermarkets on Wall Street. And these two worlds of corporate monopoly networks have become codependent collaborators. They fuel each other's wilding and keep the secrets the public and investors need to know. And, in both cases, it is political wilding in Washington that lets this wilding blossom, despite the best efforts of muckrakers like Jon Stewart.

George W. Bush, Barack Obama, and the Corporate State: Bailouts, Deregulation, and Political Wilding in Washington

Americans elected President Barack Obama to make changes to help ordinary people, not the rich. But when Obama took office, one of the first things he did was dish out hundreds of billions more to bail out Wall Street, a policy started under President Bush. Obama also approved more than a trillion dollars of credit, which was infused into Wall Street by the Federal Reserve. And Obama promised to buy up many of the banks' "troubled assets" in a public-private "bad bank," in which the government took most of the risk, although big private investors could reap most of the benefits. Nobel laureate economist Joseph Stiglitz called it "cash for trash."[46]

Obama put $170 billion into AIG alone, effectively making the government an 80 percent owner of AIG, but didn't take control of the company to ensure that it worked for the public. This helps explain why AIG paid bonuses and funneled bailout money to the big banks that had bought AIG credit swap default "insurance" but had not yet acknowledged or put a figure on their losses. Likewise, Obama bailed out Citigroup with $50 billion, enough to own more than 35 percent of the company, but again backed away from any meaningful nationalization or public control.[47] Such coddling of banks—bailouts for the Wall Street elites rather than the little guy, a policy bordering on wilding—hardly seemed like the change Americans had voted for.

This wouldn't have surprised anybody who looked at Obama's economic team. His chief economic advisor, Lawrence Summers, was a protégé of former Citigroup Chair, Robert Rubin, with numerous other lucrative ties to Wall Street. In 2007, Summers earned over $5 million as a director, working one day a week, with D. E. Shaw, a hedge fund on Wall Street.[48] Summers has received nearly $3 million in speaking fees from Wall Street firms that received bailout money; he also called Senate Banking Chair Christopher Dodd to request the removal of caps on executive fees for CEOs of banks receiving bailout funds. Obama appointed Timothy Geithner as his treasury secretary. Geithner was a protégé of Summers and the chair of the New York Federal Reserve. He had spent most of his professional years hobnobbing in the elite suites of Wall Street executives. Geithner had worked closely with George W. Bush's secretary of the treasury, Hank Paulson, formerly

a Goldman Sachs CEO, to devise the original bailout for the banks. There was
no reason to believe that this team would bail out the hard-pressed workers or
homeowners rather than the Wall Street titans, nor would one expect this to be
a team that would impose nationalization, stringent bailout conditions, or tough
regulations on Wall Street.[49]

Anybody who knew a bit of history might also have expected this kid-glove
treatment of Wall Street by Washington, a treatment that actually enabled much
of the wilding leading up to and through the crisis. Political scientist Thomas
Ferguson has described an "investment theory" of politics; those who invest in
and fund political candidates will see a return on their investment in terms of
friendly policy.[50] Wall Street has been an equal opportunity investor, lavishly pour-
ing money into the campaign coffers of both the Republican and Democratic
parties. This helped turn the federal government into a corporate state, with both
parties enabling their corporate "investors" to go wild in search of big profits at
the expense of the general public.

The corporate state took its modern form with the election of Ronald Reagan
in 1980 and surfaced in clearest public view in the administration of George W.
Bush.[51] After the Enron crisis hit the headlines, George W. Bush proclaimed that
corporate criminals would go straight to jail, but then he appointed Harvey Pitt
as head of the chief watchdog agency, the Securities and Exchange Commission.
Pitt was a lawyer for accounting firms, well known for protecting the rich. The
Pitt appointment was just the tip of the iceberg of the political protection system
that both Republican and Democratic administrations have lavishly supported.
The Bush administration, with a cabinet drawn almost exclusively from the big-
business community, was the pure embodiment of the corporate state, which is
a melding of corporations and the political class that pursues profit over people.
The corporate state helps fuel systemic wilding today, and it continues to grow
under both Republican and Democratic presidents.[52]

The era from Reagan to Bush institutionalized systemic wilding and enabled
both the 1980s savings and loan crisis and the Enron meltdown by deregulating
Wall Street and breaking down the "Chinese wall" that had historically separated
commercial from investment banking as well as banking of both types from research
and analyst services. After the 1929 financial crash, where similar crony relations
had contributed to loss of faith in the markets, President Franklin Roosevelt signed
the Glass-Steagall Act and other regulations that prevented commercial banks from
engaging in investment banking, brokering sales, or other financial services. During the 1990s bubble, these regulations were systematically dismantled and new
financial giants such as Citigroup and Merrill Lynch gobbled up business on both
sides of the toppled Chinese wall. The only answer to this particular component
of systemic wilding on Wall Street: Rebuild the wall.

The corporate state is indifferent to whether the donkey or the elephant is
sitting in the White House. Consider that Enron in 2002 had contributed to 71
of the 100 senators as well as to 187 members of the House. The top recipients
included Senator Charles Schumer, a Democrat from New York, and Senator
Joseph Lieberman of Connecticut, who ran for vice president in 2000 on the
Democratic ticket with Al Gore.

Moving forward to the 2008 Wall Street crisis and the election of President Barack Obama, the corporate state is still intact, despite the anger of the public toward the banks and the decisive rejection of the Republicans who had been aiding and abetting Wall Street's wilding. We have seen that Obama's economic team differs little from that of Clinton, who operated more or less comfortably within the corporate regime.[53] The bailouts and broader recovery measures for Wall Street, as of this writing, involve changes in political rhetoric but no dramatic shift from the favorable treatment of the banks that they have enjoyed for decades, despite the huge cost to ordinary Americans that their financial wilding has caused.

Because of the gravity of the financial crisis and economic meltdown, however, and widespread public anger at the giant banks and mortgage companies, it appeared that Obama might be forced to reform the corporate state and move the nation on a different course. Despite the Congressional passage of the Dodd-Frank financial regulatory law, signed by Obama, the evidence is that Wall Street and the corporate state have largely gone unscathed, and may, in fact, be returning to the same practices causing the crisis. First, as of August 2013, Obama has given massive bailouts to the biggest banks, such as AIG, Goldman Sachs, and J.P. Morgan Chase, without prosecuting criminally any of the banks or their top executives involved in the bundling and selling of toxic mortgage-backed securities that precipitated the meltdown. Second, he has taken no antitrust action to break up monopoly banks "too big to fail." Third, he has failed to help implement large parts of the Dodd-Frank regulatory framework, partly because of Congressional obstruction and also because of failure on his part to go to the public and hold Congress' feet to the fire. Fourth, he has failed to follow through on new regulation of large sectors of the "shadow banking" sector that operates without any public scrutiny or accountability. Fifth, he has implemented new "free trade" treaties that permit U.S. corporations to outsource jobs and engage in the global wilding discussed in Chapter 4. Lastly, he has failed to fight Citizens United, the 2010 Supreme Court decision that gutted campaign finance laws restraining big money in politics, while also failing to contest the idea of corporations as legal persons that helped legitimize the Citizens United decision and empowers corporations with many new political rights.

Moreover, Obama has failed to follow through on the most hopeful parts of his economic agenda; notably full employment policy through major public financing of green jobs and a new green energy, transit, and urban infrastructure, as well as large-scale investment in education, social welfare programs, and housing help for the millions "underwater" on their mortgages. Given all the disappointments suggesting Obama's embrace of much of the corporate state, the prospects at this stage, for all these critical changes, which are essential to ending systemic wilding and building a new economy, depend on the rise of citizen action and social movements that mobilize the population against the wilding of the corporate state.[54]

The consequences are clear. Five years after the crash in 2008, as of this writing in 2013, the biggest banks are bigger, wealthier, and more powerful. Economic recovery has taken place only at the very top, because the state has protected them while abandoning the population. We are left with even more extreme inequality, as reported by Krugman: "The data in question have been compiled for the past decade by the economists Thomas Piketty and Emmanuel Saez, who use I.R.S. numbers to estimate the concentration of income in America's upper strata. According to their estimates, top income shares took a hit during the Great Recession, as things like capital gains and Wall Street bonuses temporarily dried up. But the rich have come roaring back, to such an extent that 95 percent of the gains from economic recovery since 2009 have gone to the famous one percent. In fact, more than 60 percent of the gains went to the top 0.1 percent, people with annual incomes of more than $1.9 million."[55]

The corporate state has become the domineering institution of our times, undermining the prospect of true democracy and running roughshod over the interests of ordinary people.[56] A marriage of corporations and the political class, the corporate state is the engine that drives systemic wilding. It shapes a political and economic system designed to reward the rich, especially those on Wall Street, at the expense of the general public. The economic meltdown exposes the wilding dimensions of the corporate state and the larger social system it creates and protects.

The solution to systemic wilding is democracy. Wall Street has been a huge unaccountable network of overwhelmingly powerful corporations, with its top executives wheeling and dealing without having to answer to anyone: not its board of directors, not federal regulators, not its own workers, and not the general public. Wall Street, however, simply symbolizes the lack of accountability built into the larger capitalist system in which it has become the central player. All the major players—the banks, other huge corporations, and politicians—work together to insulate their collective wilding from public view or control.

How can such a system be made accountable? Only if the public decides that enough is enough and begins to take the constitutional creed of democracy seriously. The corporate state will continue to be an engine of wilding—siphoning power and wealth from ordinary citizens to the rich—until people turn off their corporate-programmed televisions, shrug off their couch-potato identities, and decide to throw the CEOs out of Washington. Then, they will face the task of rebuilding a true democratic system—something that will require imagination, hope, and dedicated activism in a new generation that may be inspired to act by the current crisis and by the ideals kindled—but not implemented—by Obama himself.

Discussion Questions

1. Did wilding cause the Great Recession?

2. What do you view as the worst form of wilding carried out by the biggest Wall Street banks during the Great Recession?

3. What caused the biggest mortgage companies and banks to go wild?

4. How would Marx explain the Great Recession, and would he describe it as a form of wilding?

5. Why was so much wilding by the Wall Street banks perfectly legal?

6. Are there regulations that could prevent the corporate wilding that helped cause the Great Recession? Why hasn't the government passed such regulations?

7. What can your generation do to help prevent another economic meltdown caused by wilding? Does the Occupy movement offer any clues?

six

Sociopathic Capitalism

Wilding Wars against Workers, the Poor, and Democracy

On July 18, 2013, the city of Detroit filed for bankruptcy. On December 3, 2013, a judge ruled that the filing was legal and that the city, officially defined as bankrupt, would move forward with bankruptcy proceedings. This unraveling of one of the largest and most important cities in the United States was an epochal event. How could Detroit, once the economic capital of America, go bankrupt and show signs of dying? The answer offers a window into the crucial forms of wilding that are built into our current capitalist system. It is leading not only to the crumbling of Detroit but to massive financial and social crises in Chicago, Philadelphia, New Orleans, and many other U.S. cities, as well as a larger major crisis in the U.S. economy and society. All this hints at the idea of sociocide, a kind of self-destruction or cannibalization by the society of itself, a wilding crisis that, taken to its logical conclusion, erodes the very possibility of civilized social life.

When Detroit filed for bankruptcy, it was $18 billion in debt. The city had 78,000 abandoned buildings and thousands of more vacant lots. In the last five years, half of its parks have closed. Forty percent of the streets currently have no lighting or electricity.[1] If your house is on fire, fire trucks may not arrive.

But in 1950, Detroit had 1.8 million residents and was the fourth-largest U.S. city. At the time of the bankruptcy filing, Detroit had shrunk to a population of about 700,000. People had died or fled to the suburbs or other states. New people were not replacing them. Large parts of Detroit had become ghost towns.[2]

Most of the people who didn't, or couldn't, leave are now in desperate conditions. More than one-third are poor, with over half of Detroit's children living in poverty. The schools are terrible, and medical and social services are badly frayed. Unemployment is skyrocketing as jobs vanish. Detroit has one of the highest murder rates in the country, with the lives of both children and adults in peril on city streets.[3]

Detroit in 2013 seemed scarily like New Orleans in 2005, when the latter was hit by the full fury of an apocalyptic Category 5 hurricane: Katrina. Many neighborhoods were destroyed and depopulated by those who could get out, leaving other people trying to survive as their homes were flooded and social and police services collapsed. But in Detroit, the hurricane that hit with full force was what I am calling sociopathic capitalism, a system of economic, social, and political wilding that can upend the biggest cities and threaten the survival of a great nation. In this chapter, I review the various forms of wilding that hit Detroit and show how sociopathic forces are now at the foundation of our economy and threaten the entire country.

Economic Wilding: Disinvestment, the Wage Squeeze, and the War on Workers

How did Detroit crumble? It was no accident—and it was not inevitable. Since the 1970s, the auto industry—the center of the city's economy—made a calculated and sociopathic decision to abandon Detroit. This was not an inevitable market decision based on steep differences in wage costs at home and abroad, although that played an important role. It was a managerial choice by automakers to maximize profits by leaving Detroit, often for areas as close as Detroit suburbs and nearby cities or as far away as Mexico and China.[4]

As early as the 1960s, the Big Three—GM, Ford, and Chrysler—began shifting production out of Detroit, driven by a shrinking market as sales of Japanese imports picked up, strong auto unions demanded better wages and benefits, and changing technology seemingly outdated the huge factories in Detroit. Managers and the best-paid workers moved to the suburbs as they embraced an overriding strategy to rebuild the auto industry on a new social contract, with workers holding the short end of the stick. Auto production facilities and jobs followed them—driving even more people out of the city to find jobs. This downward spiral continued over several decades, leaving the empty shells of old auto factories littered around the city. When the auto industry collapsed in 2009, there were just a few GM and Chrysler facilities left in Detroit and only GM still had corporate headquarters there.[5]

Detroit grew up as the auto capital of the world. The auto industry's investment in the city and in good-paying jobs made it one of America's premier urban centers in the first half of the twentieth century. But the massive disinvestment by the Big Three also was key to the bankrupting of the city. Executives abandoned the city and lacked either the managerial vision or the social responsibility to keep the city alive. Lacking that strategy, the industry took what seemed the easy way out in a classic form of capitalist wilding: wage war on the workers that had built the industry and on the city that had supported it. Disinvest in the workers' jobs, create new jobs that paid far less, and eliminate as many jobs as possible, either through globalization or robotic technology. Attack the unions that had negotiated good wages and benefits, and tear up the old labor contracts to write punitive new ones. The new regime was designed to drive labor costs down as fast and far as possible, to sustain big profits even as the industry declined.

The Detroit strategy is important because it models a wilding war against workers that has been unfolding in the U.S. economy as a whole. In the second half of the twentieth century, global competition began threatening the monopoly that post–World War II U.S. corporations enjoyed in the 1950s. Like the auto companies, corporations in every industry embarked on a sociopathic solution: wage war on U.S. workers and their unions to regain high levels of market share and profitability, whatever the harm of this strategy to the U.S. labor force and American communities.[6]

The war took two central forms. One was the decision to disinvest in the infrastructure and jobs of the United States, as production abroad was seen as a way to reduce labor costs and boost profits. This disinvestment in U.S. jobs—not only in manufacturing but in many service and high-tech professional sectors—was a momentous decision. It hollowed out the U.S. economy, substituting short-term high corporate profits for a viable long-term or sustainable economic base in the United States. Jobs disappeared, leading to a new mass population of unemployed, underemployed, and temporary and part-time workers, making up the core of what I have called a population of "surplus people."[7] In 2013, only about 59 percent of working-age adults were in the labor force, with a large percentage of the rest essentially surplus people.[8]

A majority of Americans already are surplus, at least during parts of their lives. A devastating survey reported by The Associated Press (AP) on July 28, 2013, is headlined "80 percent of U.S. Adults Face Near-Poverty, Unemployment." The article opens bleakly: "Four out of 5 U.S. adults struggle with joblessness, near-poverty or reliance on welfare for at least parts of their lives, a sign of deteriorating economic security and an elusive American dream." The explanation is based on survey data pointing to "an increasingly globalized U.S. economy, the widening gap between rich and poor, and the loss of good-paying manufacturing jobs as reasons for the trend."[9] "I think it's going to get worse," says Irene Salyers, 52, of Buchanan County, Virginia, who lives mostly on disability checks as she tries to survive with her boyfriend by working for a pittance at a small fruit and vegetable stand. "If you try to go apply for a job, they're not hiring people, and they're not paying that much to go to work."[10]

The data are depressing, reflecting record corporate profits as unemployment remains at very high levels, hinting at the wilding involved. While official unemployment is declining as the Great Recession recedes, at 7.3 percent in August 2013, this understates the surplus population, including the underemployed, involuntary part-time workers, temps, and those who have lost hope and dropped out of the labor force. None of these latter groups are counted among the officially unemployed, and when we count them, the "real" surplus or jobless rate rises to at least 25 percent, supporting Nobel Prize–winning economist Paul Krugman's argument that we have been going not through a Great Recession but a Great Depression.[11]

In 2013, the second front of the war on workers became more visible to all, with mass strikes of fast-food workers. In scores of cities and towns across the country, in a series of repeated walkouts over several months, workers at McDonald's, Burger King, Taco Bell, Pizza Hut, Kentucky Fried Chicken, and other fast-food chains went on strike and into the street. Paid around the minimum wage of $7.25 an hour, a wage that keeps a full-time worker in poverty at about $15,000 a year, these workers, the majority of whom are not teenagers but adults trying to support families, are calling for a new civil rights movement for workers. As the *New York Times* editorialized in support of the fast-food workers, "As lower-wage occupations have proliferated in the past several years, Americans are increasingly unable to make a living at their jobs. They work harder and are paid less than workers in other advanced countries. And their wages have stagnated even as executive pay has soared."[12]

CEOs at McDonald's, Taco Bell, and other fast-food companies are, in fact, among the highest-paid corporate leaders, and these companies are among the most profitable.[13] McDonald's made $5.5 billion in profits in 2011. They can afford to pay workers more—including the $15 an hour striking workers are demanding—but instead are driving them into poverty, much as Detroit auto executives did, to pad their own paychecks. This is economic wilding because it creates avoidable mass suffering caused by greed. McDonald's executives and their colleagues could have chosen to make very different choices and remain comfortable, but their wilding impulses led them to choose the corporate "low-road." As *U.S. News & World Report* wrote, "And why can't a company making billions of dollars in profits every year pay its workers a livable wage, anyway? The answer is greed."[14]

Workers from many other industries, equally desperate, are joining fast-food workers on the streets. On Sept. 6, 2013, walkouts by Walmart workers in at least 15 cities led to at least 100 arrests among thousands of Walmart workers who protested their minimum wage.[15] Walmart, the biggest employer in the world, with 2.2 million workers, is famous for its low wages, which average between $8 and $9 an hour, and has called any increase in the minimum wage a form of Soviet-style Communism. Walmart's low wages are wilding since, as with fast-food, there is an alternative strategy alleviating worker suffering, embraced to some degree by rival Costco, which pays its workers better than Walmart but still remains profitable.

The wilding war against worker wages is sweeping industries across America. The Department of Labor projects that as corporate profits soar, six of the top ten occupations projected to add the most jobs by 2020 pay low wages similar to those in the fast-food industry.[16]

Over the last three decades, the average wage has stagnated or declined for about half the U.S. population.[17] And even as the average worker works longer hours in a household where spouses are more likely also to work, household income shows the same pattern of stagnation of middle- and especially low-income workers.[18] The result is that worker wages, by 2012, made up the lowest percentage of the gross domestic product (GDP), or the national economy, since 1929. Wages made up only 44 percent of GDP while corporate profits after taxes in 2013 rose to about 10 percent of GDP, even higher than the previous record set in 1929.[19] In 2011, 99 percent of the population received only 7 percent of the growth of national income (see Chapter 1, pp. 13–14).

Low wages are a key source of high poverty, officially at about 15 percent of the population, or about 45 million Americans. One of every four or five U.S. children lives in poverty. About 70 percent of adults in poverty work, often full-time or at more than one job. The reason for their poverty: rock-bottom wages, which also explains the high rates of people who are hungry, homeless, or unable to heat their homes in the winter.[20]

This reflects, again, not market inevitability but an economic wilding strategy by the largest corporations, backed by their political allies in Washington since the

Reagan Revolution. What has driven down wages so long and so much? A calculated profit-driven decision by U.S. corporate leaders to eliminate the last vestiges
of the New Deal social contract that viewed workers as stakeholders deserving
to see their wages rise with their companies, and their productivity levels.[21] In
the early 1970s, in what I have called a "regime change," huge U.S. corporations,
working together in organizations such as the Chamber of Commerce and the
Business Roundtable, decided to launch all-out war on the unions and the New
Deal benefits they had helped deliver, which created the U.S. middle class but
modestly restrained profits. This meant an attack not only to wipe out unions
and slash union wages but to cut or eliminate pensions (which may be paid pennies on the dollar to Detroit city workers in bankruptcy settlements and have been
slashed by corporations all over the country), medical benefits, and any form of
job security.[22] Corporations have reaped huge profits with this strategy, but by undermining jobs and driving millions of Americans into poverty, they are engaging
in one of the fiercest forms of economic wilding in U.S. history, rivaled perhaps
only by the ruthless practices of the appropriately named corporate robber barons
of the nineteenth-century Gilded Age, such as John D. Rockefeller and Andrew
Carnegie, who frequently called their own goon squads to shoot protesting workers or beat them senseless.[23]

A war against workers is entirely predictable from a neo-Marxist sociological
perspective. Marx foresaw that capitalists would seek to create millions of surplus
people—what he called the "reserve army of the unemployed"—to make workers
afraid and more compliant. Cutting labor costs was the key to capitalist profit, so
Marx also foresaw that capitalist economies would drive down labor costs as far
as possible, leading to the extreme inequality that we are seeing today between
the ownership class and the workers.[24]

Marx saw class warfare as integral to capitalism. He viewed class warfare as
precisely the war by capitalists against workers and the poor that we have begun
to describe. Marx foresaw a continuous globalizing of production and increasingly
intense exploitation of workers as capitalism matured, leading toward social unrest
and capitalist self-destruction. When low-wage workers are unable to buy more
goods, tendencies toward stagnation and overproduction intensify. Workers who
go into debt to survive or "keep up with the Joneses" will add to an unsustainable
private as well as public debt in advanced capitalism. Their inability to buy what
businesses produce will ultimately crash the economy.[25]

Capitalist economists argued that market competition would keep capitalists
from waging such a ruthless war, since workers could migrate to companies that
treat them better and consumers might favor those companies. But Marx argued
that, as capitalism developed, competition would decline as companies merged
and used their political connections to create quasi-monopolies, giant companies
"too big to fail." The biggest companies would use both their political influence
and market power to drive out smaller or better-paying competitors whose higher
wages might lead to more efficiency. Marx's view seems more credible, in the light
of our current monopoly capitalism, where, in almost every sector, from banking
to fast food to agribusiness to aviation to big box retail, a tiny number of companies have taken control of their respective markets. It is Walmart, not the mom

and pop stores, that dominate sociopathic capitalism, and the giants do not face the kind of competition that might prevent their sociopathic war on workers.[26]

Class Apartheid and Social Wilding: The Secession of the Rich and the Segregation of America by Wealth

The Detroit collapse has not bankrupted all areas of Detroit. Parts of downtown, where investors see new opportunities for "Renaissance Detroit," are being revitalized. Old and new businesses alike are making good money in the city, including the federally bailed-out giant GM headquarters. However, many of the executives and top managers who work at the new GM and Chrysler in Detroit use the city's resources and infrastructure even though they live in wealthy surrounding suburbs.

Detroit has been restructured geographically into at least three cities: the abandoned and impoverished local neighborhoods, the downtown center where corporate headquarters and political elites still do much of their business, and the affluent suburbs, where the corporate managerial classes and political leaders live the high life. This is not entirely new. Mitt Romney, whose father ran an auto company, grew up in luxury in the Detroit suburb of Bloomfield Hills as the auto companies were driving thousands of workers into poverty. In 1990, Bloomfield Hills ranked as the second-richest town in the United States and in 2012 ranked as the fourth richest.[27]

Bill Clinton's Labor Secretary, Robert Reich, argues that the Detroit bankruptcy represents a "secession" by the rich, who have succeeded in working in downtown areas and using resources of the city while escaping tax burdens to support the city by moving out of Detroit. They have redefined political and social geography in a way that enriches themselves at the expense of everyone else, a clear form of social and political wilding. Reich writes, "If 'Detroit' is defined as the larger metropolitan area that includes its suburbs, 'Detroit' has enough money to provide all its residents with adequate if not good public services, without falling into bankruptcy." Reich notes that if you redrew the map so that the suburbs were included tax-wise in "Greater Detroit," there would be no bankruptcy. Greater Detroit "is among the nation's top five financial centers, the top four centers of high-technology employment, and the second-biggest source of engineering and architectural talent."[28] Reich also writes that, "Politically, it would come down to a question of whether the more affluent areas of this 'Detroit' were willing to subsidize the poor inner-city through their tax dollars and help it rebound. That's an awkward question that the more affluent areas would probably rather not have to face."[29]

Reich observes, "But there's a more basic story here, and it's being replicated across America: Americans are segregating by income more than ever before. Forty years ago, most cities (including Detroit) had a mixture of wealthy, middle-class, and poor residents. Now, each income group tends to lives separately, in its own city—with its own tax bases and philanthropies that support, at one extreme, excellent schools, resplendent parks, rapid-response security, efficient transportation, and other first-rate services; or, at the opposite extreme, terrible schools, dilapidated parks, high crime, and third-rate services."[30]

The secession of the rich is part of the wilding war on workers and the poor. Economic apartheid—or social segregation of the nation—by income is partly a way to create social distance, so the rich no longer feel a common bond with those who aren't rich, the vast majority of the country. In sociopathic capitalism, a wilding cycle of accelerating secession and inequality takes on its own momentum. The rich secede and use their economic and political power to make sure their taxes aren't used to support ordinary workers and the poor. This increases inequality and creates further secession and social distance, leading to more economic and political policies that assault the living standards of most nonrich Americans, thereby increasing inequality and triggering another cycle of secession. The process never ends.

As a sociologist, Marx foresaw economic and social polarization emerging in capitalism with the secession of the rich being one way of carrying forward the class struggle against workers. For Marx, capitalists and workers would increasingly occupy different social worlds, as class warfare cleaved society into rich and poor, with little connecting them. That this would lead to geographical segregation was not something that Marx highlighted, but it is consistent with his view that capitalism was a system sociopathically dividing society into separate and antagonistic groups, one subjugated by the other.[31] Social segregation based on wealth was a logical extension of capitalist inequality and would help restructure the political system to ensure that the capitalist class remained far on top.

Sequesters and the Slicing of the Safety Net: Austerity, Triage, and Political Wilding

One of the most emotionally charged issues in the Detroit bankruptcy is the fate of the pensions of the city's long-time workers—teachers, social workers, police, and firefighters, among others—who contributed money throughout their careers for their retirement into city pension funds. Without these pensions, most of these workers will have no way to survive in their "golden" years. Michigan's Constitution actually prevents these pensions from being cut or eliminated. But the bankruptcy has raised the prospect that wealthier creditors who bought city bonds will be paid before pensioners, and that city workers may actually lose some or all of their pensions.

For ordinary workers in Detroit, this is perhaps the cut that will draw the most blood. We have already noted that social services throughout Detroit—offered by schools, hospitals, social welfare agencies, police, firefighters, garbage collectors, and other providers—have been severely cut. Taken together, these cutbacks are destroying Detroit's safety net and its larger social infrastructure, creating an emergency in the provision of jobs, affordable housing, and the social services required to sustain the social fabric.

Tragically, Detroit is reflecting a national political dynamic that is threatening the social infrastructure and social safety net of the entire country, pointing toward potential sociocide. The national social infrastructure—consisting of federal economic and social welfare programs that ensure employment, health care, food, and housing for all—is the safety net that keeps us socially connected and alive. For the last three decades, since the Reagan Revolution of the 1980s, this infrastructure has been politically targeted by ruling elites, one of the most severe and important forms of political wilding in the United States.[32] In the Great Recession, the social infrastructure is melting away more rapidly, not just for the long-suffering poor but for many millions of working and middle-class Americans.

The scope and harshness of this national political wilding became visible in 2013, when Congress enacted the infamous sequester, an indiscriminate massive cut made on March 1, 2013, in the federal budget. Unless reversed, the cut will hack more than a trillion dollars out of the budget between 2013 and 2021. The cut is divided equally between defense and social programs, cutting in 2013 almost $30 billion in domestic social programs, the federal money that supports the social welfare and very survival of millions of Americans, especially workers and the poor.[33] It is such a brutal cut that the program was put in place initially to force a compromise in Congress on deficit reduction, based on the view that politicians would never wage this severe an attack on their own constituents and on America's social infrastructure. But this is just the political side of the broader wilding war on workers and the poor that we have documented above, and there appear to be no limits, as Tea Party Republican House members and other conservative politicians are pressing for even deeper cuts, including in Social Security, Medicaid, and food stamps that are currently exempt from the sequester.

Sequester is a dry abstraction but it gets more real—and sickening—when we look at the concrete cuts. In 2013, there were 25,000 fewer breast and cervical cancer screenings for low-income and high-risk women; 4 million fewer meals for seniors who depended on them; 540,000 fewer vaccinations for at-risk children and adults; 424,000 fewer HIV tests by health departments; 30,000 fewer poor children of working parents getting child care assistance; 6.6 million fewer special education students in educational programs, with 7,400 of their teachers and aides laid off; 70,000 fewer kids in Head Start programs along with 14,000 teachers and staff who lost their jobs; 1 million poor students impacted due to cuts to their school districts and teacher layoffs; 100,000 poor people losing rental vouchers for housing; and 100,000 fewer homeless people receiving housing assistance.[34] This doesn't include hundreds of thousands of others who lost access to public defenders in the justice system, suffered loss of medical benefits from Medicare, lost benefits of science and health grants for research on diseases, and were deprived of health and educational programs for veterans. Just in 2013, the National Institutes of Health's funding was cut by $1.6 billion, Head Start by $406 million, airport security by $323 million, public housing by $1.94 billion, and FEMA disaster relief by $375 million. Some academics estimate a total of 2.14 million jobs will be lost.[35]

The sequester shows that the U.S. political elite is engaged in a form of triage.

Triage is a term originally used in military medicine for the decision to abandon terminally ill or horribly injured patients in order to save others who were less time consuming or costly to treat. Triage, defined sociologically, means the sacrifice of the socially weakest sector of the society: the poor, the homeless, the hungry, the unemployed and underemployed, and those without health care. The politics of triage over the last several decades has meant that the New Deal social infrastructure that protected most of the poor and working class has been systematically dismantled, leaving a huge sector of the population to suffer job loss, financial ruin, loss of their homes, and sickness from lack of access to health care. Triage is political, economic, and social wilding woven together in a massive crisis of the commons that we need to ensure our collective social welfare.

How can the sequester cuts and broader triage be justified when they represent a wilding spear aimed at the heart of U.S. civil society? The sequester is part of a broader politics associated with the idea of austerity. Austerity is a political agenda rooted in neoclassical economics, as developed in the work of Nobel Prize–winning economist Milton Friedman, who described the federal government as coercive and destructive to a market economy, which should be self-regulating and free of political intervention. At austerity's heart is the idea of cut, cut, and then cut some more government spending, especially on discretionary social programs that benefit working and poor Americans. As the federal government expands, and budget deficits grow, neoclassical economists and their current political allies, such as Wisconsin Representative Paul Ryan, the Republican House chair of the budget committee and Republican vice presidential candidate with Mitt Romney in 2012, have taken Friedman's ideas to an extreme that even Friedman, who believed in government monetary policy to help manage business cycles, would likely find remarkable. Beyond the sequesters already enacted, Ryan has written austerity into his GOP House 2014 and 2015 budget proposals, which decimate social spending on everything from health and education to poverty programs, all in the name of balancing the budget. And Tea Party leaders, such as Kentucky Republican Senator Rand Paul, would go even further and dismantle large sectors of the U.S. government, as well as Social Security and Medicare.[36]

The corporate and political elites of sociopathic capitalism have grabbed on to the concept of austerity, in the context of growing public and private debt, as a weapon to wage the wilding war against workers and the poor in the name of efficiency and growth. Nobel Prize–winning economist Paul Krugman has demonstrated in influential columns and books that austerity is a senseless political club wielded by conservatives and wealthy elites, to transfer wealth to themselves in the name of debt reduction and economic revival, an illusion and a clear form of political wilding. Krugman shows that dramatically increasing government stimulus and job spending, even when it increases short-term debt, is the main way to grow the economy and permit repayment of long-term debt, since it puts income into the hands of millions of needy Americans who then can buy products necessary to revive U.S. companies and sustain private investment and long-term growth.[37] Austerity actually prolongs recessions and has been proved to be a false and failed remedy, with European nations who practiced it following 2009 going deeper into recession. The sequester has reduced U.S. economic growth, according to the nonpartisan Congressional Budget Office (CBO), by more than 1 percent annually.[38] Moreover, austerity is hypocritical since it has not cut "corporate welfare," which is government subsidies and tax breaks to agribusiness, the pharmaceutical companies, Big Oil and Big Coal, military companies, and the large Wall Street banks that have been bailed out. In practice, austerity has actually meant simply redirecting government money and help from those who need it most—workers and the poor—to those who need it least—the largest corporations and wealthiest Americans. This can only be viewed as gross political and economic wilding.[39]

Marx was an early prophet of these developments. As explored more in the next section, Marx saw government in capitalist societies as the executive committee of the bourgeoisie. As class warfare subjugated workers and created increasing inequality, capitalists would use their money to take control of the state. Money can buy anything, even politicians or, indeed, a society's entire system of politics. But even Marx might not have foreseen the amount of money that would pour into politics in the United States and turn it into a capitalist fiefdom.

The War on Democracy: Money, Voter Suppression, and Extreme Political Wilding

The situation in Detroit is a powerful symbol of the rising crisis in democracy. In 2012, Rick Snyder, the Tea Party governor of Michigan, used powers in a law he had crafted that allowed him to replace elected officials in cities with severe financial crises and appoint his own "emergency manager." These emergency managers would take over all the powers vested in the city council and mayor and run the city like a dictator. Elected officials would lose all their power.[40]

In 2012, Governor Snyder appointed a bankruptcy lawyer and turn-around artist, Kevyn Orr, as his emergency manager to run Detroit. Orr immediately took over all political control of the city, giving Detroit's mayor and city council some limited decision-making but making them powerless over big decisions, including the filing of bankruptcy itself. After only a few months, Orr decided that the city was unable to manage its financial crisis without filing for bankruptcy. While this was a highly controversial decision, with some believing it gave Detroit a way out and others seeing it as a death sentence, nobody could call the decision democratic. Orr acted unilaterally, without any popular or elected politicians or citizen groups able to stop him.[41]

The war on democracy is a national pattern. While it is not usually quite so blatant as in Michigan, it is driven nationally by two forces, each a major form of political wilding. One is the flooding of Washington by corporate money, aided by political and judicial decisions that have opened the floodgates. The second is the explicit effort to suppress, rig, or deny voters their right to vote, through changes in state and federal voting laws, redistricting, and other not-so-subtle changes, reminiscent of the old Southern poll taxes that prevented freed slaves from voting, all to restrict the right of millions of Americans today, mostly the poor and minorities, to vote.

In 2010, in a case known as Citizens United that will go down in history as one of the great acts of judicial political wilding, the Supreme Court effectively ruled campaign finance reform as unconstitutional. Most limits on corporate political spending were ruled a violation of the First Amendment, based on the view of corporations as "legal persons" and political contributions or money as a form of "speech." Citizens United has been compared to the Dred Scott case, a dreadful decision in which the Supreme Court said that slavery was constitutional. Many view Citizens United as the twenty-first-century Dred Scott decision, ensuring a form of political control by the wealthy and large corporations that enslaves the rest of the population. At the very least, Citizens United gives the wealthy a level of political power that seriously endangers meaningful democracy. This form of political wilding was exacerbated by the court in a second campaign finance case, McCutcheon vs. the Federal Election Commission, decided on April 2, 2014, that eliminated any cap on the total amount a donor could give to political parties, PACs, and candidates in a given election season. The sky is now the limit.[42]

Before the Citizens United and McCutcheon cases, a series of Supreme Court decisions had affirmed the constitutionality of laws restricting campaign donations by individuals or corporations. The laws did not prevent corporate money from dominating campaigns, but they allowed a measure of countervailing influence. After Citizens United and McCutcheon, when key campaign finance regulations were struck down as violating the free speech of corporations, the last restraints broke down and permitted a small number of billionaires and giant corporations to give literally hundreds of millions of dollars to elect the president and Congress, typically through Super PACs or secretive 501(c)(4) organizations that are under no obligation to limit or disclose identities or amounts of individual or corporate donors. In the 2012 elections, $6 billion to $7 billion dollars, largely from the wealthy and big banks and corporations, were spent on electing the president and Congress. Not surprisingly, former U.N. Secretary-General Kofi Annan, in a report of the Global Commission on Elections, Democracy and Security, singled out the United States as the example of a trend of "uncontrolled, undisclosed, illegal, and opaque" campaign financing.[43]

Some of the biggest donors were billionaires such as David and Charles Koch, extremely conservative Texas oil magnates who are among the top ten richest Americans, and Sheldon Adelson, another activist billionaire who personally committed to spending several hundred million dollars to elect his preferred candidates. In 2012, Adelson personally spent millions to keep Newt Gingrich in the Republican primary, and then shifted to supporting Romney, drawing on his network of far-right, ultra-rich supporters. Using 501(c)(4) organizations, a billionaire or giant corporation is legally empowered to spend as much as they want, without disclosure, even if it dwarfs all other contributions to the race. This ability of big money to drown out millions of small contributors and thus dilute their voice was one of the original rationales for the campaign finance laws that were struck down in the Citizens United and McCutcheon decisions.[44]

Both major parties have become dependent on corporate money in the new environment, since it dwarfs the second-largest source, union money, by more than 7 to 1 in campaign contributions. In 2008, Obama received contributions from small donors, but the majority of the total amount he got came from Wall Street and other giant corporations. The dependency of both major parties on corporate money creates what I call "corpocracy," the illusion of democracy by maintaining elections while both major parties are largely controlled by the huge amount of money given by corporations. Corpocracy is the institutionalization of systemic political wilding.[45]

Corpocracy—a sham that is the ultimate political wilding—is precisely what Marx predicted 150 years ago. Marx saw democracy as a necessary illusion, a way to divert attention from the control that the capitalist class inevitably exercised over government through its wealth and connections. Marx understood that, despite their antigovernment rhetoric, big business depends on corporate welfare for vast government subsidies and is willing to invest because of the stakes—and return on investment—that control of the state delivers.[46]

As with the Citizens United case, the Roberts Supreme Court was important in a second front in the war on democracy. In 2013, the Court gutted the key provision of the 1965 Voting Rights Act that allowed the federal government to screen in advance and prevent changes to voting laws that had discriminatory intent or effects on minorities. The Voting Rights Act, one of the signal accomplishments of the civil rights movement, overcame historic Jim Crow barriers to African-American and other minority and poor voters. According to Georgia Representative John Lewis, one of the few surviving civil rights leaders involved in the fight for the Act, the 2013 Court decision "stuck a dagger in the heart of the Voting Rights Act"—and was "personal."[47]

Even prior to the Court's decision, the 2010 midterm election that swept conservative Republicans into the statehouses and legislatures of 30 states, had launched an all-out war against democracy. The war was ongoing in key battleground states such as Florida, Ohio, Pennsylvania, Michigan, Wisconsin, and many southern and western states. Conservatives introduced new, burdensome photo identification requirements, reduced voting hours, closed many polling places, eliminated same-day registration, banned votes on the weekend prior to elections, gerrymandered voting districts, and excluded ex-felons from voting, among many other restrictions. In 2012, there were pictures of long lines of voters in Ohio, a pivotal state, on Election Day, especially in minority or poor voting districts; people were waiting in the rain for 7 or more hours, just to get in and try to vote. There were also extensive reports of other groups—such as seniors and students—who found it extremely difficult to vote because of the new rules. All this was done in the name of eliminating voter fraud, although legislators passing the new laws could not document more than a handful of fraud cases, often none at all, in their states.

In July 2013, North Carolina, a critical battleground state, passed the most restrictive voting law in the country. The bill mandates strict voter ID (no student

ID or public employee ID permitted); eliminates same-day registration, cuts 7 days of early voting, and includes these other restrictions:

- The end of pre-registration for 16- and 17-year-olds
- A ban on paid voter registration drives
- A provision allowing voters to be challenged by any registered voter of the county in which they vote rather than just their precinct
- Elimination of straight party ticket voting
- Authorization of vigilante poll observers, lots of them, with an expanded range of interference
- An expansion of the scope of who may examine registration records and challenge voters
- A repeal of out-of-precinct voting
- A repeal of the current mandate for high-school registration drives
- Elimination of flexibility in opening early voting sites at different hours within a county
- A provision making it more difficult to add satellite polling sites for the elderly or voters with disabilities
- New limits on who can assist a voter adjudicated to be incompetent by a court
- The repeal of three public-financing programs[48]

This is just a sample of the restrictions in a law that includes almost every voting hurdle passed in states around the country. It includes other provisions that make it easier for corporations to finance and influence election outcomes, as well as redistricting or gerrymandering that minimizes prospects for minority or poor people to elect their own candidates. Representative Mickey Michaux, the most senior North Carolina state legislator and civil rights activist, said this about the bill: "I want you to understand what this bill means to people. . . . We have fought for, died for and struggled for our right to vote. You can take these 57 pages of abomination and confine them to the streets of Hell for all eternity."[49]

Voter suppression is political wilding taken to an ugly extreme. It evokes awful memories of the days of slavery and Jim Crow, when African-Americans were in some areas lynched and, elsewhere, forced to pay unaffordable poll taxes if they tried to vote. The contemporary disenfranchisement is less physically violent, but it includes banning ex-felons from voting for life, pioneered in a period when incarceration of millions of African-Americans is a vast national scandal, a form of political apartheid. Voter suppression and the war on democracy is the dark political side of the broader war against workers, minorities, and the poor.

Marx himself recognized that the capitalist class used race as a vehicle in their political wars against workers and the poor. Marx, a close observer of American politics and a regular columnist for the *New York Tribune*, wrote President Lincoln after his Emancipation Proclamation, commending him for issuing one of the most liberating changes in history. Marx understood that corpocracy grew not only out of the money of corporate elites, but of the ideology that divided white and black workers and prevented a united working class from confronting the capitalist elites.[50]

Marxist sociology lays bare—and offers the most coherent explanation—of the war on workers and democracy, in an age when Marxism has largely been discredited. It will take a revival of a new neo-Marxist sociology to educate the public about sociopathic capitalism. And it will take a new generation of educated students, of all incomes and races, to take up the fight to move beyond sociopathic capitalism toward a just and community-based economy that eliminates economic, social, and political wilding.

Discussion Questions

1. Is the bankruptcy of Detroit a result of wilding? Does Detroit's collapse suggest we are heading toward sociocide, or collapse of society?

2. Are the low wages and job insecurity of workers and the poor a form of economic wilding by corporations?

3. Is economic wilding growing worse in the United States? Why?

4. Is capitalism inherently sociopathic, a wilding system? What would Marx say? What do you say?

5. Is the minimum wage paid to most fast-food and Walmart workers a form of economic wilding? Does it make you want to see more unions and an increased governmental role in protecting workers?

6. Does wilding cause a growing inequality between rich and poor?

7. Is political wilding destroying democracy? In what way? Who is at fault?

[seven]

Vigilante Society

Guns, Profits, and Race in the New Wild(ing) West

On February 26, 2012, in Sanford Florida, George Zimmerman, a 28-year-old Neighborhood Watch coordinator, fired a shot heard around the world. The target was a 17-year-old African-American boy, Trayvon Martin. Martin was killed instantly. Martin was returning to his father's apartment from a 7-11 store where he had bought a soft drink and a bag of Skittles. He was unarmed and had committed no crime. He was walking back in the soft rain of an early Florida evening to his home when Zimmerman followed him and confronted him. Zimmerman was carrying a concealed Kel Tec 9 pistol, and killed Martin with one bullet through the heart.[1]

Trayvon Martin's death led to one of the most charged trials in U.S. history. The case brought together the explosive issues of gun violence, race, public safety, and social justice. Although Zimmerman was acquitted of second-degree murder and manslaughter charges, he became a symbol of the vigilante in America who shoots first and thinks later. He was protected by "Stand Your Ground" laws. These laws were pioneered in Florida and permit anyone to shoot rather than retreat when they feel threatened. It is a profound, dangerous change in the concept of self-defense. Florida itself became the symbol of the vigilante society, where an angry and armed population confronts each other on the streets, prepared to take the law into their own hands.[2]

Zimmerman was to the vigilante culture what Bernie Madoff was to the greed-is-good Wall Street culture. He personified those twenty-first-century gun-toting Americans, viewing themselves as vigilantes protecting the public and themselves. Zimmerman was an angry young man. He had recently joined Kokopelli's Gym, advertising itself as the "most complete fight gym in the world." Prior to the shooting, Zimmerman had been slapped with a restraining order for domestic violence and been arrested and charged for assaults on an undercover alcohol agent. In another case, several months after his acquittal, on September 9, 2013, he was arrested for domestic violence alleged by his wife against her and her father. A few months later, on November 18, 2013, police arrested Zimmerman and jailed him after a fight with his new girlfriend, Samantha Schiebe. Authorities charged him with an aggravated assault felony and other domestic battery charges, after he allegedly threatened to shoot Schiebe with a shotgun and then physically threw her out and barricaded her house when she asked him to leave.[3] He had been required a few years earlier to take anger management courses. Yet, he had taken on the trappings of a respectable citizen focused on community safety and well-being. He aspired to be a policeman and judge, and he had helped initiate the Neighborhood Watch group—ultimately becoming the main "Watcher" in the gated community in which both he and Trayvon Martin were living at the time of the shooting. In the weeks before shooting Martin, he had a record of calling police multiple times while trailing "suspicious" strangers.[4]

Zimmerman's behavior suggests a profile of ultimate wilders discussed in Chapter 2, linked to narcissism, anger, bullying, lying, and feeling entitled to harm others while making the rules. He had a quick, ugly temper and viewed others as threats, especially if they challenged his authority. His sense of self-importance and desire for attention was reflected in his going on Sean Hannity's national television show when advised not to by his attorneys, lying to a judge about his financial situation, and starting online sites about himself, for self-publicity and to raise money for himself. After his acquittal in 2013 of criminal charges, when stopped for speeding on a Texan highway with a gun in the glove compartment, Zimmerman, in a bragging way, asked the trooper if he recognized him and knew who he was dealing with.[5]

Zimmerman is important as a symbol of the wilder-as-vigilante. A society of Zimmerman clones—defined by their love of weapons, anger, and self-appointed policing—are turning the streets and many of America's public squares into Hobbesian jungles. And the Zimmerman case helped make the Stand Your Ground and other permissive gun laws the symbol of the rising national wilding and vigilante culture. Senate Democratic leader in the Florida legislature Chris Smith, referring to the Zimmerman case and the Stand Your Ground law, spoke of the larger wilding implications:

> "This bill actually encourages people to shoot their way out of situations and that's not how we live in a civilized society," Smith told a news conference. "It's a mentality that has permeated the state of Florida. It's a mentality of shoot first, and we should not have that in a civilized society."[6]

Smith was hinting at the return of the "Wild West," a theme that recurred frequently in the commentary on the case. In a 2013 opinion piece in *U.S. News & World Report*, Benjamin Todd Jealous, former president of the NAACP, wrote:

> Over the last decade, "stand your ground"-style laws have fundamentally redefined the concept of self-defense and justifiable homicide in the United States. . . . George Zimmerman took this concept to its logical conclusion last year when he notoriously stalked unarmed 17-year-old Trayvon Martin in his gated Florida community. Zimmerman approached Martin, shot him in the heart and yet won an acquittal after arguing the teenager's attempt to fight back made him fear for his life. The fact is that Zimmerman never needed to claim "stand your ground" as a defense because Florida's "stand your ground" law had already redefined self-defense in the state: Whoever lives to walk away, wins. It's the law of the Wild West.[7]

Jealous wrote that, "Only now are Americans beginning to understand how these new laws threaten community safety and cohesion."[8] This is crucially important, because the real sign of a sociopathic society is when laws and social norms encourage or cause wilding—with our gun laws a vivid example of sociopathic rules. But the gun laws are just one element of the rise of a twenty-first-century wilding culture of vigilantism that Zimmerman's killing of Trayvon

Martin brought into public view. This evolving culture is itself a product of larger forces and broader social, economic, and political wilding in America, a culture of capitalism in violent decline, as well as of a more specific economic wilding by gun manufacturers and sellers. All of this also reflects systemic political wilding by legislators who have aided and abetted the wilding of the gun companies and the NRA, who are working to put guns in the hands of every citizen. The political wilding underlying vigilantism is also heightened by the crucial dimension of race and is most fierce in Florida and throughout the South and West, where the legacy of gun violence and vigilantism cannot be separated from the history of racism.

Armed, Angry, and Afraid: Social Wilding and the Arms Race at Home

After a jury declared George Zimmerman not guilty of murder or manslaughter in July 2013, the *New York Times* ran a lead editorial sounding this alarm:

> Amid all the furious debate generated by gun tragedies like the Trayvon Martin shooting in Florida, citizens in too many states have been quietly, legally arming themselves at alarming rates that offer scant optimism for reining in the nation's runaway gun culture.[9]

The *Times* went on to point out that during the Zimmerman trial, Florida had issued 173,000 new permits to people seeking to carry concealed weapons (as Zimmerman himself did). This is double the rate of 5 years ago and brought the total of gun-ready citizens in Florida to more than one million. The same rush to arm was found in more than 20 states, "prodded by the gun lobby into loosening their concealed-carry laws."[10] After Florida passed the first "Stand Your Ground" law in 2005, more than 30 states by 2013 had passed "Stand Your Ground" laws, permitting people to carry guns in classrooms, churches, and even bars, helping fuel what the *Times* called a senseless "Arms Race at Home."[11]

The *Times* minced no words about the social wilding consequences of this "arms race," including the "Wild West implications . . . when police officers respond to a nightclub disturbance involving cocky drinkers armed and ready to draw." An armed population—often angry and fearful—is a recipe for escalation of what President Obama's Attorney General Eric Holder, in characteristic understatement, called "dangerous conflict in our neighborhoods."[12] In fact, the mass sale of arms connected to the loosening of gun laws and new definitions of self-defense fuel fear and violence, as each person sees in any new social encounter both the possibility of lethal engagement and the entitlement to shoot first rather than retreat. Everyone gets an invitation and incentive to become a vigilante policing his or her own social world, a license to go wild.

The social wilding dimensions of the crisis involve both expressive and instrumental wilding. The expressive dimension involves shootings out of rage or a desire for control, both significant factors in the Zimmerman case. The instrumental dimension involves motives stemming from economic insecurity and desires for fame, money, and career advancement, factors also at play in the Zimmerman case.

The sensational publicity surrounding the Zimmerman case reflected the larger context of horrific shootings, wilding acts that get perhaps the greatest media attention. In the few years preceding and overlapping with the Zimmerman trial, multiple massacres in classrooms, workplaces, and on the streets dominated the headlines. Perhaps the most frightening was the mass shooting at Sandy Hook Elementary School in Newtown, Connecticut, on December 14, 2012. Adam Lanza, 20, used a military-style semiautomatic Bushmaster .223-caliber rifle to murder 20 innocent and beautiful young children and six adults and then kill himself. Lanza first killed his middle-class mother at home, who herself was a gun enthusiast and collector and had brought Adam to shooting ranges many times during his childhood, essentially teaching him the values and skills that he would later use to kill her.[13]

About 6 months earlier, on July 20, 2012, James Holmes, 24, who was also from a well-to-do family and had earned a Master's degree but had not found a job, committed a horrific massacre. Dressed in a gas mask, ballistic helmet, and black body armor, he opened fire in a movie theatre in Aurora, Colorado, at an audience of people viewing a midnight screening of *The Dark Knight Rises*. The total number injured and killed was 71, with 12 dead, one of the largest civilian domestic massacres in U.S. history. Holmes, like Adam Lanza, used an arsenal of military-style semiautomatic weapons—including a Colt AR 15—that allowed him to fire scores of bullets in seconds without stopping to reload. He had left his apartment booby-trapped, a double sneak attack on those hunting him, a hint of the rage driving his horrifying wilding act.[14]

Holmes' murderous assault was preceded on January 8, 2012, by yet another gun, this time by wilder Jared Loughner, 22, who fired a bullet into the brain of Democratic Congresswoman Gabrielle (Gabby) Giffords at a constituent meeting outside a Safeway store in Tucson, Arizona. Giffords survived but many at the meeting did not, with a total of 6 dead and 12 wounded by Loughner, who also used semi-automatic weapons. While the attack on a congresswoman did not have any apparent affect on Congress, which has failed to pass a single new gun control law, it did lead Giffords and her husband, Captain Mark Kelly, an astronaut and gun owner himself, to launch a gun control campaign reflecting the will of millions of shocked and frightened American citizens.[15]

While there were scores of such massacres over recent years, including the notorious Columbine and Virginia Tech school killings, the more significant forms of gun wilding were the thousands of individual shootings in workplaces, community buildings, and on the streets. The most heart-rending are the thousands of shootings each year involving children, such as when a 5-year-old boy in Cumberland, Kentucky, in April 2013, accidentally shot and killed his 2-year-old sister with a .22 Cricket rifle for kids (nicknamed by the manufacturer, Keystone Sporting Arms, "My First Rifle"). It was given to him as a gift by his parents, and it was the fourth such shooting by a child of a sibling or parent in the few weeks preceding the tragedy.[16] The Cumberland police reported that, "One of the parents was at home at the time of the shooting . . . She was cleaning and stepped outside to empty a mop bucket."[17] She didn't realize the gun was loaded and forgot about it. The wilding in these types of accidents is mainly in the "family fun and family safety" marketing strategies of gun companies and the broader gun culture encouraging the arming of parents and children.

The character of the gun culture—with its inherent cycle of fueling more guns, anger, and fear that lead to more shootings—is evident on the highways, with each incident of road rage now tied to the possibility of escalation to a shooting. Harvard Professor of Public Health and director of Harvard's Injury Control Research Center, David Hemenway, a prominent scholar of gun violence, reports a telling example:

> Two women, aged thirty-four and forty, were driving home from work when one cut the other off on a congested highway. Their rage escalated as traffic crawled for miles and the women flashed their headlights and hit their brakes. Both vehicles left the interstate, heading for home. At the first traffic light, one woman left her car and approached the other, perhaps to end the confrontation. The woman in the car shot the approaching woman in the face, killing her.[18]

These were not hardened criminals but ordinary commuters. The shooter was recorded saying, "Oh, my God, I shot her. Oh my God, I can't believe I shot her. Oh my God, I can't believe she's dying."[19]

This reflects how decent citizens can get transformed into a new breed of semiconscious vigilantes taking control of routine stressful situations by using their guns at hand to shoot and survive. Most drivers know the feeling of rising anger at other drivers seeming to disrespect them. With a gun in their belt or glove compartment, the wilding impulse to take control, revenge, or simply let one's rage be fully vented can morph into a violent "high noon" standoff. Gun owners who are not clinical sociopaths can easily commit vigilante gun violence, with some, like the shooter woman above, expressing remorse afterward. But many others feel a sense of moral righteousness, adding insult to the injury of their wilding act.

Gun violence occurs at a rate far higher in the United States—about eight times the rate in other nations of comparable high development, including all European countries and Japan. In 2009, the rate of gun homicide in the United States was 3 per 100,000 people annually. In Great Britain, where handguns are prohibited, the rate was .07 per 100,000, 40 times lower than the United States. In Germany, it was .2 per 100,000, more than ten times lower than the United States.[20] This pattern of the United States as an outlier on gun violence has been true for many decades up to the present day.

Gun availability and ownership across countries is not perfectly correlated with gun violence, as some countries, such as Sweden and Switzerland, have relatively high gun ownership based on hunting and sporting traditions but very low gun violence. Nonetheless, strict gun control has a major impact on gun violence. *Developed countries with strong gun control laws have virtually eliminated gun violence.*[21]

The level of gun violence in the United States threatens the social infrastructure that sustains civilized life. Society requires safe streets, parks, schools, highways, workplaces, and public and private places where we can walk, mingle, and connect without fear or rage. Gun wilding thus urgently requires an analysis of causes and roots, leading us to a solution essential to sustaining civil society and avoiding societal collapse.

The most obvious and proximate cause is the easy availability and widespread ownership of guns. In 2009, the Congressional Research Service estimated that there were 310 million guns in the United States not owned by the military, including 115 million handguns, 110 million rifles, and 86 million shotguns.[22] This suggests that there are as many civilian guns as people in the United States, although gun ownership is concentrated within certain households, regions, and states. In 2004, about 36 percent of Americans said they had a gun in their home, which is about 44 million gun owners.[23]

The difference in gun ownership and gun violence across states and regions within the United States is striking—and proves to be very important. The highest rates of both gun ownership and gun violence are in southern and western states where approximately 60 percent own guns.[24] The most armed states in the United States in 2009 were Kentucky, ranked number one in per capita gun ownership, followed by Utah, Montana, Wyoming, Alaska, West Virginia, South Dakota, North Dakota, Arkansas, Alabama, Tennessee, and Oklahoma. The lowest ownership rates—about 30 percent of people owning guns—are in the Northeast, with the lowest armed states including Massachusetts, New York, Rhode Island, and New Jersey.

While data on the relation between gun ownership and gun violence in the United States have been controversial, one fact is clear. States in the highest quartile for gun ownership had homicide rates 114 percent higher than states in the lowest quartile of gun ownership.[25] High gun murder–rate states include Louisiana (ranked the highest), Alabama, Georgia, South Carolina, Florida, Missouri, Arizona, and Oklahoma, all southern or southwestern states with high gun ownership. Oklahoma's gun violence got international attention when three young men in a car in Duncan, Oklahoma, killed an Australian college baseball player, Christopher Lane, running on the streets, because they were "bored . . . and had nothing to do," leading the former Australian deputy Prime Minister Tim Fischer to recommend that Australians "think twice" before traveling to the United States because of its lack of gun control. "I am angry," Fischer said about the "thrill killing," because "it is corrupting the world, this gun culture of the United States."[26]

States with low gun murder rates include Vermont (ranked lowest in gun murder rates), Massachusetts, Rhode Island, New Hampshire, all in the Northeast; and Hawaii, Washington, and Oregon on the West Coast. Some high gun-ownership states, such as South Dakota and North Dakota, have low gun violence, and some low gun-ownership states, such as Delaware, have high gun violence rates.[27] But these tend to be exceptions to the pattern of gun ownership connected to gun violence and are consistent with the finding that economically developed high gun-control or gun-prohibition countries have almost eradicated gun violence. Important research by Harvard's David Hemenway and others showing that in the United States, "guns are used far more often in the home to intimidate and frighten intimates than to protect against intruders" supports this finding.[28]

In U.S. vigilante society, guns are legitimated for self-defense but are more likely to be used to attack and control. Moreover, the line between self-defense and attack is tragically but deliberately being blurred, a process integral to the social wilding dimensions of vigilantism. Social empathy and solidarity, essential to social interaction and society itself, are eroded as people on the streets and in schools, restaurants, and any public or private place, learn to approach each other as potential adversaries in a shoot-out.

Gun Profits: How Corporate Wilding Helps Drive Our Gun Culture

Economic wilding is at the heart of the deeper causes driving our gun culture and wilding in the streets. The simplest form involves the profits of the gun companies. The more complex economic roots involve the dynamics of economic insecurity and political sociopathy in our racially charged capitalist system.

America's gun culture is driven by vast profits, especially for the huge gun companies and manufacturers, such as Freedom Group (which owns Remington, Bushmaster, and others), Colt, Smith and Wesson, and U.S. Repeating Arms. The NRA is essentially a trade association of these massive and politically potent gun corporations, funded by the industry to protect their right to sell all their brands of guns, ammunition, and other accessories. In 2005, the NRA formed its Ring of Freedom program to attract funding from the big gun companies, and more than 50 firearms companies gave about $15 billion to that NRA program alone from 2005 to 2013.[29]

Bushmaster, which manufactures the semiautomatic AR .223-caliber rifle used by Adam Lanza at Newtown, is owned by Cerberus Capital Management, a giant Wall Street hedge fund. Cerberus created Freedom Group, which also bought Remington and Advanced Armaments. But Freedom Group is just one of several Wall Street firms buying up giant gun firms.[30] *New York Times* reporter Andrew Ross Sorkin wrote after Newtown that, "It is often overlooked, but some of the biggest gun makers in the nation are owned by private equity funds run by Wall Street titans," whose interests are not in sports or hunting but maximizing profits at a Wall Street scale and pace.[31] After the Newtown massacre, though, Wall Street groups such as Freedom Group considered selling the gun companies when big institutional investors like the California Teachers' State Pension System announced it was considering disinvesting in Freedom Group.

The gun companies, as they have melded with Wall Street, have operated much like not only greedy banks but like the tobacco companies. They are among the most sociopathic corporations, putting profits over the most socially harmful products. With billions of dollars at stake, the gun manufacturers and their Wall Street masters have been among the leading forces driving the gun culture and gun violence, working with the NRA to prevent any meaningful gun control legislation.

Much like the tobacco companies, they see recruiting new young shooters as "imperative to the survival of the industry" and have moved aggressively in recent years to capture the youth market, sponsoring gun programs for elementary and high schools, the Boy Scouts and Girl Scouts, 4-H groups, and even church groups.

They encourage family trips to the gun range and gun show for fun, learning self-defense, and as an aid to character development. The marketing targets include children as young as 4 or 5 years old, although the prime marketing, carried out through industry-supported print media such as Junior Shooters, targets children and teens between 8 and 18 years old, with the older kids seen as "peer ambassadors" to enlisting younger siblings or friends. Industry-supported magazines discuss the imperative of getting youngsters involved early in "shooting anything," perhaps moving from archery to firearms, including semiautomatic weapons. One ad in a sports shooting industry–funded magazine directed at kids says, "Maybe you'll find a Bushmaster AR-15 under your tree some frosty morning," the semiautomatic high-capacity-magazine gun used by the shooters at Newtown, Aurora, and Columbine.[32]

The NRA, as one of the nation's most powerful lobbying groups, symbolizes the political sociopathy of gun violence in sociopathic society. Polls show a majority of the public favors stronger gun control laws, including bans on semiautomatic weapons and on high-capacity magazines. Yet, even after Newtown, while President Obama proposed limited bans, Congress was incapable of any serious gun control legislation banning the sale of even military-style assault weapons. The failure to pass such laws epitomizes political wilding, since political elites prioritize the profits of their corporate patrons over the safety of children and the larger public interest.

Sociopathic Capitalism and Survivalism: Systemic Wilding and the Structural Roots of Our Gun Crisis

Behind the corporate wilding of gun companies lie deeper, systemic economic and political causes of our wilding gun culture. Consider the following four apparently disconnected facts. First, many prominent vigilante shooters are losers in the job market. George Zimmerman was rejected when he applied to be a policeman. James Holmes, the Aurora theatre killer, had been unable to find a job despite his Master's degree. Second, the highest gun violence is in urban inner cities and rural areas that are marked by extreme poverty and joblessness. Third, gun violence is highest in the U.S. states hit hardest by the Great Recession. Fourth, gun violence is also highest in U.S. states with the strongest history of racism and racial tension.

These four facts point to two fundamental systemic causes of gun wilding in the United States today. The first is the rise of intense economic insecurity in the general population. This sociopathic capitalist trend—which is today's core systemic form of economic wilding—creates a survivalist mentality brewing violence in a surplus population that is increasingly stressed, angry, and afraid. Second, such survivalism in a society with a long history of racial conflict leads to new racial tensions and scapegoating, generating a pattern of vigilantism against racial minorities in what I call the Weimar Syndrome, an especially scary form of political and social wilding.

The relation between economic insecurity and violence is most obvious in the deepest pockets of poverty and hopelessness, whether in U.S. inner cities or rural regions with high unemployment. The gun-murder rates in U.S. cities like Chicago, Detroit, Washington, D.C., Philadelphia, and Los Angeles, while reduced significantly since the early 1990s by new community-based development and policing strategies and other factors still being debated by criminologists, rose in 2012 and 2013 and remain tragically high. Chicago, often dubbed the murder capital of the nation, had 512 murders in 2012 and exceeded that number in 2013. Detroit, as it moved closer to bankruptcy, had a 20-year murder rate high in 2012.[33]

Journalist and sociologist Alex Kotlowitz observes that, "many of these shootings are over what are such petty matters." Kids with weapons too often react violently to another person coming to their street corner, which they consider to be their clique's "territory."[34] In many neighborhoods, it is never safe to walk in the streets, and children are terrorized, prompting mayors and community leaders to view their communities as war zones.[35] Gangs and guns seem the only path to survival in the inner cities populated by the poorest minorities and abandoned by the corporations, helping to explain why there are more young African-Americans in the prison system than in the school system.

The overwhelming impact of economic insecurity created by systemic economic wilding in sociopathic capitalism is also evident in the striking contrast between the high gun-violence rates in states most impacted by the Great Recession and the states least impacted. A 2012 study by Yale political scientist Jacob Hacker and the Rockefeller Foundation found that the Great Recession severely impacted almost every state in the country, but it created the greatest economic insecurity in the Southeast and West and the least insecurity in the Northeast.[36] The study found that the states where the highest percentage of people suffered severe economic losses and the most economic insecurity were Mississippi, Arkansas, Alabama, Florida, and Georgia.[37] These states all suffered high rates of gun violence in 2013. In contrast, the states with the lowest percentage of economically impacted people included New Hampshire, Connecticut, Washington, and Minnesota, all states with relatively low rates of gun violence in 2013. Modest differences between these two groups of states existed earlier, reflecting the fact that even before the Great Recession, the high gun-violence states were among the most economically insecure while the low gun-violence states were the most prosperous and economically secure.

This takes us back to the regional differences in gun violence, with the South, especially the Southeast, having the most homicides and the Northeast having the fewest. This difference has long corresponded with regional differences in economic insecurity, with the southeastern states suffering higher poverty and unemployment, lower wages, and more economic insecurity than the northeastern states. People in the South have been economically harmed by their lack of unions and by their conservative state governments—from Georgia and Florida to Alabama and Mississippi—that deregulate corporations and offer large corporate subsidies while dispensing few social welfare programs for their citizens. In contrast, northeastern states are more unionized, pay higher wages and benefits, and tend to have more liberal state governments that are disposed to greater corporate regulation, more progressive taxation, and more robust safety nets for workers and the poor.[38]

These variations in the forms of capitalism in the South and the North explain the regional variations in economic insecurity and help cause the corresponding differences in gun culture and gun violence and wilding. Survivalism and vigilantism are national phenomena but are far stronger in the South and West, consistent with the economic disparities and the intensity of economic wilding in the South. The regional differences are strong evidence of the role of economic insecurity and corporate wilding in creating homicidal gun wilding.

☐ Race and Vigilantism: The Weimar Syndrome in the United States

The regional differences also highlight the role of race in gun violence and the causes of our gun crisis, which are tied to what I have called the Weimar Syndrome. The Weimar Republic was the German government in the 1920s. After the harsh reparations treaty with the Allies following World War I, Germany suffered a severe economic crisis, with hyperinflation, high unemployment, and extreme economic insecurity for much of the German population.

Angry and often violent right-wing political groups grew rapidly, including the Nazi party led by Adolf Hitler. These groups blamed the economic crisis on the Jews and other non-Aryan people, such as Gypsies and Slavs, living in Germany. While left-wing groups also grew and gained power in German cities and in the federal Weimar Republic, the right-wing groups, waging a charismatic and violent vigilante-style of politics, attracted strong support in rural areas and small towns that were long exposed to anti-Semitic ideology and a "Volk" or "folk" ideology of racial purity.[39]

In the global Great Depression after the 1929 crash, the Weimar Republic's left-leaning government failed to solve the deepening economic catastrophe. This bred mass public discontent with the German Social Democrats, Socialists, and Communists, and increased the popularity of the right-wing groups such as the Nazis. Hitler gained increasing popular support among a deeply insecure German population, as he offered an easy explanation of their problems and a simple solution. The Jews and other racial and ethnic minorities were parasites and traitors plunging the nation into debt and national collapse. Germany could revive its great national heritage only by exterminating the Jews and building a racially pure Aryan German nation, a process that Hitler began in the 1920s by turning his Nazi brown-shirted supporters into armed vigilantes who would shoot traitors and any political opponents.

The failure of the Left and the growing resonance of Hitler's message and vigilantism to an economically insecure and angry German public led the German corporate and aristocratic elites to help broker Hitler's ascension to power in the early 1930s. This was the decisive stage of the Weimar Syndrome. The

Syndrome, a horrific form of political wilding, can be defined by these elements: (1) a severe and intensifying economic crisis, (2) a failure of liberal or left-wing groups to solve it and, (3) the rise to power of right-wing populist groups who blame the crisis on racial minorities and the Left, and, once in power, carry out a vigilante agenda stoking anger and homicidal violence against racial minorities and political opponents.[40]

The vigilantism and gun violence in the United States today, despite significant differences, has some eerie similarities to that seen in Weimar Germany in the 1920s, a parallel highlighted by the South at the center of U.S. gun culture and vigilantism. Economic insecurity following the intensification of sociopathic capitalism, and the onset of the Great Recession has hit the southern (and secondarily western) states most acutely, where right-wing political forces, steeped in a long history of racial prejudice and violence, have gained control. As in Weimar Germany, a conservative populist movement linked to financial elites has gained traction in the most racially charged and gun-centered region of the United States, where economic insecurity and racial conflict have long been intense and intertwined.

The key to the Weimar Syndrome is the rise of mass economic insecurity in a state with historical ideologies and practices of racial hatred and violence, exploited by ruling elites to divide and conquer. The U.S. South, with its lengthy history of slavery and segregation, is the region of the United States most vulnerable to the Weimar Syndrome in economic crises, since racial ideologies and practices were so deeply imprinted into the southern way of life and are sustained by contemporary social patterns of job and housing discrimination and partisan politics, even as the ideological legitimacy of overt racism has waned.[41] Moreover, while guns and violence have always been a distinctive national phenomenon in the United States, it is in the South and West that gun culture has been and remains the most powerful and most politicized in vigilante style.

Southern states are now politically polarized by race, with whites voting overwhelmingly Republican and Blacks and Hispanics voting overwhelmingly Democratic. The Republican Party gains support among whites by speaking to the economic anxieties of white workers in the Weimar spirit, blaming their economic problems on immigrants and racial minorities living off big government and the welfare state. The rise of the Tea Party, a grassroots group strongest in the South that feels intense anger, and hatred toward "aliens" or "illegals," suggests racialized political wilding. Its association with survivalist and white supremacist groups and its passionate defense of guns and vigilante take-no-prisoners approach evokes the populist and racialized spirit of the Far Right groups in the Weimar Republic. The corporate national elites and the Republican Party establishment have seen these groups as their most important political base, and they have been willing to fund them despite the fact that many hold their nose while doling out money to them. Their assumption, which proved wrong in Germany, is that they can control the Far Right and the anger and violence to which they are prone, while using them to grab and gain state and national power, an assumption that some mainstream Republican groups, after the 2012 re-election of Obama and a Democratic Senate, began to question.

When economic insecurity reaches crisis levels, corporate elites, in their need to divert popular anger from themselves, blame the crisis on minorities and "aliens" supported by elitist liberals. This style of Weimar politics, a horrific form of political wilding, is played out on the national stage, but gains its greatest support in a southern and western population saturated with guns and racial divisions. The scapegoating of minorities and illegal immigrants is a crucial means by which sociopathic capitalism legitimates itself in a crisis, and it involves, especially in the South, the breeding of a culture and politics of racially charged vigilantism. One can see this most clearly in the politics of immigration on the Mexican border, where ordinary citizens, almost all white, are being deputized all along the border to discourage illegal immigrants from entering, and searching out those already here to deport them. They are being supported by an army of federal Immigration and Customs Border Control agents, backed by drones, tanks, and advanced weapons, which have turned the border, as the *New York Times* reported in a particularly vivid exposé, into a war zone.[42]

The economic and political wilding here is particularly dangerous and frightening. The war against workers and the poor, and on democracy itself, is, as discussed in the last chapter, wilding enough, breeding insecurity and violence. The Weimar Syndrome bolsters this systemic sociopathy with another particularly vicious layer of wilding built around racial scapegoating and vigilante racial politics. Racial prejudice is a terrible but potent means of reinforcing and intensifying the vigilante wilding bred by economic insecurity in an armed population. And racialized politics is being exploited in the South to help build the national conservative movement seeking to take over the White House and institutionalize sociopathic economics.

Stand Your Ground: Political Wilding and the Politics of Gun Control

After the Newtown massacre of those young, innocent children at Sandy Hook Elementary School, polls showed a national surge of support for stricter gun laws. More than two-thirds of the country favored universal gun registration and background checks. Pluralities also supported more safety devices on guns, such as trigger locks, serial numbers that can't be effaced, bullets that can't pierce police armor, or new technology that would make guns inoperable except by the owner, and restrictions on military-style semiautomatic weapons that can fire scores of bullets with one pull of the trigger. Gun control advocates felt in 2012, the year of horrific gun massacres, that this might be their time, finally supported by a public majority that might allow them to beat back the NRA's overwhelming success in opposing all gun restrictions.

At this writing in late 2013, though, the majority will has been denied. The federal government has passed no new gun control laws at all a year after the Newtown and Aurora massacres. The same is true of state governments, which, in fact, have moved in the opposite direction. While a small number of states, such as Connecticut and Colorado, the sites of the Newtown and Aurora massacres, have passed modest gun control laws, the majority of states are further loosening gun regulation and passing laws legalizing unfettered gun access and carrying of weapons, whether concealed or carried openly, by people on the streets and in parks, sports fields, schools, churches, restaurants selling liquor, and—remarkably—bars.

The NRA, as discussed above, is the de facto trade association and lobbyist for the gun companies, which fund it lavishly. The NRA does more than politically lobby; it helps shape the vigilante gun culture and molds public views about the virtues of gun ownership for all. After the Newtown massacre, NRA Executive Vice President Wayne LaPierre helped launch a major campaign to arm teachers in public schools, with the assertion, made in 2012, that "the only thing that stops a bad man with a gun is a good man with a gun." This kind of argument has helped support not only the laws being crafted to put armed teachers in every school but the myth that every home should have a gun for self-defense, when academic research shows that a gun in the house more often results in the increased risk of suicide, lethal accidents, and lethal domestic violence.[43]

The NRA has also been a major force behind the conceal-carry laws, permitting carrying of hidden weapons in schools, bars, workplaces, and most other spaces, as well as a force behind the Stand Your Ground laws, passed by more than 30 states, as noted earlier. Florida's first such law in 2005 used the same specious argument that guns offer self-defense when research shows that they actually create higher risks of aggression and violent, lethal confrontation.

The scholarship, however, gets little attention by Republican Congressional representatives and Republican governors and state legislators in red (Republican-majority) states, where the NRA is king. Republicans see the gun control issue as one of their primary ways to win power, particularly in the South and West where Weimar-style political wilding strategies are very effective. Since 2010, when Republicans took control of 30 state legislatures as well as the House of Representatives, they have fought to eliminate all gun control at both the federal and state level, with startling success.

About 20 southern and western Republican-dominated states have made significant changes to weaken or eliminate gun control.[44] In Alabama, citizens can now carry a loaded gun in their cars to work if they have a concealed-carry permit. In Arizona, a new law banned any record of "the identifying information of a person who owns, possesses, purchases, sells, or transfers a firearm." In Arkansas, a new law permits guns in church, and licensed professors and staff at public universities can carry concealed handguns, while employees of bars and liquor stores with concealed-carry permits can bring their guns to work. In Kansas, federal gun legislation will no longer be enforced. In Kentucky, people can now carry guns into formerly prohibited venues, including the State Capitol, city halls, zoos, libraries, parks, and community centers.[45] In Wyoming, judges can now carry guns into a courtroom.

These laws are evidence of a political system and society gone wild. As the population becomes fully armed in private and public, and as self-defense becomes redefined as the right to shoot when people feel subjectively threatened, civil society morphs into a Hobbesian jungle and the Wild West. Every social interaction carries increased risk of armed confrontation, and feelings of empathy and community will give way to a cold war at home while eroding any prospects of community and social solidarity.

In Florida, after George Zimmerman was acquitted of criminal charges in the killing of Trayvon Martin, a group of mainly students and minorities calling themselves "Dream Defenders" carried out a sit-in protest at the Florida State Capitol, demanding repeal of the Stand Your Ground law.[46] They stayed for 31 days and promised to return when the Florida legislature reconvened in the fall. This kind of bold political response points to the response needed to counter the wilding unleashed by today's vigilante culture. Young people and minorities are among those most likely to lead a new national movement for gun control, as they learn that the many developed societies that have banned guns have largely eliminated gun violence. But since vigilantism and gun violence in the United States reflect systemic wilding embedded in our sociopathic capitalism, a full solution to the gun crisis will require a challenge to our current model of corporate capitalism and its hyperindividualism and racial biases.

Discussion Questions

1. Was Trayvon Martin a victim of wilding?

2. Is George Zimmerman a wilder? If so, why was he acquitted of Martin's murder?

3. Are U.S. gun laws a form of wilding? Is Stand Your Ground legislation political wilding?

4. The U.S. Supreme Court has ruled that owning guns is a constitutional right. Does that mean that gun ownership should not be treated as a form of wilding?

5. Is the NRA an economic and political wilder?

6. What explains the high level of gun violence in the United States, compared with other countries? Does wilding help explain this problem?

7. Does gun violence reflect a return to the "wild west?" What kind of wilding is at the root of this crisis? What is the role of race and racism in gun wilding?

[eight]

Wilding against the Environment:
Climate Change and the Ultimate Tragedy of the Commons

The natural environment, including the earth's air, water, forests, plants, and soil, is the ultimate commons on which all civilization and the very survival of humanity depend. As the United States and other societies burn more oil, coal, and other fossil fuels, we are spewing out catastrophic levels of greenhouse gas emissions, which act like a blanket, trapping heat in the atmosphere and heating up the planet. As one of the world's most eminent climate scientists, Columbia professor and director of NASA's Goddard Institute for Space Studies, James Hansen, told Congress in 2008, if we do not act decisively now, global warming will escalate into a "perfect storm," creating a "global calamity," endangering human civilization as we know it.[1]

Environmentalist Bill McKibben has called 350 the most important number in the world.[2] This is because Hansen and many of his fellow scientists now believe that a concentration of carbon dioxide in the atmosphere exceeding 350 parts per million (ppm) is like a cholesterol level greater than 350, almost certainly likely to kill us, sooner rather than later.[3] In 1850 and for centuries earlier, before the Industrial Revolution took off, the number was 286 or lower. It is, at this writing, about 400 and rising each year, helping to explain why our current carbon concentrations in the atmosphere and average global temperatures are higher than in hundreds of thousands of years.

Global warming is the ultimate tragedy of the commons. It ranks with all-out nuclear war as an existential threat to human survival. As each company and nation follow their own profits and growth, the fates of our children and our children's children are increasingly undermined. This is action taken consciously for short-term interests. It constitutes the ultimate wilding against future generations and nature.

Weather Gone Wild: Heat, Rain, Hurricanes, Floods, and Fire

In 2012, *National Geographic* published a memorable feature article called "Weather Gone Wild." The opening sentence reads, "Rains that are almost biblical, heat waves that don't end, tornadoes that strike in savage swarms—there's been a change in the weather lately. What's going on?" The rest of the article delivers the answer: Climate scientists in the Intergovernmental Panel on Climate Change (IPCC) had predicted in their alarming reports from the early 1990s to 2009 the faster and more catastrophic global warming that awakened the world to the changing weather nightmare.[4]

Examples of "nature gone wild" include a record-setting rainstorm in Nashville on May 1, 2010, which dropped 13.3 inches of rain, double the previous record set by Hurricane Frederic in Nashville in 1979. Brad Paisley, a country singer and local Nashville farmer, marveled that, "It came down harder than I've ever seen it rain here. You know how when you're in a mall and it's coming down in sheets and you think, I'll give it five minutes, and when it lets up I'll run to my car? Well, imagine that it didn't let up until the next day."[5] The storm was so fierce that it picked up a large mobile building, part of a local school complex, and sent it floating on water down an interstate highway. A local anchorman reported, "We've got a building running into cars."[6]

Described by officials as a "once in a millennium occurrence," it happened about a year before the November 2013 monumental Typhoon Haiyan in the Philippines, one of the most ferocious storms in human history, with sustained winds of about 200 mph (far higher than during Katrina) and storm surges 20 feet high that killed over 10,000 people in just one province and left millions homeless. The Nashville storm also happened at roughly the same time as a torrential rain storm in Rio de Janeiro, Argentina, that created mud slides that buried hundreds of people, floods in Pakistan that affected 20 million people, and floods in Bangkok, Thailand, that submerged hundreds of factories and crashed computers around the world.[7] Not long after these startling events, Superstorm Sandy hit the East Coast with a ferocity only second in U.S. history to legendary Hurricane Katrina, which destroyed much of New Orleans. In October 2012, Sandy, which lashed the entire East Coast, killed hundreds of people and destroyed the homes, businesses, power grids, roads, bridges, and job prospects of thousands of survivors. The total cost of damages is estimated at $80 billion.[8]

As these hurricanes were destroying communities around the world, unprecedented drought was taking place across many continents, including in Texas, Australia, and Russia, as well as in East Africa, where tens of thousands of people without water were forced into refugee camps.[9] Along with the global drought crisis, the world is witnessing horrifying fires from spontaneous ground fires in Russian forests and massive wildfires burning down thousands of acres of forest in American national parks, as well as residential land and homes in the western United States, including California, Oregon, Utah, Idaho, and Montana.

Meanwhile, in the years from 2010 to the present, the National Climate Data Center of the American Meteorological Society reported in its 2012 "State of the Climate Report" that sea levels reached a record high, threatening millions living on global coasts; Arctic ice caps melted at record levels, with 97 percent of Greenland's ice sheet showing some form of melt; and ocean heat content hovered at near record levels, as did ocean salinity.[10]

Climate scientists are unequivocal that a leading contributor to this extreme weather is global warming, associated with increasing concentrations of greenhouse gases in the atmosphere. According to the American Meteorological Society, the 2012 carbon dioxide concentration rose to a record 400 ppm in periods during 2012 and averaged 398, substantially above the levels just a few years ago and well above the "red zone" of 350.[11] Climate scientist Gerald Meehl, at the National Center for Atmospheric Research, explains that rising greenhouse gases are the trigger of extreme weather. "Picture a baseball player on steroids," Meehl says. "This baseball player steps up to the plate and hits a home run. It's impossible to say if he hit that home run because of the steroids, or whether he would have hit it anyway. The drugs just made it more likely." He says that, "greenhouse gases are the steroids in the climate atmosphere." "By adding just a little bit more carbon dioxide to the climate, it makes things a little bit warmer and shifts the odds toward these more extreme events."[12]

This conclusion of the overwhelming majority of climate scientists—that our new plague of costly and deadly natural disasters and extreme weather are caused by human-created global warming—is supported by the heat records in the United States and globally. The hottest year in recorded U.S. history was 2012. The top ten hottest years averaged across the entire world all happened, as of 2012, in the 14 years after 1998. By virtually every way of measuring average temperature in the global atmosphere, we are suffering the hottest temperatures in many centuries.[13] But this heat wave, unlike any other, is an existential threat that could end civilized society as we know it. Since humans have created it, governments and corporations bear responsibility and are doing far too little to stop it, and many of the elites in the United States are actually denying the grim reality they have constructed (as discussed below), this must be seen as the ultimate wilding against humanity.

Big Oil and Big Coal: Corporate Wilding and Climate Change

In his 2008 Congressional testimony, NASA climate scientist James Hansen dropped a bombshell, saying that the top executives of the biggest oil and coal companies should be tried in the International Court in the Hague because they are undermining the world's fight to stop global warming. He did not mince words: "CEOs of fossil energy companies know what they are doing and are aware of long-term consequences of continued business as usual. In my opinion, these CEOs should be tried for high crimes against humanity and nature."[14]

Top energy executives are guilty of extreme wilding. Their economic wilding includes a catastrophic disinformation campaign designed to confuse the public about the reality of the global warming emergency and to preserve company profits. Hansen told Congress that "[s]pecial interests have blocked transition to our renewable energy future. Instead of moving heavily into renewable energies, fossil companies choose to spread doubt about global warming, as tobacco companies discredited the smoking-cancer link. Methods are sophisticated, including funding to shape school textbook discussions of global warming."[15] The analogy to the tobacco executives is apt, since top oil executives, to preserve their profits, have lied repeatedly and funded for decades right-wing foundations and a tiny minority of scientific dissenters linked to the tobacco companies.[16]

As late as 2006, long after virtual unanimity among the world's climate scientists had been recorded in the U.N.'s IPCC reports, Exxon continued to fund climate change–denying groups and to reject global warming as a scientific truth. But in the face of blunt criticism from both Democratic and Republican senators to "stop the denial," Exxon shifted to what I have called a "Stage 2" Denial Regime.[17] On June 19, 2007, Kenneth Cohen, the top global spokesperson for Exxon, announced that the corporation had "evolved" in its understanding of climate change. "We're very much not a denier," Cohen said. Anticipating new worldwide and American initiatives on global warming, he said Exxon is now "very much at the table with our sleeves rolled up."[18]

This can be seen as the symbolic date of the Denial Regime's shift from Stage 1 to Stage 2. In Stage 1, big oil and big coal companies simply lied outright, denying that global warming existed or was caused by humans. But in Stage 2, the oil and coal companies took a more sophisticated stance, now acknowledging that human-caused global warming was real and must be addressed. But, they said, the shift to clean energy had to be gradual and required continued core reliance on oil and coal, thus seeking to wring profits from catastrophic pollution for as long as possible.[19]

Stage 2 denial is corporate whitewashing, symbolized by British Petroleum renaming itself BP (or "Beyond Petroleum"). This rebranding would become the symbol of Stage 2, making a major oil company a self-pronounced leader in the search for alternative energy. Exxon, BP, and other Stage 2 energy firms began investing in some forms of renewable energy. But rebranding themselves as green is clear "greenwashing," which an environmental group, Friends of the Earth, defines in this humorous vein:

Green*wash: (gren-wôsh) -washers, -washing, -washed 1) The phenomenon of socially and environmentally destructive corporations attempting to preserve and expand their markets by posing as friends of the environment and leaders in the struggle to eradicate poverty. 2) Environmental whitewash. 3) Hogwash.[20]

The corporate greenwashers—including a majority of global corporations today—proclaim in their mission statement their commitment to fight global warming, and they show colorful charts measuring environmental performance and highlighting a reduced carbon footprint in their annual reports. But BP shows this is, for the most part, economic wilding, since it was determined from the start to remain an oil company. Lord John Browne, BP's former CEO, made clear that despite the rise of renewables, "the oil industry is going to remain the world's predominant supplier of energy . . . alternatives will take a greater share of the energy market as we go into the next century. But let me be clear. That is not instead of oil and gas. It is additional."[21] Exxon, Duke Energy, and all big oil, gas, and coal companies now talk clean energy but produce oil, gas, and coal as the core of their dirty business—and plan to do so for decades to come.[22]

As in the case of the tobacco companies, the big oil, gas, and coal companies decided to embrace the cause of protecting public health and the environment while producing as much of their dirty products as possible to maximize short-term profits before they are taxed, capped, or rationed. In the last few years, they have reaped the biggest profits in corporate history, while endangering the future of civilization.

☐ Capitalism, Consumerism, and Climate Change: The American Dream and Ultimate Systemic Wilding

The wilding that is causing global warming is not restricted to big oil and coal. The hard truth is that the capitalist system itself is a major cause of climate change, especially the U.S. capitalist model. The exceptionally high U.S. carbon footprint is hardly surprising, considering that the American Dream is built around a religion of extreme consumerism, with a lifestyle organized around carbon-spewing cars, freeways, suburbs, exurbs, large, air-conditioned homes with chemically treated yards, and huge malls.

The relationship between capitalism and climate change is emerging as one of the most important issues in sociology today, and it points to the most extreme form of systemic wilding, as Karl Marx predicted.[23] The capitalist drive for profit requires ever-greater production, growth, and consumption: Capitalism is a system based on "me" and "more." It rejects limits; without more and more consumption, profits will fall and capitalism will decline. But nature has its own limits, which create inherent tensions between capitalism and a sustainable world.

Capitalism generates crises of overproduction and debt-induced consumption that threaten the environmental commons. The wage paradox discussed in the introduction and Chapter 5 leads each profit-seeking firm to produce as much as possible while reducing workers' wages. But when all firms do this, workers collectively lack the money to buy all the goods stocked on the shelves. As seen in the current Wall Street crisis, capitalists respond by creating easy credit and encouraging workers to go into extreme debt to keep consuming beyond their means, thereby threatening the sustainability of both the economy and the environment.[24]

The U.S. capitalist model poses special threats to the environmental commons. American capitalism enshrines self-interest as sacred, protecting the rights of property owners, including big oil, gas, and coal, to "drill, baby, drill" and seek profit at whatever the cost to the environmental commons. Likewise, U.S. consumers feel they have a God-given right to drive a Hummer or use the dirtiest carbon-burning lawn mower, viewing this as the very definition of freedom in America.

Keeping in mind the current Wall Street crisis and the Great Recession, we can see at least six ways that U.S. capitalism inherently creates climate change and is a catastrophic form of systemic wilding:

1. U.S. markets "externalize" or ignore environmental and social costs, forcing others to pay the true costs to health and life, since the corporations can spew carbon emissions into the air or water without paying for them.

2. Low wages, driven down by the core capitalist drive to maximize profits, create a work-and-spend cycle that is unsustainable.

3. Big business, the advertising industry, politicians, and economists create a religion of unlimited growth and unsustainable consumerism; Madison Avenue makes us all believers.

4. Wall Street grows like a cancer, creates "financialized capitalism," and promotes extreme short-term business and consumer thinking, undermining the culture of stewardship needed to prevent climate change.

5. Big corporations intertwine with political elites and dominate Washington, with both parties promoting profits over people and the environment.

6. American consumer capitalism becomes entrenched in a fossil-fuel intensive lifestyle based on cars, highways, suburbs, and malls and is ultimately justified by capitalist values of hyperindividualism.[25]

Mainstream economists largely ignore this analysis of inherent capitalist contradictions and the system's built-in environmental unsustainability, which are greatly exacerbated by the United States, the current crisis, and the global economy. Global U.S. firms push down wages far more easily by outsourcing jobs and exploiting billions of impoverished workers in Asia, Latin America, and Africa. Global sweatshops and pollution created by transnational companies in poor nations strip naked for all to see the crises of the global economy and the environment as intertwined systemic capitalist time bombs.

Capitalist conflicts between labor and capital—and the squeeze on U.S. workers facing competition in a globalized labor market—create declining consumer demand, growing inequality, slack productive investment, financialization, speculation, and accelerated financial transactions, credit, and debt. The aim is to speed up short-term consumption in order to buttress a stagnating real economy and feed the financial services industry that produces the easy credit and loose debt as well as the last great profit opportunities for big business. The debt system and the short-term mentality of easy credit fuel madcap environmentally unsustainable consumption, which leads toward even more debt that is economically unsustainable and brings the economy to its knees. At the same time, workers are induced into the short-term thinking of the consumer culture that redefines excess (bigger, carbon-intensive houses and cars, more "stuff") as happiness while burning up the planet.[26] This all might be called "capitalism's bonfire," a real-world variant of what novelist Tom Wolfe called "the bonfire of the vanities."[27]

Systemic capitalist wilding against the environment involves political and social as well as economic wilding. In the United States, politicians act as handmaidens to the corporations that pay for their campaigns, putting profit and their own power above people and the environment. The refusal by all presidential administrations before President Obama's to admit and act against climate change is the political component of capitalist wilding against the environment. Politicians have refused to tax fossil fuels (for example, institute a gas tax) or put in strict carbon regulations that would preserve the environmental commons. Political wilding also involves creating the legal framework and economic policies that favor unlimited fossil fuel–driven growth and consumption; subsidizing business expansion with tax deductions, loopholes, and direct giveaways; facilitating cheap extraction of oil and coal; and fighting wars for oil in the name of the war on terrorism.

While global warming will affect every individual on earth, it will most severely harm the poor and vulnerable. Global warming will create hundreds of millions of environmental refugees, most immediately in Asia, Africa, and Latin America.

Our failure to act is thus an extreme act of triage, wilding by the more affluent to preserve their carbon-intensive lifestyle at the expense of the poor, making global warming a crisis of global justice.[28]

The American Dream that equates big money and what economist Thorstein Veblen called "conspicuous consumption" with success is a script of extreme social (or cultural) wilding against the environment.[29] Our own addiction to "stuff" makes us all complicit in climate change and in wilding against the planet. True, much of our consumerism is "coerced," since even if we don't like to drive, the lack of good public transportation makes it nearly impossible for many of us not to rely on cars; similarly, extremely sleek and sophisticated advertising techniques and salesmanship help make us consumer addicts.[30]

But in addition to coerced consumption, we each play our own wilding role by buying into the American Dream with the idea that our self-worth and value are best measured by how much money we make and spend. Our life story becomes what filmmaker Annie Leonard calls "the story of stuff." [31] The accumulation of overstuffed closets and oversized cars that end up ultimately in landfills is not the legacy we want to leave behind.

[□] Keystone XL and the New Environmental Movement

Since we are all complicit, and because global warming threatens all of us and our children, we can solve this terrifying wilding crisis only by taking action into our own hands. Part of this involves individual change in lifestyles to reduce our own personal carbon footprint. We can drive an electric, hybrid, or "smart car"; walk, ride bikes, eat less meat and more vegetables, or use public transportation more often; turn down the heat or air conditioner; recycle; buy less "stuff"; take shorter showers; insulate our homes; and buy green products. These changes can make you happier and healthier and save you money.[32]

But the truth is that such personal changes will not solve the problem, which will require major changes in the American system. These changes in the U.S. capitalist model, now being globalized throughout the world, can only be brought about by strong international agreements to cap and tax greenhouse gases at sustainable levels—backed by grassroots global social movements that force national leaders to act. The United States—pushed by environmental, consumer, and labor movements—must take the lead, since it emits by far the most carbon emissions per capita and, along with other Western countries, is mainly responsible for the global industrialization and consumer culture of the nineteenth and twentieth centuries that contributed to climate change.

In his 2008 campaign to become president, Obama advocated forceful measures to solve the climate crisis. He rejected the climate denial of many leading Republicans and appeared to recognize the gravity of the crisis, promising that he would seek to move the country toward a clean energy economy to reduce global warming. "What we can be scientifically certain of," said Obama, "is that our continued use of fossil fuels is pushing us to a point of no return. And unless we free ourselves from a dependence on these fossil fuels and chart a new course on energy in this country, we are condemning future generations to global catastrophe."[33]

In his first year, Obama moved beyond rhetoric, proposing and signing a $787 billion green stimulus bill to create green-collar jobs and invest in clean energy as his main way to end the Great Recession and rebuild the economy on a new foundation. And with Obama's strong support, backed by a brilliant team of energy advisors focused on the dangers of climate change, in June 2009, the House of Representatives passed the Waxman-Markey Bill, the first climate change bill passed by either house of Congress in U.S. history. It capped carbon emissions and allocated billions of dollars to spur wind and solar energy production and employ workers in green-collar jobs. Much of the world celebrated, thinking that it would help bring the United States to the global climate table, with Obama leading the nation and world toward international carbon caps and other climate treaties.

But big business lobbied heavily to water down the bill, significantly weakening the carbon cap, allowing big oil and coal companies to pollute freely for many years, and relying on dubious "carbon offsets" that allow companies to continue spewing out carbon emissions while claiming to offset them with unverifiable green initiatives such as planting trees in the rainforest. Even in a weakened form, the bill was opposed by House Republicans and barely passed, setting the stage for the eventual defeat in the Senate. From that point, with the landmark Republican takeover of the House of Representatives in 2010, Congress abdicated any responsibility for doing anything about climate change, and Obama barely mentioned climate change again in his first term, thus joining with Congress in one of the most serious forms of political wilding in history.[34]

After his reelection in 2012, Obama promised once again to act in the face of Congressional resistance, using his bully pulpit and executive powers to move the country toward clean energy. But while he issued new car mileage rules and helped spur his EPA to announce that it would regulate carbon as a form of air pollution, Obama has not followed through with the passion and leadership required to get meaningful change. On critical issues, including the building of the Keystone XL pipeline that carries Canadian tar sand oil across a huge swath of U.S. environmentally sensitive terrain, from the Canadian border to the Gulf Coast, the environmental community is, at this writing, losing hope that Obama will do the right thing. The pipeline extracts some of the dirtiest oil on the planet, a process that sends many polluting chemicals into the ground waters and releases methane, the most potent greenhouse gas, into the air, creating one of the greatest climate threats. Crossing one of the United States' most important aquifers, the pipeline is vulnerable to poisonous spills that could pollute much of the country's clean drinking water and agricultural irrigation. Obama indicated that he would take climate change into account in his decision, but his State Department said that it had no objection to the pipeline. The silver lining in this is that Obama's failures to deliver urgent major climate change initiatives and policies have helped create the new grassroots climate activism essential to saving humanity.

In 2013, concerned Americans realized they had to take matters into their own hands. A new climate movement began to take shape. Made up mainly of young people, including students, and a new breed of environmental activists, the millennial generation may make global warming its own civil rights movement, one that will determine future generations' prospects of survival.

The new movement is different from earlier environmental activism and organizations. It sees the environment not just in terms of conservation of natural resources but as a social justice issue focused on humans and all natural species. Earlier environmentalists were almost all white and affluent; the new movement is multicultural and led by poor as well as labor unions and middle-class and affluent communities. Its focus is on a social transformation agenda for cities and the economy. It seeks less to simply conserve and more to transform the U.S. economy and way of life.

The movement gained national visibility in 2013 with its demand to shut down the Keystone XL pipeline project and the radical tactics it proved willing to use. On February 13, 2013, 48 leaders of the new movement were arrested in front of the White House for civil disobedience, including Julian Bond, former head of the NAACP, Bill McKibben, author of the best-selling *End of Nature* and founder of the global activist group 350.org, and Michael Brune, the Executive Director of the Sierra Club. McKibben, whose website 350.org has helped spearhead the new U.S. movement, asserted, "We really shouldn't have to be put in handcuffs to stop KXL—our nation's leading climate scientists have told us it's dangerous folly, and all the recent Nobel Peace laureates have urged us to set a different kind of example for the world, so the choice should be obvious. But given the amount of money on the other side, we've had to spend our bodies, and we'll probably have to spend them again."[35]

Michael Brune's presence was significant, because it brought the most important established national environmental organization into the fold of the new movement. Brune proclaimed, "For the first time in the Sierra Club's 120-year history, we have joined the ranks of visionaries of the past and present to engage in civil disobedience, knowing that the issue at hand is so critical, it compels the strongest defensible action." The Sierra Club may now help move mainstream environmentalism toward the social justice activism and radicalism required to cope with climate change.[36] Julian Bond's presence, as a Black civil rights icon, was also important, symbolizing the transformation of environmentalism into a social justice movement, where an African-American civil rights leader is willing to challenge an African-American president.

☐ Fracking

The pipeline fight is tied closely to another key issue animating the new movement: fracking. Fracking, or hydraulic fracturing, is the process used by fossil fuel companies to extract oil and gas from shale or other rock deep underground. It mixes water and sand with chemicals to blast open the rocks, spewing dangerous pollution, including methane—the most toxic greenhouse gas—into surrounding earth and water. Tar sands oil to be piped down the Keystone XL pipeline is extracted by fracking, as is much of the natural gas that U.S. energy companies and political leaders have defined as the "clean energy" of the twenty-first century, which can make the U.S. energy-independent and provide the world with bountiful new green fuel.

The movement against fracking will continue long after the Keystone project is settled. The turning of big energy companies and U.S. political elites toward natural gas—rather than truly clean energy sources such as wind or solar—as the solution is unsupportable, and it will become a major issue of the new climate movement, to preserve safe drinking water and food, prevent poisonous ground pollution, and reduce a huge amount of methane and carbon emissions. The antifracking movement will grow because so many communities will be harmed by the massive fracking required to create the natural gas revolution, and because the toxic role of natural gas in increasing global warming will continue to grow. Hundreds of local communities have already passed fracking bans.

The antifracking movement is in its early stages, but it is both global and local, embodying many features of the new environmental activism. It is community-based, fearless, morally passionate in ways similar to civil rights activism, and is led by grassroots activists, such as Jill Wiener, who has spent much of the last five years fighting to keep fracking from being legalized in her state, New York. Wiener is an artist and farmer who works with a group called Catskills Citizens for Safe Energy, an all-volunteer citizens group who make decisions by consensus and have successfully worked with other New York State groups against fracking. Wiener, whose moral convictions motivate her, explains, "I don't have kids. It's not like I'm fighting for my own children. But there is right and there is wrong. And, boy, I really hate wrong."[37]

Divestment

Another part of the new climate movement is the divestment campaign to force universities—as well as cities, churches, and pension funds—to divest their portfolios from fossil fuel companies. Modeled on the divestment campaign of the 1980s that succeeded in getting universities to stop investing in companies doing business with the South African apartheid regime, this initiative brings the movement directly to the home base of the millennial generation of students, the greenest in history. By July 2013, students in 300 colleges and universities, including Harvard, MIT, Princeton, and Boston College, had formed divestment groups to push their administration to act.

This divestment manifesto hints at the antiwilding sensibilities of the new student movement. It forthrightly challenges the corporate wilding that is creating and perpetuating the crisis. It is also a call for social solidarity, a recognition that global warming affects everyone and essentially unites them in a global common struggle for survival. The new activists seek to supplant the individualistic American dream of money and success with a sustainable life based on community.

The divestment movement, with its focus on exposing corporate sociopathy and changing economic behavior and values, reflects a key aspect of the new environmentalism: its connection to other social justice groups such as the labor movement, the civil rights movement, and the peace movement. The new activist students—whether focused on Keystone, fracking, divestment, or the increasing corporatization of the university—are dealing with corporate power and the corporate state and has no option but to partner with unions, civil rights groups, and citizen action community groups also forced to target corporate power and malfeasance.

The link to civil rights has been the most successful, since African-Americans from Oakland, California, to Washington, D.C., have become environmental leaders in organizations and campaigns such as Green for All, founded by the African-American writer and political organizer Van Jones. In his work in Oakland, Jones realized that it was impossible to improve the lives of urban minorities without simultaneously overcoming the jobs and environmental problems plaguing the inner city. In his best-selling book, *The Green Collar Economy*, written in the depths of the Great Recession, Jones argued that investment in green jobs is the solution to both the economic and climate crisis, a vision that drives Green for All and new partnerships between the new environmentalism and the labor movement.[38]

The breakdown of the traditional barrier between the environmental and labor movements is crucial. Historically, they were enemies, with unions seeing environmentalists as job-killers and environmentalists seeing unions as environment-killers. The new environmentalists and progressive unionists are now doing a U-turn, as they move toward turning themselves into social movements that must deal with corporate wilding and social injustice. As minorities and women have entered the labor market, with their historic struggles for social justice, they are also helping to unite together the various movements in the face of climate change's overwhelming threat to all of us. Might a common enemy—in this case, global warming—be the tool that can bring us out of the individualistic silos that help fuel wilding and limit our ability to end it?

Beyond green jobs, many other economic concerns are critical and must be taken up by the new environmentalists in partnership with unions, civil rights groups, and women's groups. The new environmentalist demand for flexibility and a choice of shorter work hours offers the hope of reducing mass consumerism while improving quality of life. It can be a healing innovation for today's stressed-out workers, especially female workers seeking to balance overwhelming demands of work and family, and to environmentalists who are seeking alternatives to the consumerist lifestyle. Unions and environmentalists in European nations such as France, have succeeded in getting shorter workweeks (35 hours in France), increasing leisure, engaging in community, and freeing up time to grow one's own food, what is now consumed from fossil-fuel agribusiness.[39]

In the end, our future is in our own hands. The political system is driven by big money, and capitalism creates huge structural hurdles to a sustainable world. President Barack Obama can help bring a real solution to the intertwined environmental and economic crises only if millions of ordinary Americans wake up to the extreme dangers and then demand systemic change—regime change at home. It will require what dedicated Americans have always done best: joining grassroots movements and organizing in their communities, workplaces, and the electoral arena to force politicians to act to solve this greatest of all planetary emergencies. As the climate scientist James Hansen said in his Congressional testimony, "Democracy works, but sometimes churns slowly. Time is short. . . . If Americans turn out to pasture the most brontosaurian congressmen, if Washington adapts to address climate change, our children and grandchildren can still hold great expectations."[40]

Discussion Questions

1. Is global warming caused by wilding?

2. Does capitalism cause global warming? Why or why not?

3. Is mass consumption a form of wilding? Are you a wilder when you buy lots of stuff?

4. Are climate deniers wilders?

5. Are the builders of the Keystone XL Pipeline wilders?

6. Are you an activist to end climate change? If not, are you a wilder?

7. What can students do to reverse climate change and stop wilding against the environment?

[nine]

War and Wilding
Iraq and the War against Terrorism

The great sociologist Max Weber defined the state as the institution with a monopoly on official violence. Hans Morgenthau, the famous political theorist, argued that states always act in their own self-interest. If states use their monopolies on violence to wage war for naked self-interest or corporate profits, this would appear to make war one of the most catastrophic forms of institutional wilding. We have already defined state violence for greed or power at home as political wilding, and in a world long bloodied by war for power and profit, it is hard to imagine a more dangerous and sociologically important species of wilding.

In this chapter, we consider two American wars: the war against Iraq and the "war on terrorism." In focusing on American-led wars, it is important to keep in mind that the United States is the greatest military power in world history and the sole superpower today. The United States spends more on the military than all the other nations of the world combined.[1] Many view the United States as an empire, exceeding in its power even the Roman or British empires. Sociologists such as Immanuel Wallerstein and Giovanni Arrighi offer a framework known as "world system theory" for understanding the American empire as a wilding system. Looking back on the last 500 years of colonialism, world system theorists argue that the world economy has been organized by a dominant or "hegemonic" power, such as Britain during the late eighteenth and nineteenth centuries, that ruled over much of the world for profit and glory. The United States is the successor hegemon to Britain, with even greater power.[2]

Hegemony, as conceived by the Italian social theorist Antonio Gramsci, is power dressed up in universal values, such as freedom and prosperity. Gramsci wrote that governments always use such soothing rhetoric as "the white man's burden" to "manufacture consent," since naked coercion is an expensive and inefficient mode of control. During the British Empire, the British claimed to bring civilization to the whole world, as did the ancient Romans to their conquered provinces. During the Cold War, the United States claimed to defend the entire "free world" against the evil of communism. Arrighi and other world system theorists observe that with the collapse of the Soviet Union, American hegemony is increasingly organized around claims to defend the whole civilized world against the evils of terror and chaos.

Hegemons increasingly turn to military force when their economic power and legitimacy begin to wane. The United States is in the early phases of hegemonic decline, associated with a long-term crisis in the global economy and the 2008 meltdown of speculative "casino capitalism" that yields short-term profits at the expense of long-term growth. We can expect that the United States may move toward increasing militarism to secure its endangered global wealth and power, leading to the kind of mayhem and wilding witnessed during the decline and fall of the Roman and British empires.[3]

☐ War in Iraq

When Baghdad fell on April 9, 2003, U.S. newspapers and TV news programs showed jubilant Iraqis dancing in the streets. Iraqis embraced and kissed American soldiers, stomped on pictures of Saddam Hussein, and with the help of U.S. Marines, toppled the huge iron statue of Saddam in central Baghdad. This was the reaction that President Bush had promised. Although no weapons of mass destruction were found, the Iraqi celebration seemed to nail down Bush's claim that this was a war of liberation, a just war destroying a barbaric regime and bringing freedom and democracy to a suffering nation.

Just after Baghdad's collapse, surveys suggested that most Americans agreed with the president. A poll released on April 10, 2003, showed that about 75 percent of Americans supported the war. Even those who had earlier protested the war were rethinking their opposition, wondering whether the end of a horrific despot justified the destruction inevitably wrought by war. One thoughtful student in my class raised his hand and said that the obvious joy of many Iraqis at the downfall of Saddam made him question whether his earlier opposition to the war was ignorant.

But while Americans watched images of Iraqis celebrating in the streets, Arabs were opening newspapers with headlines blazing, "Humiliation!" and "Colonialism Is Back!" The images Arabs saw were of dead Iraqi children killed by bombs; starving Iraqi families screaming at U.S. soldiers for water or food; Iraqi soldiers lying dead on the highway; hospitals without electricity or medicine, overflowing with wounded Iraqi civilians; widespread looting and mayhem; and fires burning out of control in many Iraqi cities. While there was no love lost on Saddam Hussein, Arabs all over the Middle East were horrified at the prospect of an American military occupation of Iraq.

Talal Salman, publisher of *As-Safir*, a leading Lebanese moderate newspaper, grieved the loss of the richest Arab civilization to a "colonial power." Iraqis, he wrote, are now moving from "the night of tyranny" under Saddam Hussein to the "night of foreign occupation" under U.S. troops.[4] Ahmed Kamal Aboulmagd, a leading pro-Western member of the Egyptian establishment and a longtime friend of the United States, said, "Under the present conditions, I cannot think of defending the United States. To most people in this area, the United States is the source of evil on planet earth."[5]

These sentiments were shared by many Iraqis, who were grateful to U.S. and British soldiers for ousting Saddam but desperate to survive in the wake of the world's most intense bombing campaigns and viscerally hostile to a new foreign occupation. The majority Shiite population in Iraq mounted huge street protests demanding that American soldiers get out of their country. Iraqis interviewed in Baghdad and Basra told U.S. reporters that they hated Saddam but equally "resented the foreign troop presence." One Iraqi Shiite cleric said the Iraqis were caught between "two fires": one, the cruel, fading power of Saddam; the other, the looming domination by the Americans. Qabil Khazzal Jumaa, an Iraqi nurse, horrified by the amputated limbs, burned bodies, and rotting corpses among the hundreds of civilians he had treated, said that this was "a brutal war. This is not just. This is not accepted by man or God." Iraq did not belong to the Americans who would now govern his country. He said simply, "This is my country."[6]

In the face of these starkly competing images—Iraqis dancing in the streets and a bombed, looted country fearing subjugation to a hegemon occupying its cities and oil fields—how does one decide whether the U.S. war in Iraq was wilding? We can start by asking whether the war was legal and then whether this was a just war. This discussion can be framed from a sociological perspective around the question of hegemony: Did the United States invade Iraq to tighten its hegemonic control over the Gulf and the entire oil-rich Islamic world?

Legality

According to Article 51 of the U.N. charter (which the United States ratified), a country can legally engage in war without U.N. approval if the war is in self-defense. Right after 9/11, on September 12, 2001, President Bush redefined "self-defense" in a more expansive way than the charter implied. Bush asserted that the United States could no longer afford to abide by conventional concepts in an age of terrorism. We must be prepared, the president declared, "to strike at a moment's notice in any dark corner of the world . . . to be ready for preemptive action when necessary to defend our liberty and to defend our lives." The president was very explicit about preemption: "We must take the battle to the enemy, disrupt his plans and confront the worst threats before they emerge."

In emphasizing that he would act against threats "before they emerge," the president was moving beyond preemption to prevention. A war is considered preemptive if it begins because a threat is imminent—for instance, when missiles or planes are detected moving toward one's shores. Preventive war is a response to threats not yet visible and suggests that one nation can use the Bush Doctrine to attack almost any other country that it mistrusts, an application of the wilding precept that "might makes right."

Bush's approach kicked up a firestorm of opposition. Former White House adviser William A. Galston said that Bush's new doctrine "means the end of the system of international institutions, laws, and norms that the United States has worked for more than half a century to build. . . . Rather than continuing to serve as first among equals in the postwar international system, the United States would act as a law unto itself, creating new rules of international engagement without agreement by other nations."[7] Princeton political scientist Richard Falk, a leading authority on international law, writes that, "this new approach repudiates the core of the United Nations charter [outlawing wars that are not based on self-defense against overt aggression]. . . . It is a doctrine without limits, without accountability to the United Nations or international law, or any dependence on a collective judgment of responsible governments."[8]

When the United States invaded Iraq, it claimed that Article 51 made the war legal. The U.N. Security Council disagreed, saying that there was more time for inspection and that the threat was not imminent, meaning that the war could not be viewed as self-defense. France and Germany, along with scores of other countries, repeatedly argued that the war undermined the U.N. charter.

Although the president invaded Iraq alleging that Saddam Hussein had weapons of mass destruction (WMD), American forces on the ground failed to find any nuclear, biological, or chemical weapons. On April 24, 2003, President Bush suggested that WMD might never be found and might not exist, raising grave new questions about the legality of the war.[9] The president's legal argument for the war had rested on the premise that such weapons existed and constituted a threat to American and global security. But after two years of exhaustive investigation, the president's own official commission on arms in Iraq, led by David Kay and Charles Duelfer, concluded in 2004 that Saddam did not have weapons of mass destruction or any imminent program to build them successfully.[10] This conclusion suggests that there was no threat and no plausible legal justification for the invasion. The clear implication is that Iraq was a war of aggression rather than self-defense.

How U.S. presidents define self-defense—and whether it serves as a fig leaf for hegemonic aggression—will be a crucial U.S. and global issue for years to come. It blazed into the headlines in September 2013, as President Obama proposed a military strike against Syria to punish it for breaking the international ban on use of chemical weapons. Obama's proposed strike, which he has not carried out at this writing, was not endorsed by the United Nations, the Arab League, or most countries and peoples around the world, including the majority of the U.S. population. But Obama claimed that he had the international legal right—even responsibility—to enforce international norms on weapons of mass destruction, and that U.S. national security was at stake. Although there was no foreseeable way that Syria had or could attack the United States, the president argued for an expansive definition of self-defense, arguing that the spread of chemical weapons could turn into an attack on American allies or on the United States itself. Obama was expanding the concept of self-defense even beyond that proposed in the Bush Doctrine, and set off a firestorm domestically and internationally about U.S. intentions and the use of illegal or overly expansive concepts of self-defense, in wars long after Iraq, as a basis for military intervention and global aggression.[11]

◻ Justice

The question of wilding goes beyond legality to the broader issue of whether the war on Iraq was a just war of liberation. While the argument that a legal war to remove a tyrant can, under some circumstances, be a just action is true, three arguments based on historical, economic, and political perspectives suggest that other goals were behind this war.

The historical argument is based on government planning documents. In a 1990 strategy document put together by a team under Dick Cheney during the first Bush administration, the United States announced that it must "preclude the rise of another global rival for the indefinite future," by building such an overwhelming military superiority that no other nation could possibly contemplate challenging American power. The Cheney document suggested that the United States needed to create a "democratic zone of peace" in which Americans would be prepared to use force if necessary to ensure "human rights or democracy," even if using force involved violating the sovereignty of another nation that posed no threat to the United States. While Iraq was the test case of the time, the idea of overthrowing Saddam was rejected after the first Gulf War because the United Nations did not authorize a regime change. The Cheney Doctrine was shelved as embarrassingly imperialistic.[12] Nonetheless, after 9/11, Cheney's vision became the centerpiece of the new Bush administration's foreign policy, and the Iraq war was a crucial first step toward securing the global dominance laid out in the earlier documentary record.[13]

A second argument that the war on Iraq involved wilding centers around the economic goals of the war. Like all prior hegemons, the United States has two economic agendas. The first is to ensure the stable operation of the world economy, including the guarantee of a cheap supply of Mideast oil. In 1990, when Saddam Hussein invaded Kuwait and threatened Saudi Arabia, the United States launched the Gulf War against Saddam to stabilize the entire global economic system, protecting the oil supply not only for itself but also for its European and Asian allies. In the 2003 invasion of Iraq, the United States again acted with broad concern for global economic stability based on securing greater control of Iraq's and its neighbors' oil supplies—still a form of wilding but different from simply grabbing more profit for U.S. oil companies.

The second U.S. economic aim, though, is closer to what the protestors had in mind as they waved their "No Blood for Oil" signs. The corporatized American hegemon sees U.S. national interests as tightly connected to the profitability of politically influential American corporations. The Bush administration, including most notably the president and vice president, was especially close to the energy industries, in which several Bush cabinet members served as corporate executives, as well as to the military-related companies rooted in Texas and throughout the U.S. Southwest. It is predictable that the interests of this sector of American corporations weighed heavily in the Bush administration's assessment of the national interest.

Evidence that profits for U.S. oil giants and other companies were part of the Iraq war aim comes from the postwar reconstruction contracts, which the U.S. Agency for International Development awarded through a closed bidding process. Halliburton, the Texas-based oil giant formerly headed by Dick Cheney, was awarded the first major contract for servicing of Iraqi oil wells and fire prevention in the oil fields, estimated to be worth up to $7 billion.

The United States also awarded a leading reconstruction role to Bechtel, the vast construction and energy company with ties to former Secretary of Defense Donald Rumsfeld and others closely connected to the Bush administration. George Schultz, former president of Bechtel and currently on its board, also sat on Bush's Pentagon's Defense Policy Board, which advised the administration about Iraq and other vital matters. Richard Perle, the former head of that same board and a hawk on Iraq, was forced to resign his chairmanship when concerns about potential conflicts of interest were raised about his own business interests. At a time when Pentagon planners and the CIA were predicting major new terrorist attacks as a near certainty in the wake of the Iraqi invasion, Perle's company stood to generate lucrative profits from Defense and Homeland Security contracts.[14]

A third argument that the Iraq war involved wilding concerns domestic political benefits reaped by the Bush administration. Bush entered office without a popular majority and only through a controversial Supreme Court decision regarding the Florida vote. Even before 9/11 and the Iraq war, critics perceived Bush as a servant of the big corporations whose campaign funding had helped propel him to Washington. In his first moves as president, Bush chose a cabinet led by other former corporate executives, including Cheney, Rumsfeld, and Paul O'Neill, his secretary of the treasury. Bush then pushed a domestic agenda centered around the biggest tax cuts to the rich in history, enhancing his image as a political stand-in for his corporate friends.

Such a corporate presidency is inherently vulnerable to a crisis of legitimacy. Bush's social and economic domestic policies were consistently opposed by a majority of the American electorate. Karl Rove, Bush's political guru, denied in public that foreign policy decisions were made on the basis of domestic political considerations, but he sent a secret memo to Republican activists during the 2002 midterm elections urging them to "focus on the war." He also acknowledged to reporters during the 2002 campaign that he liked the slogan circulating among Republican strategists, "Are you safer now than you were four years ago?"[15]

▣ Occupation as Wilding

On March 11, 1917, British troops captured Baghdad. That day, the British commander Lieutenant General Sir Stanley Maude promised the Iraqis, "Our armies do not come into your cities and lands as conquerors or enemies but as liberators." Maude was not telling them the truth, since the British stayed more than 40 years. The real British aims were to take over Iraq after the crumbling of the Ottoman empire, to control trade routes to India and the Far East, and, as the occupation unfolded, to control the newly discovered oil fields. Although Iraq won formal sovereignty in 1931, the British ruled the country through puppet regimes until a coup in 1958 formally drove them out after a long, popular insurgency. T. E. Lawrence, better known as Lawrence of Arabia, wrote in 1920 that the British public was "tricked" into supporting occupation "by a steady withholding of information. . . . Things have been far worse than we have been told, our administration more bloody and inefficient than the public knows. We are today not far from a disaster."[16]

The parallels to the American role in Iraq are painful. The United States also built permanent bases around the country to secure Iraq as a nation friendly to the United States and to American oil interests. Iraq also offers a staging ground for keeping military pressure on Syria, Iran, and other Middle Eastern nations, and for securing other major oil fields as far away as the Black Sea and the Caucasus.

The U.S. public was misled in the same manner as the British. Lawrence wrote that the British public had been suckered "into a trap from which it will be hard to escape with dignity and honor." British leaders, Lawrence observed, were not honest about their aims, and occupations are, by their nature, "bloody and inefficient." President Bush proclaimed, "Mission accomplished," in the spring of 2003, after U.S. Marines reached Baghdad, saying American troops would be showered with roses. But taking Baghdad created inevitable insurgencies that led the occupiers to fight the people they rescued. The truth is that occupations are almost always systemic political wilding, evoking popular resistance that requires more and more violence against civilians to suppress. The war to save Iraq became a war that killed thousands of Iraqis, pitting Sunni, Shiite, and Kurdish ethnic communities against each other in bloody sectarian conflict, while also bringing new Al Qaeda fighters into Iraq.

The wilding by American occupation forces in Iraq became painfully clear during the U.S. invasion of the Sunni stronghold in Fallujah in 2004, which was seen as an epicenter of the insurgency. Heavily armed American forces demolished whole neighborhoods as they systematically ransacked the city. A quarter million residents evacuated, and the whole city burned in a hell-storm of lethal destruction. Doctors in Fallujah hospitals reported "melted bodies," victims of poisonous gases sprayed by U.S. planes. One resident, Abu Sabah, spoke of "weird bombs that smoke like a mushroom cloud. . . . The pieces of these strange bombs explode into large fires that burn the skin even when you throw water over them," which suggested the possible use of napalm by U.S. forces, expressly prohibited by the United Nations in 1980 after its use in Vietnam.[17] The United States has denied using napalm but admits using white phosphorus as an incendiary weapon against insurgents, contrary to its previous claim that it was used only for illumination purposes. White phosphorus, which has a similar effect to napalm upon contact with the skin, is a lethal substance banned by international treaty for use against civilians, although the United States is not a signatory to that treaty.[18]

The most famous symbol of the wilding created by occupation is the horrific images of torture at Abu Ghraib, which led to convictions against military guards Charles Graner, Lynndie England, and five other Americans. Most Americans can still remember the photo seen around the world: an Iraqi prisoner held by the U.S. military, hooded and with electrical wires attached to his arms and genitals. Also circulated on the Internet were photographs of naked Iraqi prisoners draped in a pyramid, forced to masturbate by their U.S. guards; pictures of U.S. military guards leading Iraqi prisoners around by a leash; and pictures of U.S. soldiers using fists or weapons to harm prisoners.

☐ The War on Terrorism

The attacks of 9/11 were a watershed event. When Al Qaeda operatives hijacked the two jumbo jets and crashed them into the twin towers in New York, they showed that the United States was vulnerable to the devastating violence that many other countries have suffered for decades. Americans have historically felt protected by the oceans and the enormous power of the U.S. military. We know now that tiny bands of terrorists can inflict horrific damage on our country, whatever the size of our military or our hegemonic power.

Is the American-led war on terrorism a form of wilding? If it is truly an international struggle to eradicate groups such as Al Qaeda, then diplomatic, police, intelligence, and military actions designed for such aims may be morally legitimate. But the history of hegemonic powers—and of the United States in particular— offers cautions. During the Cold War, many wars fought in the name of anticommunism, such as the 1954 overthrow of Guatemala's elected president Jacobo Arbenz Guzmán, had more to do with protecting the United Fruit Company's banana plantations than fighting communism. The 1953 CIA overthrow of another democratically elected leader, Iran's president Mohammed Mossadegh, was also an imperialist war. It was called an anticommunist war, but it was waged mainly to protect U.S. oil interests. The Cold War developed into a form of hegemonic wilding, involving scores of greed- and power-driven military interventions by the United States to build the American empire, as well as wars by the Soviet Union to build its own empire.[19]

What, then, are the real motives driving the U.S. "war on terrorism" that began after 9/11? One is undoubtedly to destroy Al Qaeda and similar violent, criminal groups that threaten the United States, and if this were its sole purpose, directed and carried out by the United Nations in coalition with the United States purely for its own and other countries' self-defense, the war might not be wilding. But just as the Soviet threat served a useful function for American leaders during the Cold War, the threat of terrorism helps U.S. elites achieve very different aims than self-defense. In fact, the U.S. political leadership and its terrorist enemies function like spouses in a long and hostile codependent marriage. They hate each other but need the marriage because it serves crucial functions for each of them. While trying to destroy each other, they also become increasingly reliant on the conflict between them to survive and achieve their own aims.

A key codependent marriage has developed between U.S. elites and Al Qaeda. Both seek to destroy the other but at the same time find each other exceedingly useful in promoting their own ends. The American empire provides Al Qaeda with its most potent tool for rallying Arab popular support and undercutting moderate

Islamic groups that could make the radicals irrelevant. Similarly, Al Qaeda offers American political leaders their most powerful case for vastly enhanced military spending and wars that bring profit, power, and political legitimacy at home.

A major covert aim of the war on terrorism is to replace the former communist enemy with a new terrorist enemy who provides the cover or justification to dominate the world. Put simply, terrorism (and the war against it) has become a powerful selling point for the global wilding policies at the heart of empire. Without Al Qaeda, the Bush administration could not have diverted so much money to expanding the armed forces, especially in an era of decline in jobs and domestic social services. Nor could U.S. leaders have explicitly proclaimed the doctrines of preemptive war and unrivalled military dominance. Al Qaeda has provided U.S. leaders with an argument to introduce American forces in scores of countries as well as to overthrow governments that have not attacked the United States, which is perhaps the defining feature of an imperial power. Without their hated terrorist partners, American leaders could not have attacked Iraq by falsely linking Saddam Hussein with Al Qaeda, or pursued so blatantly the new politics of preventive war and empire.

The war on terrorism was the answer to the political problem posed by the inevitable public opposition to the domestic agenda of the corporate state. Bush's political vulnerability at home would be shared by any president, Democrat or Republican, who presided over the corporate state, since such a government is structurally committed to policies that do not benefit the majority of Americans. If new corporate presidents continue to rely on the war on terrorism for their political survival, we may be faced with one wilding war after another, fought in the name of antiterrorism for economic and political benefits abroad and at home. After the fall of Baghdad, rumors surfaced almost immediately about new potential confrontations with Syria, North Korea, and Iran. Fighting even one war for domestic political gain is a horrific form of political wilding; fighting a whole generation of such wars is systemic wilding on a grand scale.

Barack Obama ran for president by opposing the war in Iraq, and he promised to bring change to U.S. foreign policy. But while his rhetoric has been very different from Bush's, with a strategic emphasis on multilateralism and diplomatic "engagement" rather than unilateral militarism, Obama never renounced U.S. hegemony, nor did he suggest he would end the war on terrorism. Even as he promised to draw down U.S. forces in Iraq, he promised in his first term a major new commitment to the war in Afghanistan, which he viewed as the epicenter of the fight against Al Qaeda and global terrorism.

In his acceptance speech at the August 2008 Democratic National Convention, Obama said, "I stood up and opposed this war [Iraq], knowing that it would distract us from the real threats we face." And then he immediately talked in tough terms about those "real threats":

> When John McCain said we could just "muddle through" in Afghanistan, I argued for more resources and more troops to finish the fight against the terrorists who actually attacked us on 9/11, and made clear that we must take out Osama bin Laden and his lieutenants if we have them in our sights. John McCain likes to say that he'll follow bin Laden to the Gates of Hell, but he won't even go to the cave where he lives.[20]

By July 2009, Obama had deployed more than 19,000 additional U.S. troops to Afghanistan—with a commitment to a total of 68,000 U.S. soldiers in Afghanistan by the end of 2009, a doubling of U.S. forces since his inauguration.[21] By mid-2009, Obama had decisively embraced his own Afghan "surge," ordering thousands of Marines into Helmand Province, long a stronghold of the Taliban. The new surge was overseen by Obama's secretary of defense, Robert Gates, who was also Bush's defense secretary, and by General David Petraeus, previously Bush's top commander in Iraq, who had conceived and implemented the surge in Iraq. Afghanistan rapidly became "Obama's War," dousing any hope that the United States would be entering a peaceful post-Bush or post-hegemonic era.

In an influential July 9, 2009, essay, Rory Stewart, a British Conservative and Director of the Carr Center on Human Rights Policy at Harvard, wrote a powerful critique of Obama's view of the Afghanistan war. It rests on "misleading ideas about moral obligation, our capacity, the threat of our adversaries, the threat posed by Afghanistan." Stewart shows that Obama's "war of necessity" is really a "war of choice" bound to fail. Al Qaeda is a threat, but it can be managed by means other than a war and occupation of Afghanistan, and does not require a secure, democratic central state in Afghanistan, which is nearly impossible. Stewart personally walked across the entire country of Afghanistan and knows what he's talking about. He supports economic development aid and small special forces, but not a massive occupation that will have a far worse outcome than even Iraq.[22]

Why is Obama pursuing a "mission: impossible" in Afghanistan? One motive is to secure U.S. economic and political interests in the region, including oil pipelines and influence in Pakistan and Iran. Another is political support at home to defend against Republican charges of weakness in both Iraq and Afghanistan. Such political calculations for war are political wilding.

Obama's foreign policy has remained that of a hegemonic nation, and he continues to pronounce the fight against terrorism as his top national security priority, one that ensures continuing U.S. militarism and interventionism throughout the world. Obama's foreign policy puts more emphasis on diplomacy than Bush's, but his aims are similar: to protect regimes friendly to U.S. economic and political interests in the Middle East and around the globe. Obama has already shown that, even as he withdraws most U.S. combat troops from Afghanistan in 2014, he has proposed keeping up to 12,000 U.S. forces in Afghanistan through 2024, as well as maintaining huge U.S. bases in the nation, a sign that he will use force to ensure continued U.S. dominance and control, a form of global wilding practiced by every empire.

☐ Drone Warfare as Wilding: Global Interventionism Masked as Antiterrorism

At the 2010 annual Radio and Correspondents' Television Dinner, President Obama joked that the band that was playing, the Jonas Brothers, better stay away from his daughters. "Sasha and Malia are huge fans," the president cracked, "but boys, don't get any ideas. Two words for you: Predator Drones. And you'll never see them coming."[23]

That joke would not have amused many Pakistanis or other people around the world who have been subjected to an unprecedented campaign of drone attacks by the United States under Obama, with thousands of civilians killed or injured as "collateral damage." Obama's joke is not funny mainly because he spoke the truth about drones. They are now his preferred method of warfare, and he is using them to wage war in any country that he thinks is harboring terrorists who might attack the United States.

Drones are unmanned aerial vehicles (UAVs) that have the capability to engage in intelligence and military strikes any place in the world, without risking the life of a U.S. pilot or crew. While drones have been around since World War I, the mass use of drones began after 9/11 in Iraq and Afghanistan. Although the United States is by far the biggest manufacturer and military user of drones, they are increasingly being developed and used, mainly for intelligence purposes, by countries all over the world, especially by Israel, Russia, and China.[24]

Until the United States and NATO attacked the Serbs in Kosovo in 1999, drones were used only as surveillance devices, but technology and new strategy permitted a rapid transition after 9/11 to use drones as weapons, capable of firing Hellfire missiles and many other advanced kill devices. The Air Force extensively used drones to attack Iraqi insurgents and the Taliban in Iraq and Afghanistan. As those wars have wound down, the CIA and another secretive military agency, the Joint Special Operations Command (JSOC), have taken over the main job of using drones (along with some private contractors), for intelligence collection and military strikes. They are redefining drones as the major instrument of global warfare by the United States in the name of antiterrorism. Journalist and peace activist Medea Benjamin wrote in her searing book, *Drone Warfare*: "And drones are not named Predators and Reapers for nothing. With no judge or jury, they obliterate lives in an instant, the lives of those deemed by someone, somewhere to be terrorists, along with those who are accidentally—or incidentally—caught in their cross-hairs."[25]

While drones may appear to be a more humane form of warfare, since they spare lives of U.S. pilots and are capable of precision strikes, drone warfare actually involves several serious forms of political wilding. As shown below, these include (1) the killing of thousands of innocent civilians, (2) the violation of international law concerning the extension of military attacks into any country chosen by the president, even if the United States is not at war with them, (3) the violation of international rights of foreigners in those countries who are killed without any declaration of war, even if their government has approved U.S. drone attacks on them, (4) the constitutional violation of the rights of Americans killed by drones without a trial or judicial oversight, and (5) the constitutional violation of the requirement of a Congressional declaration of war.

First, the killing of innocent civilians (those who are not militants or terrorists) has grown rapidly as the use of drones has accelerated, with the largest number in Pakistan. Studies show that in 2009 alone, U.S. drone strikes killed over 900 innocent Pakistani civilians, and that between 2004 and 2010, there were 1,065 civilian deaths, including people who have gone in to try to rescue drone victims or are attending funerals of those attacked (all figures are estimates that vary because the CIA doesn't report numbers).[26] In 2012, another round of strikes killing many more innocent civilians created a political firestorm in Pakistan and bred enormous hatred of the United States, with many Pakistani politicians leading campaigns to demand that the United States stop all drone attacks.[27]

Meanwhile, in 2012, 30 U.S. drone attacks on Afghan homes led President Karzai to demand that the United States put an end to all drone attacks on Afghanistan, and former president Jimmy Carter critiqued U.S. policy, saying, "We don't know how many hundreds of innocent civilians have been killed in these attacks . . . This would have been unthinkable in previous times." He said the United States is "abandoning its role as champion of human rights. . . . It is disturbing that, instead of strengthening these principles, our government's counter-terrorism policies are now clearly violating at least 10 of the [U.N. 1948 Human Rights] declaration's 30 articles, including the prohibition against 'cruel, inhuman or degrading treatment or punishment.' "[28] Meanwhile, in Yemen, a frequent target of drone strikes in 2012 and 2013, the BBC reported this quote from a father whose young son and daughter were hurt, along with other children, when they were all hiding in a school basement from drones—a constant source of terror—overhead: "When the smoke cleared, I saw my son's leg was bleeding, and my daughter was hit on the back of the head," he said. His son survived but his 8-year-old daughter bled to death on the way to the hospital. "As she bled, she went yellow. She actually started to shrink in my arms," he said. Mr. Bagash asked a question for the person who ordered the drone strike: "What did my daughter ever do to them? She was only 8 years old." He continued, "They think we're rats. We're not. We're human beings."[29]

The terror felt by civilians as drones hover overhead for hours and strike in unpredictable patterns, particularly in countries such as Pakistan and Yemen that are not at war with the United States, leads many Muslims to view the United States as the real terrorist nation. The United States now operates 7,000 drones, with another 12,000 on the ground, that have been used in many countries beyond Iraq, Afghanistan, Pakistan, and Yemen, including Somalia, Libya, Algeria, and Iran. The United States is violating international law by bombing countries, such as Pakistan, Libya, and Yemen, that are not at war with the United States and are, in some cases, important allies, such as Pakistan and Yemen. This is a major form of political wilding, since it suggests that the United States has the right to bomb any country it pleases, a position that the Obama administration has officially embraced. John Brennan, the president's top counterterrorism adviser, argues that the United States has the right to unilaterally strike terrorists anywhere, including any areas or countries not in combat zones: "Because we are engaged in an armed conflict with Al Qaeda, the United States takes the legal position that, in accordance with international law, we have the authority to take action against Al Qaeda and its associated forces," he told a conference at Harvard Law School last year. "The United States does not view our authority to use military force against Al Qaeda as being restricted solely to 'hot' battlefields like Afghanistan."[30]

If this is legal for the United States, then it would entitle the United States to unilaterally bomb Berlin or London, and would also allow Israel, Russia, or China to bomb New York City or Chicago or any other American city on the grounds that they also have Al Qaeda youth who might be threats, a rather clear indication of the wilding implications for a world without constraints on any drone attacks that political leaders see as necessary. As the ACLU put it in 2010 in a letter to President Obama: "The entire world is not a war zone, and wartime tactics that may be permitted on battlefields in Afghanistan and Iraq cannot be deployed anywhere a terrorism suspect happens to be located."[31]

In some cases, such as in Pakistan and Yemen, there were periods where the leaders of those countries, both U.S. allies, may have implicitly or explicitly given permission to the United States for these strikes. But even such permission does not end the wilding involved because of the violation of the legal rights of the victims, including innocent civilians, who are killed. Mary Ellen O'Connell, a law professor at Notre Dame, testified before Congress that, "Drones are not lawful for use outside combat zones" where "police are the proper law enforcement agency." O'Connell continued that foreign leaders "cannot, however, give consent to a right they do not have. . . . States may not use military force [or authorize other nations to do so] against individuals on their territory when law enforcement measures are appropriate."[32]

A Justice Department "white paper" helps justify U.S. drone strikes anywhere by expanding the definition of self-defense as retaliation against actual or imminent attacks. It refers to "a broader concept of imminence" that does not require actual intelligence about any ongoing plot against the U.S. homeland, consistent with the Bush administrations shift from preemptive to preventive war discussed earlier. This white paper, however, is explicitly used to justify drone attacks targeting and killing American citizens who have not been given a trial or any judicial rights—all in the name of antiterrorism.

The issue of killing Americans became a major topic after the United States launched a Predator drone attack on September 30, 2011, in Yemen against Samir Kahn and Anwar al-Awlaki, both American citizens who were killed by Hellfire missiles shot from the Predator while in their car. The United States never presented any evidence against al-Awlaki.[33] This, in itself, is a serious form of political wilding, since it violates the most fundamental right of U.S. citizens to a trial before being detained or killed. But under the new rules drafted by the Obama administration, had any evidence been presented, it would not require showing—to a court or anyone else—that the targeted American was actively involved in a terrorist plot against the United States or even had committed a crime. As Michael Isikoff, a national senior investigative NBC reporter, said on MSNBC's *The Rachel Maddow Show*, an "informed high-level" official may himself determine that the American involved has been "recently" involved in "activities" posing a threat to the

United States and that "there is no evidence suggesting that he has renounced or abandoned such activities." The term "recently" and "activities" are not defined.[34]

The Justice Department white paper discussed by Isikoff makes clear that the president has made himself accuser, judge, jury, and executioner. This is the highest form of political wilding, a violation of the Constitution and of our most basic rights as U.S. citizens. It makes the war on terrorism "extrajudicial," since in the name of pursuing terrorism suspects, it strips U.S. citizens of any judicial rights to self-protection in the face of potential deadly attacks by their own government.

The president not only concentrates judicial powers in himself when attacking citizens, whether U.S. or foreign, with drones, but he violates the sacred Constitutional mandate that only Congress can declare war. The president's authorizations of thousands of drone attacks on countries around the world have in most cases been taken without congressional authorization and usually without even the knowledge of most senators or representatives of Congress. In 2007, Obama himself said that, "the president does not have power under the Constitution to unilaterally authorize a military attack in a situation that does not involve stopping an actual or imminent threat to the nation."[35] The president is skating on extremely thin ice, using very broad congressional resolutions after 9/11—as well as the Patriot Act and a reinterpretation of the 1973 War Powers Act regarding what is an "imminent threat"—to do whatever he sees fit to fight terrorism or other national security threats. This concentration of executive presidential power is frightening and constitutes extreme wilding. Its ultimate purpose and consequence is to facilitate U.S. military intervention wherever the president wants, expanding U.S. hegemony in the name of the war on terrorism.

Drones are not the only means of doing this, but they are especially useful. Since they don't usually put U.S. soldiers at risk, the use of drones may not seem to be military or war actions, and their use may be a source of comfort, though a false one, for most Americans who don't want the United States at war everywhere. Despite their "unmilitary" look and feel, drones are also extraordinary devices for building global power. As one military analyst put it: "Drones are an incredible weapon because of their ability to project power. Without ever actually putting a person in peril, the U.S. military has expanded its kinetic and reconnaissance reach to previously unseen limits."[36] Drones have become the new weapon of choice for the twenty-first-century empire, a military and political instrument that George Orwell would undoubtedly have incorporated into his dystopian visions of the high-tech militarized future.

Torture and State Terror

Torture at Abu Ghraib in Iraq was the tip of the iceberg. U.S. military officials have used "waterboard" torture in Afghan detention centers, where a prisoner is strapped down to a board, immobilized, and has water poured over his or her face, inducing a feeling of drowning. In Afghanistan and Guantánamo Bay, other reports of U.S. torture include dog attacks that created severe wounds and leg beatings that led to the death of at least one prisoner. Based on Defense Department data, the ACLU reported on October 25, 2005, that U.S. guards and intelligence officials had murdered at least 21 prisoners in their custody in Iraq and Afghanistan, a form of wilding by any definition. The deaths occurred during or after interrogation from "strangulation" or "blunt force injuries."[37] In 2005, a large-scale hunger fast at Guantánamo by prisoners protesting abusive treatment led to harsh force-feeding that many attorneys called prisoner abuse itself.

Official torture became part of broader U.S. state terrorism inside and outside Iraq—*all in the name of the war against terrorism itself.* During his 2005 Senate confirmation hearings, then Attorney General Alberto Gonzales refused to renounce torture. In 2002, as White House counselor, Gonzales had written that 9/11 had rendered the old rules obsolete—such as the Geneva Conventions—that forbade torture. Senator Ted Kennedy argued that the new thinking "has been used by the administration, the military, and the CIA to justify torture and Geneva Convention violations by military and civilian officials."[38]

Prominent British journalist Jonathan Steele has written that the Bush administration incorporated torture and other "state terrorist" methods into U.S. policy worldwide. Steele writes, "that the administration sees the U.S. not just as a self-appointed global policeman, but also as the world's prison warder. It is thinking of building jails in foreign countries, mainly ones with grim human rights records, to which it can secretly transfer detainees (un-convicted by any court) for the rest of their lives—a kind of global gulag beyond the scrutiny of the International Committee of the Red Cross, or any other independent observers or lawyers."[39] Confirming Steele's report, in October 2005, the *Washington Post* revealed that the CIA maintained at least eight secret "black site" prisons around the world to hold prisoners indefinitely, without formal charges, and without any restraint on torture or inhumane treatment. These prisons are not subject even to military tribunal review.[40] Beyond these charges are those that American soldiers desecrated and burned the dead bodies of Taliban fighters in Afghanistan, using loudspeakers to taunt Islamic soldiers in nearby villages that they were "ladies" fearful of coming to protect their dead colleagues.

In February 2007, the International Committee of the Red Cross issued an authoritative report confirming that the CIA had been sending detainees to "black box" prisons in Afghanistan, Poland, Romania, and at least five other countries around the world and subjecting them to many forms of torture, including suffocating prisoners using water, enforcing prolonged standing in stress positions, beatings that involve the use of a collar, beating and kicking, confining prisoners in a box, using prolonged nudity, depriving prisoners of sleep and using loud music to torment them, keeping prisoners in handcuffs and shackles for prolonged periods of time, and threatening them.[41]

Prisoners brutally tortured in several black box sites included Abu Zubaydah, a suspected associate of Osama bin Laden, who told the Red Cross that "one of the interrogators wrapped a towel around my neck, they then used it to swing me around and smash me repeatedly against the hard walls of the room. I was also repeatedly slapped in the face."[42] Another detainee, Walid bin Attash, told the Red

Cross that he was repeatedly stripped naked and placed "in a standing position with my arms about my head and fixed with handcuffs and a chain to a metal ring" for "about ten days. . . . During the standing I was made to wear a diaper" that was not replaced and "so I had to urinate and defecate over myself."[43] Attash continued, "Every day for the first two weeks I was subjected to slaps to my face and punches to my body. . . . Also on a daily basis during the first two weeks a collar was looped around my neck and then used to slam me against the walls of the interrogation room."[44]

In a 2009 detailed review and analysis of the Red Cross report, Mark Danner, a leading researcher on torture and former reporter for the *New York Times*, observes that the Red Cross described these as "standardized treatments." But while CIA agents, such as John Kiriakou, witnessed the waterboarding of Zubaydah and helped validate the truth of the detainee allegations, President George W. Bush told the country that "the United States does not torture. It is against our laws and it's against our values."[45] Danner assembled detailed evidence from the Red Cross report and CIA sources that the torture sessions were approved in phone calls to the CIA in Washington, and that the overall policy was approved by President Bush and Vice President Dick Cheney. Danner sums up three central conclusions:

1. Beginning in the spring of 2002 the United States government began to torture prisoners. This torture, approved by the President of the United States and monitored in its daily unfolding by senior officials, including the nation's highest law enforcement officer, clearly violated major treaty obligations of the United States, including the Geneva Conventions and the Convention Against Torture, as well as U.S. law.

2. The most senior officers of the U.S. government, President George W. Bush first among them, repeatedly and explicitly lied about this, both in reports to international institutions and directly to the public. The President lied about it in news conferences, interviews, and, most explicitly, in speeches expressly intended to set out the administration's policy on interrogation before the people who had elected him.

3. The U.S. Congress, already in possession of a great deal of information about the torture conducted by the administration—which had been covered widely in the press, and had been briefed, at least in part, from the outset to a select few of its members—passed the Military Commissions Act of 2006 and in so doing attempted to protect those responsible from criminal penalty under the War Crimes Act.[46]

Fear that torture was damaging America's image led the Senate in October 2005 to pass a bill, sponsored by Senator John McCain, prohibiting prisoner abuse, including torture. The Bush administration sought an amendment to exempt the CIA and other counterterrorist agencies, the first time that Bush openly claimed that the United States needed to use torture, something that McCain rejected as failing to produce intelligence and endangered American lives.[47] However, when the president finally signed the bill, he issued an "interpretive" signing statement, indicating that he would not comply with the law when he believed his "constitutional authority" was being infringed, essentially saying he would obey the law only when he viewed it as appropriate.

In 2009, when President Obama came into office, he officially renounced waterboarding and other forms of torture, even as former vice president Dick Cheney repeatedly went on air to justify torture as the only way to protect U.S. security.[48] Cheney's pronouncements finally made clear that the use of torture in the Bush years was official policy approved at the highest level.

Obama promised that American national security would never again come at the cost of torture or other subversion of proclaimed American values. But while he promised to end torture and shut down Guantánamo, Obama, at this writing, has refused to launch official investigations into the Bush administration's use of torture, to show pictures of tortured detainees, or to end the use of unconstitutional military tribunals.[49] He also has failed to close Guantánamo and announced that he would continue to hold some detainees without trial for an indefinite period. Many people now believe that by refusing to support investigations of the Bush administration's torture regime, Obama himself is involved in a cover-up. Public demand for accountability and justice, in the United States and around the world, is legitimate, and bringing to justice those responsible for torture is the only way to prevent it in the future.

The Surveillance State: The NSA, Political Wilding, and Presidential Powers in the Era of Permanent Warfare

The Bush administration used 9/11 to launch a horrific assault on American constitutionalism, arguably the most serious form of political wilding that is now completely intertwined with the war on terrorism itself. At the core of the matter is unchecked executive power. The president was using "emergency powers" during crises to gut civil liberties and constitutional protections held sacred under the Bill of Rights. "The most profound issue," wrote eminent *New York Times* legal affairs journalist Anthony Lewis, "is presidential power. Since Sept. 11, 2001, [former] President Bush and his lawyers asserted again and again that the 'war on terror' clothes the president as commander in chief with extraordinary, unilateral power—the power, for example, to designate an American citizen as an enemy combatant and imprison him indefinitely, without trial or a real opportunity to demonstrate innocence."[50]

In June 2013, Edward Snowden, the now famous 29-year-old private contractor and whistle-blower working for the National Security Agency (NSA), released a treasure trove of documents showing that the U.S. government was secretly collecting billions of bits of information on the e-mails, web-surfing, phone calls, online chats, and Skype conversations of every U.S. citizen, as well as foreign citizens and governments. While President Obama defended the program as integral to the war on terrorism, and justified under the 2002 Patriot Act passed after 9/11, Snowden's revelations unleashed a national and global controversy about the right of the U.S. government to collect such voluminous "metadata" in the name of protecting from terrorism the very citizens it was spying on. Millions of U.S. citizens and many politicians on both the Left and Right were outraged, and the American Civil Liberties Union sued the NSA for violating the Fourth Amendment constitutional right to privacy, one of the bedrocks of U.S. constitutional democracy and liberty. Wisconsin Republican Senator James Sensenbrenner, the lead author of the 2002 Patriot Act, claimed he never intended that the Patriot Act be used to justify such mass invasions of privacy:

> The administration has collected the details of every call made by every American, even though the overwhelming majority of these calls have nothing to do with terrorism. Since first learning of the program this spring, I have been a vocal critic of such dragnet collection as a gross invasion of privacy and a violation of Section 215 [the section of the Patriot Act that authorizes surveillance of business phone records if there is reason to believe it is relevant to an ongoing terrorism investigation].[51]

While the Snowden leaks reinforced the accusations of those who refer to Obama's war on terror as "Bush on Steroids," the seeds of this "surveillance state" began long before either Bush or Obama. The United States has a long history of spying on its citizens, most notably with former FBI director J. Edgar Hoover's spying on anyone he regarded as communist, and President Nixon breaking into private files to dig up information on people on his "enemies list," including breaking into the office of the psychiatrist of Daniel Ellsberg, who released the "Pentagon Papers" that disclosed secrets about Vietnam. New intrusive surveillance came to light more recently in November 2005, when Americans learned for the first time that "national security letters" issued by President Bush had authorized the FBI to search the phone records of more than 30,000 Americans.

In a major story in late 2005, the *New York Times* revealed that President George W. Bush had approved National Security Agency (NSA) surveillance of ordinary Americans without court approval for over four years. According to official sources,

> The volume of information harvested from telecommunication data and voice networks, without court-approved warrants, is much larger than the White House has acknowledged, the officials said. It was collected by tapping directly into some of the American telecommunication system's main arteries, they said. As part of the program approved by President Bush for domestic surveillance without warrants, the NSA has gained the cooperation of American telecommunications companies to obtain backdoor access to streams of domestic and international communications, the officials said.[52]

Many critics, both Democrat and Republican, believed that Bush broke the Foreign Intelligence Surveillance Act (the "FISA" law), passed in 1978 specifically to prevent such spying on Americans without review by a special secret court set up by Congress (FISC). In a major address on January 16, 2005, former vice president Al Gore said, "What we do know about this pervasive wiretapping virtually compels the conclusion that the President of the United States has been breaking the law repeatedly and persistently." Gore went on to say:

It is this same disrespect for America's Constitution which has now brought our republic to the brink of a dangerous breach in the fabric of the Constitution. And the disrespect embodied in these apparent mass violations of the law is part of a larger pattern of seeming indifference to the Constitution that is deeply troubling to millions of Americans in both political parties.[53]

President Bush claimed that inherent executive powers and the initial authorization by Congress to respond to 9/11 with force entitled him to act on his own to prevent terrorist acts, essentially claiming that as commander in chief, he was above the law and that presidential powers could not be limited by Congress when it came to preventing terrorism.[54] But Congress specifically excluded the right to wiretap Americans in its post-9/11 authorization, and many constitutional lawyers and political leaders, including then-Republican-senator Arlen Specter, chairman of the Senate Judiciary Committee, were deeply troubled by Bush's claim, with Specter convening Senate hearings to investigate whether Bush had broken the law or violated the Constitution by authorizing the NSA surveillance, and with John Dean, a Republican counselor to President Nixon, saying that Bush had admitted to "an impeachable offense."[55]

Many believed that President Barack Obama, a constitutional law professor, would take a new approach, since Obama had campaigned on promises to end the war in Iraq and reexamine the executive powers exercised by President Bush in the name of fighting terrorism. But Snowden's revelations showed that Obama followed Bush's lead and built the NSA and other secret intelligence and counter-terrorism agencies into a far more expansive and invasive apparatus. Four years before Snowden's stunning revelations, prominent Washington law professor Jonathan Turley said in 2009 that the Bush administration should proclaim "mission accomplished," because, in Turley's words, they "have Barack Obama adopting the same extremist arguments and, in fact, exceeding the extremist arguments made by President Bush."[56]

Many observers view Snowden's revelations about NSA surveillance as the most significant leak of government data in U.S. history. It reveals an astonishing array of secret programs forcing telecommunications companies such as Verizon, Internet companies such as Google, software companies such as Microsoft, and online communication sites such as Skype to transfer their records of billions of private communications of Americans and foreigners to the NSA. Without a court warrant, the NSA is able to analyze, store, and investigate anything that virtually anyone in the United States or the world had communicated online or by phone in the name of stopping terrorism. One of the major programs is PRISM, which is the NSA surveillance system that forces Internet companies, including Google, Yahoo, and Microsoft, to share data about anyone using the Net on their search engines: what web sites they surfed; the content of their Microsoft Word documents; whom they communicated or chatted with; and what they said to friends or colleagues in e-mails or text messages. Snowden's leaks showed that a Foreign Intelligence Security Court (FISC), created by Congress in 1978 as a check against wiretap abuses by the government, had vastly expanded the NSA surveillance powers and approved almost all of the thousands of spying requests by the Obama administration, although it ruled in 2011 that some of what the NSA was doing was illegal, as well as forcing the NSA to pay the companies for the considerable costs involved in complying with the NSA demands.[57]

The scope of the NSA surveillance was unknown to most members of Congress, with the possible exception of a handful of senators and representatives heading congressional intelligence committees. Republican Senator Rand Paul, from Kentucky, argued that no degree of congressional insight could fix these problems, which, he said, "I fundamentally think are unconstitutional." The Founding Fathers, he said, wrote the Fourth Amendment to force the government to get a distinct court warrant to "look at any specific individual and [make clear] what you want to look for." But the NSA, he said, "are looking at all the cell phones in America every day," with no warrant at all.[58]

Paul accused the president of not understanding the constitutional checks on presidential power, and called for congressional hearings, supported by his colleagues on both sides of the aisle. But Obama insisted that the programs were constitutional under his presidential authority to protect the country and said that the programs "are not abused . . . the checks are in place," and alleged abuses "are against the law and against the orders of the FISC court."[59] But Obama's claims that NSA bureaucrats would not go on fishing expeditions to look at the content of individual American citizens' private communications is contradicted by documents released by Snowden showing thousands of examples of exactly such intrusive snooping. Oregon Democratic Senator Ron Wyden said the documents revealed a "loophole" to Section 702 of the Foreign Intelligence Security Act, permitting "backdoor search" of individual Americans. "Once Americans' communications are collected, a gap in the law that I call the 'back-door searches loophole' allows the government to potentially go through these communications and conduct warrantless searches for the phone calls or e-mails of law-abiding Americans."[60]

The violation of Americans' civil liberties and their constitutional rights to privacy are a grave form of political wilding. It permits the president to target without warrant or congressional approval perfectly innocent American citizens, and subject them to investigation, intimidation, and prosecution. Those picked out as suspected terrorists may be journalists, such as James Rosen, the Fox News Washington Bureau Chief, who talked to, and reported on a story from, a North Korean source who said North Korea might respond to further sanctions by accelerating its nuclear program. Rosen had his private e-mails read and was then subjected to criminal prosecution by the Obama Justice Department for breaking the law simply for reporting the story.[61] Glenn Greenwald, the British newspaper the *Guardian's* main contact with Snowden and the primary reporter disclosing the Snowden documents, has had his personal partner and main professional colleague on the Snowden case detained and stripped of his computers and other material in airports, and Greenwald is fearful of arrest if he returns to the United States. The *New Yorker's* Jane Mayer says that the attacks on investigative journalists "[are] a huge impediment to reporting, and so chilling isn't strong enough, it's more like freezing the whole process to a standstill."[62] Surveillance, intimidation, and prosecution of journalists, a horrific form of political wilding, threatens a free press, as does the circumventing of both Congress and the courts in snooping on individual citizens, evoking the image of a tyrannical Big Brother immortalized by novelist George Orwell in his great dystopian work, *1984.*

The "surveillance state"—and the staggering scope of the NSA spying program—is part of a broader pattern of abuse of executive power that threatens democracy, freedom, and civil society. In the name of protecting national security, Obama's Justice Department has continued to use the "state secrets" doctrine to stop many of the lawsuits that could expose Bush-era abductions, detentions, and torture. Obama is reported to be considering a new prison and court complex in the United States that would allow suspects to be held indefinitely without trial.[63] Obama has failed to renounce the use of "signing statements," allowing him to continue Bush's practice of enforcing only those parts of laws he views as constitutional. Former Department of Justice official Bruce Fein has spelled out many Obama acts that create "an emerging pattern of mightily expansive claims of executive authority" that are part of "President Barack Obama's claim to czarlike powers in a perpetual war against international terrorism."[64] Other NSA documents released by Snowden show the NSA spying on the United Nations and major U.S. allies, such as Germany (including bugging the personal cell phone of German Prime Minister Angela Merkel as well as 35 other world leaders), Brazil, and Mexico; this has kicked up an international firestorm against the United States and its claims about respecting constitutional democracy and international law.

In 2014, after a nasty battle between the Senate Intelligence Committee, headed by Senator Diane Feinstein of California, and the CIA, which involved the Senate body and the CIA accusing each other of illegal hacking or spying on the other, the political outrage escalated to the point that President Obama finally acknowledged the need to reexamine the warrantless collection of metadata on the U.S. population authorized by the PRISM program. He directed the NSA to stop collecting much of this data and to keep what they did collect stored with Verizon, Google, and other private companies for a shorter period. But it was too little too late, since Obama had essentially already institutionalized the surveillance state whose known wilding dimensions keep expanding with each new Snowden revelation.

[□] Fighting Terrorism without Wilding

Nations around the world *do* need to come together to try to prevent terrorism. It is precisely because the threat is real and frightening that it is such a powerful tool for manipulating public opinion. In the face of a very real threat, we need a more effective and honest approach to stopping terrorism. What would such an approach look like? We must begin with something like a political Hippocratic oath—the oath to do no harm—by the U.S. government to end its own practices of state terrorism described in detail in this chapter. The United States must immediately renounce the use of torture, the breaking of international treaties such as the

Geneva Conventions, and the waging of illegal and unjust wars and occupations. A country that practices state terrorism loses all credibility to lead a global war against terrorism. Moreover, when it uses the war on terrorism as a pretext not only to use terror but also to justify its pursuit of empire—in the codependent strategy discussed above—its credibility collapses entirely.

Beyond taking the political Hippocratic oath, which ultimately requires renouncing the use of terror and pursuit of empire by the U.S. government, a just global antiterror campaign would be based on the following principles. First, it would be directed by the United Nations and the international community rather than by the United States. Second, it would attack the root causes of terrorism, requiring major changes in U.S. foreign and economic policy. This would include a far more balanced American approach to the Israeli–Palestinian conflict, the most explosive issue in the Middle East. The United States could do more to end terror by pushing Israel more forcefully to end illegal settlements and accept a viable Palestinian state than by taking any other step, since this would erode support for Hamas and other Palestinian extremist groups. Ending U.S. military occupation of the region and withdrawing U.S. support for the brutal monarchies and sheikdoms are also essential. This could take place only if the United States renounces its aspiration for global hegemony, acknowledging that empire is incompatible with its own democratic ideals as well as with global peace.

An effective antiterror strategy would imply changing the rules of globalization—which is now the economic expression of American hegemony—such that poor people in the Middle East and around the world are not forced to bear the burden of debt while being denied the means to shape their own development policies. As long as the United States imposes a globalization that does not help the 2 billion people who eat fewer calories a day than the ordinary American's cat or dog, we are going to have more anti-American terror.

A war on terrorism that is not wilding would be political, economic, and diplomatic, rather than military. Police and other agents of coercive force may be required to root out violent groups, but the most effective way to do so requires enacting just global policies and involving the full cooperation of other nations and of publics all over the world. Stopping terrorism depends on winning the hearts and minds of the people.

What You Can Do

Problems related to torture, drone warfare, and the erosion of civil liberties, including unconstitutional spying, in the fight against terrorism are only likely to get worse. This is another issue that should mobilize people of good conscience everywhere in the country. Students on campuses have a major responsibility here, and they should play a crucial role in stopping this particularly horrific part of the political wilding crisis.

The issue of torture may be a catalyzing one for students. Whenever I have discussed the question among my own students, most are horrified that their own government engages in torture or aids other governments that do. When they read the actual accounts of prisoner abuse at Abu Ghraib in Iraq, at Guantánamo, or in Afghanistan, they experience revulsion. They want it to stop and never happen again.

All kinds of interventions are possible. Students can go on the Internet to learn about organizations, such as Amnesty International and Human Rights Watch, that provide information about prisoner abuse. They can "adopt" particular prisoners and write letters to their congressional representatives and the Pentagon to stop the abuse. They can stage demonstrations on their campuses, educating their peers about the abomination of torture practiced by American military officials. One of my own students made national headlines when he put on a cloak, donned a hood, attached military wires to his arms and legs, and stood out in front of a local military recruitment station. He was arrested, but the charges were later dismissed, as mass media reports concentrated on the horrors of torture in Iraq at Abu Ghraib, and the importance of young people—who are, after all, the soldiers carrying out the abuse—standing up against these practices.

The issues of civil liberties, more broadly, is arguably the most critical topic for students to address. The university is the one institution in U.S. society based centrally on free expression and critical thinking. If you shut down free speech or dissent on the campus, you doom these principles everywhere in society. Unfortunately, in past historical eras when civil liberties have been threatened, such as the McCarthy Era, many universities did nothing or, worse, even collaborated with McCarthyism by singling out left-leaning faculty and students as "communist" and expelling them from campus. Students cannot allow this to happen again.

This issue of civil liberties and the Patriot Act, as well as the burning issue of the NSA and mass surveillance, is very much alive on campuses today. Right-wing groups are targeting professors critical of the war on terrorism, paying students to monitor the classrooms of professors for any sign of liberal "bias," and some campus administrators are giving in to the pressure. Campuses are making it more difficult for student groups to protest, moving in the direction of shutting down the most basic First Amendment rights that students, and all of us, depend on for our freedom.

On my own campus, students are required to secure permits for any kind of protest, and a group protesting the presence of a military company, Raytheon, at a career fair were prevented from carrying out a silent theatrical "die-in" as a protest. This action stirred up a major storm on campus; the next day many students went to their classes with a piece of tape over their mouths, symbolizing their belief that they had been censored. They sponsored a forum on campus within the week to discuss protest, censorship, and curtailment of civil liberties on campus. The question of whether students should have to get a permit for passing out literature in dormitories, for assembling peacefully on campus to protest, or for inviting media on campus is critical. If students want to stop political wilding, there is nothing more important that they can do than to get active on their campuses to make sure that free speech and civil liberties are not destroyed in the name of fighting terrorism.

History tells us that political leaders can successfully attack student activists and other dissenters at home only by linking them falsely to enemies abroad and disguising the pursuit of empire in the name of a war against terrorism. Students must respond on both fronts. They must show that by protesting torture, drones, illegal spying, and other violations of the Constitution by the president, they are not aiding "the enemy," but instead expressing patriotism.

Most important, they must become part of the new global peace movement that is trying to reveal the war against terrorism for what it really is: the American pursuit of empire. The fight to preserve the Constitution at home is inseparable from the fight to end the pursuit of American empire abroad. Students on campuses must organize new peace movements for the complete withdrawal of American forces from Iraq and Afghanistan, the stopping of drone attacks on scores of countries by the United States, preventing interventions in civil wars such as in Syria, the removal of American soldiers from bases in Saudi Arabia and other Arab countries, and the prevention of new attacks on Iran, Syria, and North Korea. There is hope in the rise of an antidrone movement on many campuses, allied with adult activists in many communities, that is going to Congress and protesting on the streets to end drone bombing all over the world. We need a new generation of dedicated peace activists who understand that the pursuit of global power and domination by the United States (or any other country) is a kind of wilding that fatally threatens not only people around the world, but also Americans and our own most cherished freedoms.

Discussion Questions

1. Is war wilding? What about the Iraq war? What about the Afghanistan war?

2. Is terrorism wilding?

3. Is the war on terrorism wilding?

4. Is the United States' current use of drone warfare a form of wilding?

5. Is the mass surveillance used by the United States to spy on citizens and leaders a form of wilding?

6. Is U.S. foreign policy, such as frequent military intervention in the Muslim world, a form of wilding?

7. What can students do to change U.S. foreign policy and end wars that are wilding acts? Are you a wilder if you do not do these things?

ten

Beyond Wilding
Resurrecting Civil Society

An injury to one is the concern of all.

—Knights of Labor motto

Wilding has taken a devastating toll on America, but it has not permanently incapacitated it. Societies, like individuals, have a powerful natural resistance and a remarkable capacity to regenerate. Although the Ik society, discussed in Chapter 1, has been destroyed, America, always resilient, has far greater economic and cultural resources to revitalize itself. To succeed, however, it will have to focus all its efforts on the task, which involves shoring up the ideal of a "civil society" at its very foundations.

Creating and supporting a civil society is the underlying antidote to the wilding virus. Civil society involves a culture of love, morality, and trust that leads people to care for one another and for the larger community. A civil society's institutions—especially its economic and political structures—nurture civic responsibility by providing incentives for people to act not just in their own interest but for the common good. Governments must provide a supportive framework, including helping redesign an economy based on cooperation and social justice, but a robust civil society cannot be simply legislated. It must arise from the cooperation and moral sensibilities of ordinary people who understand that their own fulfillment requires thriving communities and an intact and just society.

Although there is no magic formula and no perfect model, a civil society rooted in a cooperative economy and fully democratic politics is the strongest and most suitable medicine for the wilding epidemic. Americans now must urgently recognize that they need to dedicate themselves unwaveringly to reconstructing their society.

The Case for Hope

More than 150 years ago, Alexis de Tocqueville worried that America was vulnerable to an individualism that "saps the virtues of public life" and "in the long run" might "attack and destroy" society itself. Tocqueville described it as an individualism "which disposes each member of the community to sever himself from the mass of his fellows" and to "feel no longer bound by a common interest." Americans must always be on guard, Tocqueville advised, against the deterioration of their individualistic culture into "a passionate and exaggerated love of self, which leads a man to connect everything with himself, and to prefer himself to everything else in the world."[1]

Tocqueville did not disapprove of the healthy self-interest that energized Americans, but he saw the thin line that separates American individualism from wilding. Without strongly developed moral codes, the restless pursuit of self-interest inherent in a market economy could at any time degrade into an egoistic menace that might destroy society. But Tocqueville, a sober observer, was also extraordinarily optimistic about the American experiment. Counteracting the wilding virus was another side of America, the strength of its civil society. One manifestation of this was the personal generosity and helpfulness that he observed in all his American travels. "Although private interest directs the greater part of human actions in the United States," Tocqueville wrote, "it does not regulate them all. I must say that I have often seen Americans make great and real sacrifices to the public welfare; and I have remarked a hundred instances in which they hardly ever failed to lend faithful support to each other." Because an American is neither master nor slave to his fellow creature, "his heart readily leans to the side of kindness."[2]

Tocqueville recognized that the kinder and gentler side of American life was grounded in the political rights and free institutions that "remind every citizen, and in a thousand ways, that he lives in society." Tocqueville marveled at Americans' propensity to "constantly form associations" of a thousand kinds in which they "voluntarily learn to help each other." Americans were constantly connecting and spontaneously creating the bonds of friendship, trust, and cooperation that lie at the heart of civil society.[3]

In the century and a half since Tocqueville's visit, the wilding epidemic has spread throughout America, but it has not totally destroyed the civil society that made such an impression on him. Much evidence suggests that Americans retain some of the openness, generosity, and moral idealism that, in Tocqueville's view, differentiated them from Europeans. Likewise, the free institutions and "propensity to associate" have not vanished. It is the sturdiness of this base, its survival in the face of the wilding onslaught, that offers grounds for optimism and a direction for the future.

While Hurricane Katrina was a cauldron of wilding, with abject failure by the government to fund necessary levees and help millions of victims, who were mostly poor and minority folks in New Orleans, it was also a symbol of the love and altruism that remains strong in our culture and people. In 2005, Americans dug into their pockets to donate billions of dollars to Katrina victims, less than a year after they had given record amounts to the victims of the tsunami in Southeast Asia. By the fall of 2005, the United Way reported donations of over $4 billion in charity in response mainly to Katrina. Thousands of other charitable organizations have collected, in total, more than $10 billion in relief funds, much of it from Americans who were struggling to make it through the week on their own diminishing wages.

Many in New Orleans were heroic in their rescue efforts, risking their own lives to save others. As two observers in New Orleans put it, the real "heroes and sheroes" of Katrina were

[t]he maintenance workers who used a forklift to carry the sick and disabled. . . . Nurses who took over for mechanical ventilators and spent many hours on end manually forcing air into the lungs of unconscious patients to keep them alive. Doormen who rescued folks stuck in elevators. Refinery workers who broke into boat yards, "stealing" boats to rescue their neighbors clinging to their roofs in flood waters. Mechanics who helped hotwire any car that could be found to ferry people out of the city. And the food service workers who scoured the commercial kitchens, improvising communal meals for hundreds of those stranded.[4]

The same hope can be seen in the 2008 economic meltdown. The high rollers at AIG who took $165 million in bonuses while bringing down the economy became the ultimate symbol of our new wilding culture. But despite the wilding storm on Wall Street that led millions to lose their jobs, many laid-off workers decided to go volunteer in places like New Orleans' Ninth Ward after Katrina to help build houses, or in Philadelphia's inner city neighborhood to help staff homeless shelters. They had lost their jobs but not their will to help others.

The New York United Way reported a large increase in the number of laid-off people volunteering their time, even though they had no money to give. The director reported a surge in people with some financial skills volunteering time to offer financial planning or tax help to low-income families. In 2009, groups from AmeriCorps to the American Heart Association to local soup kitchens, homeless centers, and tutoring clinics around the country reported increases in the number of people seeking to volunteer. The Peace Corps reported a 16 percent surge in applications. In 2008, 441,000 more young Americans volunteered than in 2007, a total of 8.2 million. In all, 62 million Americans put in 8 billion hours of service in 2008.[5]

The Occupy Wall Street movement represented another form of moral renewal and civic responsibility. Thousands of protesters, animated by social justice and concern for workers and the poor, engaged in civil disobedience and risked jail to help create a more social and just economy. We shall see that politicized, morally inspired behavior is key to reconstructing the now-sociopathic systems in our economy and politics. Meanwhile, it is worth noting that after the movement took down its tent cities in New York and many other cities, thousands of Occupy protesters went into the areas of New York and New Jersey where Superstorm Sandy did its worst damage and helped survivors to rebuild their homes and communities.

Meanwhile, thousands of people in all 50 states, not necessarily involved with Occupy Wall Street, organized "Economic Recovery House Meetings," an idea suggested originally by President Obama. In these meetings, neighbors get together to discuss Obama's economic policies and to help each other ride out the economic storm. Claire Anderson, an organizer of one of these house meetings in Seattle, Washington, said that "bad times make good neighbors." She said that Seattle folks were creating barter networks, community gardens for food, and mutual lending support networks. People in Seattle now "make more dinners" for their neighbors. Anderson says, "Now I wouldn't think of making a big pot of stew without taking it to my neighbors."[6]

President Obama spoke of such social responsibility and community service as the nation's new morality. In his August 28, 2008, acceptance speech to the Democratic National Convention, Barack Obama said:

> That's the promise of America, the idea that we are responsible for ourselves, but that we also rise or fall as one nation; the fundamental belief that I am my brother's keeper; I am my sister's keeper.[7]

As a former community organizer, the president's moral philosophy, as expressed here, was a clear rejection of selfish individualism. He promised to build a new economy around the values of cooperation, interdependence, and community itself.

As I argued in Chapter 1, America is simultaneously host to a wilding culture and a civil culture, with sectors of the elites increasingly immersed in wilding and a vast number of ordinary Americans uneasily straddling the two cultures. Most Americans' lives are a struggle to reconcile wilding impulses with a nagging conscience that refuses to die. Many succumb to wilding pressures at the office but rediscover their humanity with family or friends. Conversely, some become wilders in their personal lives but express their conscience in admirable careers dedicated to constructive professional or business enterprise, public service, or social change.

The stubborn persistence of civil society and moral commitment—surfacing even in the midst of an economic collapse brought on by extreme wilding—provides a fertile seedbed for social reconstruction. The way to stop the wilding epidemic is to bolster all the empathic and moral sensibilities that Americans already display. Although these need to be fortified and mobilized with new visions and structural transformation of our political economy, the project is more akin to catalyzing the surviving immune system of a weakened patient than transplanting a new immune system to a patient whose own defenses have been destroyed.

But solving the problem will take serious cultural and institutional change. As I have argued, wilding grows out of an American individualism, driven by our economic system, that is deeply rooted. Even in the Obama era, much of the country's leadership and many of its major institutions increasingly fuel Americans' wilding side and provide serious disincentives to their less egoistic inclinations. We need to cultivate the culture, economics, and politics of a civil society, where the rules of success encourage attention to morality and the common good of which Obama speaks so eloquently. To move from rhetoric to reality we must rewrite the current sociopathic rules of the game so that those who neglect the collective interest will not prosper and those who take it into account will realize their just rewards.

Rethinking the American Dream: A New Communitarianism?

The American Dream has not always been a cultural template for wilding. As we consider rewriting the Dream for a better future, we have the consolation that we can look to our history for guidance. Through most of America's past, the purely materialistic and individualistic side of the Dream has tended to be balanced by a moral and community-oriented side, preventing the Dream from transmuting into a wilding recipe. Moreover, the Dream has been inclusive, defining a set of common purposes to which all Americans could aspire. These historical features of the Dream need to be recaptured in order to fortify civil society and purge the wilding epidemic.

The individualistic Dream dominating the present has its roots in the mythology of the self-made man and, as historian James Combs argues, "stems from the ideology of capitalism and the myth of unlimited abundance." The materialistic dimensions of the Dream have become so dominant that most Americans have forgotten that there was once another side to the Dream. America has traditionally defined itself in terms of a set of high moral ideals, including democracy, equality, and tolerance. Values growing out of the religious and political foundations of the country, including the Puritan zeal for religious community and the American Revolution's idealization of civil democracy, helped shape another dream, one that mythologized family, community, democracy, equality, and civic responsibility. Throughout most of American history, the materialistic Dream prevailed, but the dream that elevated community values, while far from creating the cooperative economy and democratic polity we need, provided a warning that success should not be achieved at any price.

The two dreams define a creative tension in American history. While at some times in our history the materialistic Dream prevailed, in the 1930s, the Great Depression mobilized Americans to rally together and fashion a collective lifeline to ride out the economic storm. President Franklin Delano Roosevelt reinvigorated the dream of moral community, using the government to affirm that in a time of desperate need, Americans would take care of one another. Three decades later, in the 1960s, a whole generation of youth plunged into social activism and communal experiments, seeking a morally attractive alternative to the materialist Dream of their 1950s childhoods. But in the decades between presidents Reagan and Obama, the United States endured perhaps the most self-centered Dream in American history. President Obama, whatever his policy limitations, has articulated a new Dream focused on interdependence and community.

The moral vision will have to be creative because of the new threats that unchecked materialism now pose. It will have to encompass an ecological morality, for we now know that the untrammeled materialist Dream is incompatible with planetary survival, being a form of wilding directed against nature itself. Global warming—the catastrophic heating up of the Earth through promiscuous use of fossil fuels—is only the most frightening of the legacies of such environmental wilding. If Americans cannot learn to live within the limits dictated by the environment, we will be engaged not only in crimes against nature but also in a form of wilding against future generations who will bear the ultimate consequences.

Americans find it hard to accept any limits on materialism, for the dominant Dream has equated freedom and fulfillment with the right to become as rich or famous as luck, talent, or hard work permits. To suggest that Bill Gates should not have been allowed to make or keep the $51 billion he now has strikes us as un-American. But a civil society must respect not only ecological limits but also those dictated by the traditional American morality of fair play and egalitarianism. Uncapping all limits in the recent Wall Street orgy of greed and deregulation has polarized the country, creating an unprecedented and morally unbearable division between rich and poor.[8]

Civil society is a society of inclusion, and the new Dream will have to script new trade-offs between individual freedom and the survival of the community. This ultimately requires reviving a moral dream of community; not necessarily the utopian vision of communes that failed in the 1960s, but something that is simultaneously more modest and more ambitious: a reawakening of the American sense of community that can mobilize the country to unify and preserve itself while building solidarity with people around the planet.

The Social Economy: Sociological Sense and Dollars and Cents

Americans have struggled to choose between the materialist dream—the individualistic self-oriented pursuit of having as much money as possible—and the moral dream—the pursuit of community and the public good. The choice requires confronting tensions between the capitalist system and community. The corporate economy has been able to deliver on the promises of the materialist dream for the privileged sectors of U.S. society, but it has been far less effective in preserving the moral fiber of society and sustaining the environment. In periods when the moral dream has come more strongly to the fore, as in the 1930s and 1960s, Americans have pioneered economic models, such as the New Deal and the Great Society, that have departed from free market scripture.

Europeans spent the decades since World War II building their own "social economy." The Swedes, Danes, Austrians, and Germans recognize that they are not playing Adam Smith's game. "We are not operating a marketplace economy," admits German industrialist Helmut Giesecke, but rather a "social marketplace economy [that] guarantees food, shelter, schooling, and medical attention to every person, not as welfare but as human rights." Government, labor, and business work together to reconcile prosperity with social justice. German business has supported this program, according to Giesecke, because "this social network really works," leading to a well-educated, healthy, and motivated workforce whose productivity keeps increasing. The German wage level is significantly higher than the American one; its educational system, especially the vocational programs for the working class, is one of the best in the world; its levels of poverty, homelessness, and hunger are far lower than in the United States.[9]

The European model is a universal welfare state in which the government shelters groups unprotected by the market, responds to the medical, housing, and social needs of the population that the market neglects, and comprehensively regulates business to ensure social responsibility. But the record of American history, as well as its current fiscal crisis, argues against the likelihood that Americans will look solely to the state even in the aftermath of the 2008 economic collapse, though there is a crucial role for government to play in stopping the wilding epidemic.

The development of an American social economy could be one of the most potent remedies for the wilding epidemic. It would provide a way to reconcile economic growth and justice and to help solve America's social and environmental problems by building on its own deepest value: democracy. It also speaks to the American moral dream of community and the public good.

The key to a social, green economy and social democracy in the United States is new institutions, both public and private, that rectify the tendency of our current market economy to write social and environmental costs and benefits out of the equation. The American market responds mainly to the desires of the individual actor—whether a person or corporation—and is largely indifferent to the spillover effects that transactions may have on the rest of society. When a factory decides to pollute, the social cost of bad air and ensuing discomfort or respiratory disease or of carbon emissions is what economists call an "externality": a real cost, but one that the factory owner can ignore, because society, rather than the factory, pays the ultimate bill. In the pure free market model, there is neither an economic incentive for the individual to help society nor a market disincentive to be antisocial; the market simply does not discriminate, operating with so-called benign neglect. As such neglect accumulates, with the market turning a blind eye to the millions of externalities that affect society every day, benign neglect becomes catastrophic social blindness, and civil society is placed in jeopardy.

A social market corrects such social blindness by writing social costs and benefits back into the equation. It is a market that seeks to internalize the externalities, thus becoming socially responsible by giving social stakeholders a voice in corporate decisions and by devising strategies to guarantee that economic wilders pay the cost of their sociopathic behavior (and conversely, that the good citizen will receive his or her just rewards). One approach, appealing to Americans wary of government and committed to democracy, involves redesigning economic institutions to be better equipped to exercise social responsibility on their own initiative. An important example is new corporate ownership and participation arrangements, in which workers and local citizens gain a voice and can speak up for the needs of the larger community. The Germans, although relying primarily on government, have also invented a "codetermination" system, which requires that every industrial enterprise with more than 500 workers select half its governing board of trustees from among its own employees. This has been successful for more than 40 years, contributing not only to the German economic boom but also to a civil industrial society in which ordinary workers have been able to ensure that their health and safety are protected, their grievances addressed, and their jobs protected by investment strategies that prioritize domestic employment and environmental protection as well as overseas profit. Codetermination is a version of economic democracy that works.

Political economist Gar Alperovitz has described the many down-to-earth ways, some already highly developed in America, to fashion a social economy that works to dissuade economic wilding and preserve civil society without resorting exclusively to government. Numerous forms of worker ownership and participation, including cooperatives, in which workers own the company, and employee stock ownership plans (ESOPs), in which employees own a piece or all of their companies through their pensions, can help compel companies to treat their employees fairly and practice workplace democracy. The cooperative, as its name implies, has the potential to turn the workplace itself into a civil society because everyone within it has equal rights, and self-interest is more closely wedded to the collective interest than in a conventional firm. Another innovation involves corporate social charters that bind businesses to designated social missions, as in the case of community credit unions that are structured to reinvest in the community and offer low-interest loans to poorer residents. Land trusts—modern versions of the early British and colonial American concept of the commons—can remove property from the commercial market and legally ensure that it is used to serve sustainable community needs. A new field of social accounting can help take stock of the social costs and benefits of corporate decisions. Social capital, such as the trillions of dollars in American pension funds, one of the largest and still-growing pots of money in the world, can be used to invest in affordable housing and community economic development.[10]

A New New Deal: "My Brother's Keeper; My Sister's Keeper" as American Morality

As soon as you start talking about any kind of new role for government, many Americans roll their eyes. After all, wasn't America founded on the principle of limited government? Hasn't America prospered by rejecting the European ideas of the welfare state and relying instead on individual initiative? The Republican Party is on a never-ending crusade to cut government (or "shrink the beast"). In the 2012 presidential race, Republican candidate Mitt Romney kept calling Obama a "European-style socialist" who would use big government to end everything good and free in America. In the 1990s, Bill Clinton, the only Democratic president since Jimmy Carter, sang a softer Democratic version of the same tune about cutting government, vowing to "end welfare" and shrink the state.

But when the raging winds of Katrina blew across the Gulf Coast and destroyed much of New Orleans, even the Bush administration insisted that government had to step up to the plate. Although Bush dismally failed to protect and save New Orleans, he traveled six times in 2 months back to New Orleans to promise that he would never let the city die. Republican Chris Christie went through the same formalities of "conversion" after Superstorm Sandy destroyed much of his state. Antigovernment Republican leaders were suddenly talking about the sacred connection between an active government and a healthy community. Whether it's a hurricane or a depression, when communities come under stress, everyone suddenly becomes aware that government and community are intertwined.

The 2008 economic meltdown created a major change in the view and role of government in America. The conservative Bush administration stepped in to rescue AIG, Citigroup, Bank of America, GM, and scores of other banks and corporations tottering on the brink of disaster. Many Republicans called their own president's bailouts of the banks "socialism." It wasn't—but it did prove that even capitalists and conservatives ultimately depend on the government to save the economy and keep it prosperous.

The 2008 economic collapse was the culmination of an extended series of crises and the rise of extreme inequality that had left ordinary working Americans feeling like they had been abandoned, and that they could use a little help from government to rebuild their communities. When millions upon millions of Americans saw their wages stagnating and their jobs shipped overseas, their homes foreclosed, their roads and bridges eroding, their public education failing their kids, and their neighborhoods straining under poverty and crime, they elected President Obama in the name of change. They wanted a shift in basic values of the corporate regime that has ruled America over the last 30 years, and while many are deeply disappointed in Obama's failures to deliver big systemic changes, they looked to him to lead an activist government that would express his moral philosophy of "our brother's keeper, our sister's keeper."

The new direction we need—one essential to ending our current wilding epidemic—is a new New Deal. It will not be a clone of Europe's welfare state or Roosevelt's own New Deal. It will not be a call for massive government or even "big government," but rather an activist government accountable to communities and to ordinary citizens rather than big business, and that intervenes selectively to meet the urgent social and environmental needs of the country. Smart government nourishes socially oriented business, and it will offer all Americans a safety net and a sustainable environment, as part of a massive new effort to reconstruct and remake the economy in the new moral spirit of "my brother's keeper."

In both his presidential campaigns against hyperindividualistic and supercapitalistic Republican agendas, Obama contrasted his moral philosophy with that of President George W. Bush and the Republican Party. The "Republican philosophy," Obama said,

> ... [gives] more and more to those with the most and hope that prosperity trickles down to everyone else. In Washington, they call this the Ownership Society, but what it really means is, you're on your own. Out of work? Tough luck. No health care? The market will fix it. Born into poverty? Pull yourself up by your own bootstraps, even if you don't have boots. You're on your own.[11]

"My brother's keeper" is the moral antidote to "on your own." The philosophy of a new New Deal, which has sometimes crept into Obama's oratory, is to wed a new social economy with a government committed to building *inclusive community*. No American will be left behind in this community—the ideal long seen as part of the American creed. From the beginning, the nation has not lived up to the rhetoric of inclusion, segregating people by race, gender, and class. But inclusion has always been the defining ideal. The creed extends the same rights to all citizens, and the Bill of Rights has evolved to explicitly guarantee the same protection and rights to everyone, whatever their race, gender, or class.

The new New Deal to end wilding must build a more social, egalitarian, and sustainable economy. It has to strengthen and build communities of workers now facing vanishing jobs and declining wages and benefits. It must help most those historically left behind, particularly those who are black, female, or poor. They were the ones most affected by the 2008 economic meltdown, and they will be the most vulnerable to the global market in this new century. As this new New Deal seeks to protect them, it will also seek to nurture those who, as political scientist Robert Putnam puts it, are now "bowling alone," without any community at all. But all Americans, even the affluent, will need protection from the environmental, economic, and social hurricanes to come. The role of government in the coming age is to bring diverse people and classes together to meet their common needs, building social infrastructure and social insurance as a big umbrella sheltering all of us against twenty-first-century global capitalism's violent economic, social, and environmental storms.

Solving the environmental crisis, especially climate change, helps to distinguish the new New Deal from the old. FDR actually promoted many environmental changes, such as creating jobs for planting trees, saving forests, and sustaining family-owned farms. But the environmental changes will have to be much more central in the new New Deal. It must be centered on the understanding that materialism and consumerism are no longer economically or morally acceptable, and that we must restructure our economy and culture, not just to grow the economy but to make sure that there are limits to the economic growth and consumption that will rapidly reduce the carbon footprint of America, by far still the highest per capita in the world.

The new New Deal must be green through and through, which involves more than creating green jobs. It must promote a cultural transformation in our way of life. This means promoting incentives for a simpler and less materialistic, less consumer-focused way of life. It means shifting America away from big suburban houses, big cars, malls, and highways to urban communities, farmers' markets, and shorter work hours, so that people have time for leisure and social pleasures to replace the privatized consumerist life.

The new New Deal sees government as just one of the many ways in which ordinary citizens in a democratic society come together to protect one another and solve these crises. Government exists to help civil society sustain itself, subject to the limits that communities place on it. Government is an instrument of the people. President Obama has highlighted this theme in his rhetoric if not his action: The government is a servant of the people and ultimately the people must take responsibility for each other. Obama has made national and community service a core principle, making clear that it is not just government but "we the people" who are "our brother's keeper, our sister's keeper."

Today, Obama, who is a centrist pragmatist with an oft-expressed faith in the "free market"—and hardly an ideological advocate of big government or so-cialism—rhetorically supports new roles for government in building community, remaking the economy, creating social protections such as universal health care, and saving the planet from climate change. One task is to remedy the crisis of job loss and insecurity caused by corporate globalization and the rise of Wall Street over Main Street. While bailing out and protecting Wall Street at the expense of workers and underwater home-owners, revealing how indebted and subservient to Wall Street his administration has become. Obama has supported small efforts to regulate the destabilizing floods of global finance, limit the speculative orgy of Wall Street wilding that led to the economic meltdown, and helped put displaced workers back to work on national clean energy and infrastructure projects through stimulus programs early in his first term. Communities can't survive without jobs, and the 2008 meltdown makes clear that capitalism without smart government cannot provide sustainable jobs for all. Obama's first budget, while far too small a stimulus, invested billions in clean energy jobs, social safety nets, and community revitalization, billing itself as much a moral as an economic document. It recognized that government is a key instrument for rebuilding a sense of common purpose and cementing the ties that bind us to one another and to the natural environment.[12]

A true "brother's keeper" philosophy—the opposite of a wilding approach—requires new and transformative government. Obama has sometimes been able to articulate—but tragically has not delivered beyond small steps—on these essential truths that must guide government intervention: that jobs are the connecting link between an individual and the larger community; that capitalism cannot provide sustainable jobs without major public investment in the real economy on Main Street; and that investment in clean-energy jobs is an important way to remake the economy and local communities while saving the planet.[13]

A new New Deal agenda can be summed up in three words: inclusive, sustainable community. Green-collar jobs bring those left out of the economy for decades—the inner-city poor, the outsourced manufacturing workers, and the underpaid workers in health care, education, and social services—into the foundation of the new economy. Green-collar jobs are a magical elixir of community economics. They offer poor and working people a living wage to weatherize and retrofit green homes in their own communities, to build public transit at the heart of urban neighborhoods, and to plant forests rather than drill for oil. These are moral solutions to the greatest challenges of our century: to create a new sustainable social order built on living wages and social safety nets for all workers; to increase community revitalization built around small, walkable neighborhoods rather than gated suburbs and exurbs accessible only by freeways; and to create a national and global economy that can save the planet from the catastrophes of climate change and global poverty.[14]

Inclusive health care and education are, along with green jobs and sustainable lifestyles, among the most important foundations of community in any twenty-first-century society. Despite his failure to deliver a truly inclusive single-payer public health care plan for all, Obama understands that the government must try to extend health care to every American, for without health care nobody can be woven into a sustainable community. Americans see how vital Medicare is for their parents and grandparents, and recognize that, with 49 million Americans with no health insurance, it is just as important for their children and themselves to be insured. His legacy of Obamacare, while rejected by conservatives and viewed correctly by liberals as tragically lacking a public option—or universal single-payer care—is a step forward toward the inclusive community that we must build.

Americans also understand that our economy and our community rest on the education of our children. Obama has argued that major federal support for liberal arts education is critical for democracy, and vocational education is one key to success in the global economy. However, the massive corporate disinvestment in America means that even the most educated Americans are vulnerable to becoming surplus people. Jobs for all who want them require broader, systemic changes in global capitalism discussed in earlier chapters. If these more systemic transformations are achieved, education can breed technical skills and also the citizenship engagement essential to jobs, democracy, and community itself. Even President Bush spoke of "no child left behind," a recognition that government had to play a key role in improving education as a precondition of both democracy and community.

But will Americans support this new activist role for government? On big public issues of jobs, poverty, health care, and community, most ordinary Americans share Obama's values. A majority, even among many who label themselves as philosophically conservative, support strong government programs on jobs, education, health care, and social security to bring us together.[15] Both liberals and conservatives yearn for some form of community as an antidote to the wilding crisis, and they are willing to support politicians who propose smart government spending to remake the economy and renew our community. When, in the name of individual initiative and the free market, Bush tried to privatize Social Security and cut back Medicare, he got clobbered politically. In 2008 and 2012, when Republicans argued for small government and tax cutting, they lost pivotal presidential elections. Despite 30 years of conservative efforts to demonize government, most Americans see that they can't survive the economic crisis, or a severe health crisis in the family, or another giant hurricane, on their own. Common sense in hard times is bringing Americans together, a first step toward rebuilding community, reactivating government, and ending the wilding crisis. The country is slowly shifting from the morality of "on your own" to "my brother's keeper."

A New Bill of Rights? The Politics of Civil Society

America's romance with individualism and the market has its virtues, but it has clouded Americans' understanding of what makes society tick. Civil society arises only when individuals develop strong obligations to the larger "us" that can override the perennial, very human preoccupation with the self. Such larger commitments bloom only under special conditions: when the community shows that it cares so deeply for each of its members that each member fully understands his or her debt to society and seeks to pay it back in full.

The Japanese and Europeans, in their very different ways, seem to appreciate this deal, or contract, that preserves civil society. Japanese corporations have historically enveloped the Japanese worker in a cocoon of secure employment, health benefits, housing, and other social necessities that make it almost impossible for most workers to imagine life outside the group. Through their expansive welfare states, the Europeans deliver their own bushel of benefits and entitlements that citizens recognize as indispensable to personal survival and happiness. Both systems possess their own serious problems and are partially eroding in the face of global economic pressures, but they continue to succeed in creating an allegiance to the larger community that fosters a greater immunity to the wilding epidemic than in the United States.

Each civil society has to find its own way of inspiring its members' devotion, but all must deliver those rock-bottom necessities essential to the pursuit of life, liberty, and happiness. These include some level of personal safety, food, shelter, and a livelihood. Social orphans deprived of these essentials are unable to fulfill any larger obligation to society, for their existence is entirely consumed by the brutish struggle for personal survival.

The concept of such social necessities leads to the idea of social citizenship, an extension of the familiar but narrower notion of political citizenship. The rights to health care, housing, and a job can be seen as social rights, parallel to our political rights to vote and engage in free speech, which are enshrined in our Constitution. Political rights apply to all citizens automatically because they are the precondition of democracy as a system. Similarly, social rights should be extended automatically to everyone, for these rights are the precondition of civil society's survival. Such social and economic rights are built into the 1948 Declaration of Universal Human Rights, the most developed document on human rights in the world and one adopted by most nations.

The Japanese deliver such social rights through a paternalistic, corporate, largely private extended family, whereas the Europeans do it through the welfare state. America will have to find its own way. Ideally, the emerging institutions of a new social and ecological economy will eventually provide a more local, democratic, and communitarian solution.

Whether an American social economy could evolve in such a direction is purely speculative, but clearly there are ways to provide social rights that are realistic, democratic, and do not require overly intrusive government. Although government is not the preferred agent in our society, it has a leading role to play in areas such as education, health care, and social welfare, as well as in creation of jobs and sustainable finance and energy, where human need rather than profit is the only acceptable moral compass. Government is also the guarantor of last resort. When people are homeless, starving, or jobless, civil society has failed, and a wilding virus is activated. Remedies to these problems are not silly idealism or bleeding-heart liberalism, but a conservative and prudent defense of the social order that requires public action.

For this reason, legal scholars, such as Columbia University law professor Louis Henkin, are pointing to "genetic defects" in our Bill of Rights that constitutionally guarantee political but not social citizenship rights.[16] Even these political rights are now in severe danger. The war on terrorism is threatening free speech, privacy, due process, and a host of other basic protections in the Bill of Rights that prevent the government from destroying our liberty. These are "negative" rights—in the sense that they tell government what it *cannot* do to infringe on our freedom, but they are at the very center of our constitutional order and are now at serious risk.

The first challenge, then, is to preserve the purely political or "negative" rights built into our Constitution. Every American citizen has a major responsibility to prevent the war on terrorism from becoming a license for unchecked governmental and presidential power. Another terrorist attack similar to 9/11 on the United States might lead any president to permanently suspend our rights in the name of protecting us, undermining the Bill of Rights and the requirement that even the president must obey the law. Protecting the "negative" rights in the Constitution is only a first, but necessary, step toward building the foundation of true democracy and community: a matrix of negative and positive—or political and social—rights. If we are not able to protect our existing rights, and are scared by our leaders into turning unchecked authority over to them, we will have no possibility to enjoy any rights at all.

But as we struggle to save our political or "negative" rights ensured in the Constitution, we must simultaneously expand our vision to build new "positive" or social citizenship rights in the United States. Chief Justice William Rehnquist, in a 1989 Supreme Court decision, argued that the Constitution confers "no affirmative right to governmental aid, even when such aid may be necessary to secure life." This led constitutional attorney Paul Savoy, former dean of the John F. Kennedy University School of Law, to point out that "our civil rights and civil liberties are rights in the negative sense" and "do not include affirmative obligations on government. We do not have a constitutional right to have the state provide us with health care, or give us shelter if we are homeless, or prevent a child from being beaten or from starving to death." A coalition of unions, environmentalists, and community groups has responded by calling for a second Bill of Rights that would entitle all citizens to the elementary social rights of shelter, food, and health care.[17]

Such social rights, as noted above, have already been embraced by most nations of the world and by the United Nations. The 1948 U.N. Universal Declaration of Human Rights explicitly embraces the right of all people to employment, shelter, education, and health care. The International Labor Organization, a U.N. agency, spells out the rights of all workers to associate freely in unions of their choice and to earn a living wage. There are also U.N. agreements on the rights of women, children, and the environment. Unfortunately, many of these rights are not enforced—and the United Nations has no mechanism to do so. To combat wilding in the global economy, it is essential that the U.S. government, a signatory of many of the U.N. human rights documents, move aggressively to support international means of enforcing social rights both abroad and at home.[18]

Social rights are not a free ride for the population, for with them come demanding social obligations. Citizenship is an intimate dance of rights and obligations, and social citizens will need to enthusiastically embrace the moral obligations that come with their new entitlements. This means not only willingly paying the taxes required to keep civil society healthy, but also devoting time and effort to community building at work, in the neighborhood, and in the country at large.

The problem with the Left is that it tends to demand rights without spelling out the obligations that have to accompany them; the problem with the Right is that it expects obligations to be fulfilled without ceding any social rights in return. Both positions are flawed because rights and obligations are flip sides of civil society's coin of the realm. We need a new politics that marries the Left's moral passion for rights with the Right's recognition of obligation.

Defending Our Lives: Getting from Here to There

But what do we do now? Americans are pragmatic people who want down-to-earth answers. Although there is no recipe or magic formula, we can act now to stop the wilding epidemic. If we want to survive with our humanity intact, we have no alternative.

Since wilding can destroy society and the environment, we are all fighting to stay alive. Obviously, if we each felt we had a desperate illness, we would mobilize ourselves to act immediately to save ourselves. But since wilding is a societal crisis, not a biological illness, individuals can feel a deceptive immunity. It is possible to feel healthy, have fun, and enjoy life as society begins to come undone.

But as the epidemic spreads, everyone will increasingly feel at risk. The personal meaning of the wilding crisis is that we each have to spend more and more time simply defending our lives, our property, our livelihood, our health, our physical safety, and our egos. This imposes a terrible burden on the individual, and it can easily fuel the "me" mentality at the heart of the problem, but it also unlocks the riddle of what to do. Not only will the illusion of immunity diminish, but the wisdom of dealing with the underlying disease, not just the symptoms, will also become more apparent.

Because the disease is social, so too must be the cure. As the social infrastructure begins to ulcerate and bleed, the rational long-term way to defend one's life is to help repair the damaged societal tissue, whether it be potholes in the road, hungry people sleeping on grates, or sociopathic competitiveness at the office. Doing the right thing, then, is defending one's life by cooperating to build up community strength and bolster personal and collective resistance to wilding. This requires no saintly sacrifice for the common good but rather a tough-minded and clear-eyed assessment of where the threat lies. When facing a wilding threat, the first question to ask is, "What in my social environment or in me is creating this threat?" Once that question is answered, the next one is, "What can I do about it?" Some cases of wilding will require purely personal change: falling back on all one's psychological and moral strength, as well as love and support from family, friends, or mentors, to counter wilding impulses within oneself or susceptibility to wilding influences in the environment. Most cases will also require acting for some form of social change to extirpate the external poison, whether at work, in the neighborhood, or in the White House; this is typically achievable only with the help of others, in social movements for justice and community.

We can begin to cure the wilding sickness by doing more of what we have always done well and doing it better: taking responsibility for our lives through civic participation. Tocqueville was amazed at the richness of America's democracy; its dense web of voluntary associations and democratic town meetings made it unique. Historian Howard Zinn, in his famous work *A People's History of the United States*, demonstrated that Americans have always been ready to join grass roots movements for justice, such as the abolitionist movement, the labor movement, the suffragette and feminist movements, the antiwar movement, the environmental movement, and the civil rights movement. These movements have built community in the service of social justice. In other words, democracy, and more democracy, is the best antidote for wilding and the most nourishing food for the social infrastructure.[19]

Americans were apathetic and indifferent to national politics over recent decades, but the economic meltdown and the rise of a progressive majority that elected an African-American president twice may represent the early stages of a still tenuous new direction. President Obama's election in 2008, marked by tears of joy among that progressive base, seemed a first step toward the return of citizen action and a national morality based on community rather than "me, me, me." Obama inspired hope of a different kind of politics, built around community and social justice.

After Obama's first term, many Americans rightly doubted whether Obama could—or wanted to—buck Wall Street, turn around the political establishment, and overcome our wilding culture. But while there are serious reasons for skepticism, and it is clear that Obama will not carry out the transformation that progressives once imagined, there is also hope, coming less from Obama than from the grassroots citizens, unions, and community and social movements that helped elect and reelect him. Remember that we have always had both individualistic and communitarian values, with political cycles in which one or the other tends to dominate. Even as we have suffered through our latest fevered wilding cycle since the Reagan Revolution and the disappointment in Obama, Americans hunger for community, and the impulse to associate and act together that Tocqueville saw as at the heart of America itself, as well as the passion for social justice and solidarity in grassroots movements, remains strong.

Millions of Americans recognize that giving back can be both fun and morally compelling, and they are serving their communities in movements to help the homeless, feed the hungry, care for AIDS patients, tutor the illiterate, protect the environment, and help organize America's workers and poor people. Many recognize that in addition to individual volunteers, we need sustained social movements that can provide the voice and muscle for ordinary citizens against the power of giant, greedy corporations and unresponsive government. This will require the renewal and expansion of a labor movement that speaks for social justice and economic democracy, linked to powerful peace, environmental, civil rights, and feminist movements.

On September 6, 2013, Richard Trumka, head of the national labor movement, the AFL–CIO, proposed a bold plan to invite nonunion members and many progressive organizations that are not unions into the labor movement, an idea that would begin the process of uniting currently fragmented community and social justice movements. Trumka proposed inviting millions of nonunion members as well as organizations such as the Sierra Club, the NAACP, the National Council of La Raza, and MomsRising. Mr. Trumka said: "It's pretty obvious to all of our progressive partners that none of us can do it alone. If we're going to change the political and economic environment, it's going to take us all working together."[20]

This is precisely what might bring together a national movement that could make a difference and begin to stop the wilding epidemic. While still, at this writing, in an experimental phase, the labor movement has been partnering over recent years with civil rights, women's, and environmental groups to achieve both local and national goals they share. Washington state has been a model, when in 2011, labor joined with women's groups, immigrant organizations, and faith groups to enact a Seattle law to require paid sick days.[21] Labor is reaching out to workers not currently in unions to join the AFL-CIO as associate members to help fight for better wages, benefits, and broad community aims.[22] Antisweatshop activists on campus have joined forces with the labor movement to end corporate wilding here and around the world. The labor movement, while demonized by many U.S. business leaders, is becoming a genuine voice for the community at large. Recall that "solidarity forever" has always been the rallying cry of the labor movement and that as corporations threaten community at home and abroad, the very concept of "union" tells us what we need: people coming together to defend human values against greed and exploitation. This lies at the heart of the changes Trumka is trying to make that could reignite and transform the labor movement into a true social justice movement.

Beyond such major changes in existing movements, which are crucially important, we need entirely new forms of social movements, because the existing organizations are each having trouble reaching out and connecting to a broader public with the visionary changes we need. One example is the Occupy movement. It sought transformative change in our sociopathic capitalism and the creating of a social and fair economy and participatory democracy

Students played a key role in Occupy, but long before Occupy, students played a major role in beginning to create a social rather than sociopathic economy and society. On my own campus of Boston College, many students who have engaged in community service work have begun to realize that service is very important and gratifying but it is not enough. While it helps individuals in trouble, it does not solve the societal problems that put people in difficulty in the first place. Students who work in soup kitchens begin to ask why there are so many hungry people, and those working in battered women's shelters ask why there is so much domestic violence. This leads them to recognize that it will take collective action—that is, social movements aimed at changing institutions—to truly solve the underlying causes of the problems that plague the people they want to help.

Young people have a special role in combating the wilding epidemic, and those privileged enough to study in colleges and universities have a special responsibility to help change our society through education and social action. Students have developed some skills of critical thinking. Students have access to the Internet, a key tool to educate oneself and their peers, and a vital springboard for social activism. And students are on a campus, historically one of the best places to come together with peers and help change the world. The possibility of moving beyond our wilding culture depends to a large degree on whether students and other young people rise to the challenge.

On my own campus, over the last decade, a network of activists called the Global Justice Project (GJP) has been an inspiring example. At this writing it is being supplanted by a vibrant new organization called the Social Justice Coalition (SJC), which is carrying on its legacy. Both GJP and SJC are made up of students who have decided that they want to make a difference. Some want to protect civil liberties and protest the Patriot Act or drone warfare; some want to promote fair-trade coffee; some seek a campus safer for female students at night; some want to end sweatshops or help organize immigrant workers in nearby hotels; some want to work against global warming and for a sustainable environment; some are passionate about peace in the world and organize activism to end the war in Afghanistan, or the carnage in Sudan; some are sick about the role of big money in politics and are working for campaign finance reform. These students are passionate about education and they sponsor talks, films, and panels on campus. But they are much more concerned with changing the world than just talking about it.

Over recent years, I have noticed three things about GJP—which also seem to be defining the rising SJC. One is that many of the students came to GJP after doing service projects, such as helping battered women, serving food in soup kitchens, or rebuilding houses in Appalachia or Nicaragua. Many realize that their service activities, though wonderful one-on-one experiences, are something like putting a bandage on deeper wounds. They will not solve the societal problems that have caused poverty in the first place until they start changing the larger economic and political system. This leads them to GJP, which is focused on understanding and changing society itself.

A second observation is that GJP's structure (and now also the SJC structure) is much like a network—indeed, much like the Internet on which they rely to publicize their activities and coordinate different protests and educational campaigns. Students who feel deeply about torture or militarism or constitutional rights organize peace vigils, protests against the Patriot Act or against spying and wiretapping by the government. They start information campaigns on campus and come to the antisweatshop group and the fair-trade subgroup or the fossil-fuel-free divestment organization and others in the broader network to get support for their peace work. And so it goes. The GJP pools the efforts of small groups in order to build a large network that has clout; each group lends support to other groups in order to build leverage for power-packed large actions that each small group could not produce on its own.

Third, GJP offers a community to activists who might burn out without a lot of support. They play music together, eat together, go to protests together, and talk late into the night. Many become close friends, live together, and support each other through personal or emotional problems. Building community is both a means and end, and both are essential antidotes to the wilding epidemic.

Other social movements are also vital for people seeking to end the wilding crisis. I discussed in Chapter 4 the post-Seattle global justice movement that is bringing together students, workers, environmentalists, feminists, and civil rights groups from around the world to forge a new world community based on human rights rather than money. In Chapter 8, I discussed the rise of the climate movements, based on campuses and communities, that are now focusing, at this writing, on stopping the Keystone XL pipeline and fracking, as well as on university divestment in fossil fuel companies. Each of these movements has its own agenda essential to combating aspects of the wilding crisis but are now joining together in multi-issue coalitions. Anyone concerned with the wilding crisis should learn about these different movements and join them. For in these movements lies the chance not only of changing the world, but of creating a new form of community for oneself.

For these movements to succeed, they must overcome their current fragmentation, attract a larger group of young and older people, and develop a clearer vision and political strategy for a new American Dream and a new political economy. The most recent movement to embody that spirit was Occupy Wall Street, a movement made up mainly of young people, and focused on Wall Street wilding and the building of a new social economy, democratic politics, and community life. Occupy had many shortcomings and failed to achieve major structural change or sustain itself in a major way beyond about two years of activism. Nonetheless, it carries important lessons, especially for students and young people, about what must be done to move beyond our wilding epidemic.

Occupy was the kind of movement that just might be a catalyst and model for new movements that can help stem the wilding tide. For one thing, it brought a new generation of idealistic young people back onto the streets, in a way that we haven't seen since the 1960s. They symbolized the hope of the millennial generation, which, while pragmatic and constrained by student debt and a poor job market, have—according to Pew and other polls—the strongest concern with saving civil society and the environment as any youth cohort in history.

Unlike the social movements of the last few decades, Occupy was focused on sociopathic capitalism, seeking a system-wide change in the structural economic, political, and cultural sources driving the wilding epidemic. Wilding on Wall Street was its bulls-eye target, but Occupy focused on Wall Street because it was the engine of the greed and competitive individualism that young people viewed as destroying their prospects for a meaningful way of life. Occupy wanted a deep change in the money-driven American Dream and a more sustainable and just economy and political system. Its demands were diffuse but it was clearly "systemic," meaning it wanted to create a new economy and society. That society would not only end the wilding of the 1 percent on Wall Street but end the inequality that created a 1 percent and 99 percent, putting in place a more just and sustainable economy based on solidarity and cooperation.

Because of its focus on "the system"—specifically sociopathic capitalism—it integrated most of the fragmented progressive movements that have been unable in recent decades to join forces in a common antiwilding struggle. The labor movement gave money to the tent cities, and one could see peace signs, feminist literature, and environmental practices, such as recycling and vegetarianism, all over the Occupy tent communities. The "system," after all, is the source of the inequalities and power hierarchies that are at the root of all the different movement struggles, whether about labor, race, gender, poverty, peace, or climate change. Like the progressive populist movements of the nineteenth century, that opposed the robber barons and Wall Street tycoons of their day, Occupy's strike against the heart of sociopathic capitalism was a way of bringing all the different dispossessed peoples under a common umbrella of dissent. A movement of the 99 percent is a movement of virtually everyone, not just of special interests or single causes. And it brings the 99 percent together to end the systemic wilding that separates even progressive groups into narrow justice visions, and instead, suggesting that there can be no justice for any group if there is not solidarity with and justice for all.

Occupy was no paradise—it made plenty of mistakes—but it walked its talk. It created practices that embodied many of its ideals: truly democratic assemblies that resisted hierarchies of any form, encouraged everyone to speak and lead, and found innovative ways to bond people together. Outsiders may have thought the strange wiggling of fingers to symbolize agreement and repetition by the whole tent city of what each person said in a meeting or "general assembly" to be a bizarre ritual. But these rituals were remarkably powerful in making everybody feel connected and empowered. As a participant myself in some General Assemblies in the Boston Occupy tent city, I was moved by the power of the experience, during which I came to feel close with people I had never met but who were showing me and everyone else a sense of affirmation and respect.

All movements succeed by creating communities mirroring the values they seek to create in the larger society. Occupy may not have known the history of earlier Occupy-style movements, but it understood that the means help shape the ends. If they didn't act in a democratic, egalitarian, and nonviolent way, and create feelings of solidarity in the tent cities, they certainly couldn't achieve these ends in the larger society. And at the micro level, on the streets of cities across America, they succeeded in creating minicommunities that were hardly perfect but were not illusory, putting into practice the cooperation and mutual aid and respect they wanted the entire economy and society to embody.

Occupy also used social media and the new technology of their generation to build community. There was constant communication with other Occupy groups around the country as well as with young people in the Arab Spring and in Canada, Europe, and Asia who were building their own Occupy movements. Occupy set up media sites in their tent cities that could get messages out to the mass media and begin connecting with the larger population.

Occupy's biggest challenge was reaching out to the larger public, socialized since the 1960s to be cynical about big change. Occupy could easily be viewed as a bunch of "spoiled kids," who had no clear vision and no concrete demands, leading to a political dead end. The idea of changing the system, even in the depths of the Great Recession where people's jobs, pensions, and houses were disappearing, was a stretch for a public that had lost hope in any alternative to the system they knew and that was now abandoning them.

When the police in most cities finally invaded and tore down the tent cities, Occupy could not sustain itself robustly. It had not built up a major support base even in its own generation, and its demands to "change the system" did not translate into concrete agendas that the public could understand. Occupy did begin to reach out, surrounding foreclosed homes to protect those about to be evicted from police attack, helping rescue people in disasters such as Superstorm Sandy, and building new connections with unions, civil rights, and peace groups. But unlike the grassroots movements of the 1930s, which occupied factories and helped build the labor movement with the support of President Franklin Roosevelt, Occupy could not institutionalize itself and build connections to President Obama and the Democratic Party that would keep its demands alive. This was not only Occupy's fault, but also the fault of a corporate-funded Democratic Party and the failures of President Obama to act in solidarity with the new community organizers who were acting as he had in his own role as youthful community organizer.

Occupy does show that there remains the possibility of a new generation coming together to say no to the wilding system and build an alternative. President Obama repeatedly said that he cannot change the sociopathic tendencies in our society by himself and that only the people can do it, forcing the president to act in their defense, to survive in a society worth living in. About this, Obama is certainly correct.

Americans' indifference to national politics over the last few decades reflected less pure selfishness or apathy than despair about leaders and the absence of real choices. Obama cannot or will not change the wilding culture on his own; it can be changed only by those passionate and morally dedicated ordinary citizens who refuse to give up. No president or Congress will solve the problems without us speaking truth to power over and over again, abandoning our identity as couch potatoes. The real burden of overcoming our wilding culture falls on "we the people," where, indeed, it ultimately belongs. When we lead, and only then, the politicians will ultimately have to follow.

Discussion Questions

1. Is there a realistic hope of ending the wilding crisis in the United States?
2. What kind of cultural change would this take?
3. What kind of economic and political change would this take?
4. Has Obama increased or decreased wilding in the United States and abroad?
5. What can you do to stop yourself from wilding acts that you might be tempted to do?
6. What can your generation do to end the wilding crisis in the United States?
7. Has this book changed your view of how to live your life? In what way?

NOTES

Chapter 1

1. Sullivan, Ronald. 1989. "Move to Kill Victim Described by Defendant in Jogger Rape." *New York Times*, November 2, p. 1.

2. 1989. "Testimony Has Youths Joyous after Assault." *New York Times*, November 4, p. 1.

3. Tye, Larry. 1990. "3 convicted of raping jogger in NYC park." *Boston Globe*, August 19, p. 9.

4. Oxford English Dictionary. "wilding." Retrieved February 5, 2014 (http://www .oxforddictionaries.com/us/definition/american_english/wilding#wilding-2).

5. Newsweek. 1989. "The Central Park Rape Sparks a War of Words." *Newsweek*, May 15, p. 40.

6. Williams, Patricia J. 2002. "Reasons for Doubt." *Nation*, December 30, p. 10.

7. Graham, Renee. 1990. "Hoax Seen Playing on Fear, Racism." *Boston Globe*, January 11, p. 24.

8. Turnbull, Colin. 1972. *The Mountain People*. New York: Simon & Schuster.

9. Ibid., p. 86.

10. Ibid., p. 153.

11. Ibid., back cover.

12. Ibid., p. 132.

13. Ibid., p. 132.

14. Ibid., p. 137.

15. I am indebted to Mike Miller for suggesting the terms *instrumental* and *expressive* wilding.

16. I am indebted to Mike Miller for his suggestion of "two Americas."

17. For an excellent book on the subject, see Taylor, John. 1989. *Circus of Ambition: The Culture of Wealth and Power in the Eighties*. New York: Warner Books.

18. Shames, Laurence. 1989. *The Hunger for More: Searching for Values in an Age of Greed*. New York: Times Books.

19. Story, Louise and Eric Dash. 2009. "Bankers Reaped Lavish Bonuses During Bailouts." *New York Times*, July 31, p. 1.

20. Ibid.

21. Robison, Peter. 2012. "Top 1% Got 93% of Income Growth as Rich-Poor Gap Widened." Bloomberg.com, October 2. Retrieved December 18, 2013 (http://www.bloomberg.com/news/2012-10-02/top-1-got-93-of-income-growth-as-rich-poor-gap-widened.html).

22. Collins, Chuck. 2012. *99 to 1: How Wealth Inequality Is Wrecking the World and What We Can Do About It*. San Francisco: Berrett-Koehler.

23. Ibid.

24. Leopold, Les. 2013. "Happy Labor Day . . . for Wall Street." *Huffington Post*. Retrieved December 18, 2013 (http://www.huffingtonpost.com/les-leopold/happy-labor-dayfor-wall-s_b_3845622.html).

25. Collins, Chuck. *99 to 1*.

26. Ibid.

27. Kroll, Luisa and Kerry A. Dolan. 2013. "*Forbes 400*." Forbes.com, September 16. Retrieved December 18, 2013 (http://www.forbes.com/forbes-400/).

28. *New York Times* Editorial. 2013. "Labor, Then and Now." *New York Times*. Retrieved December 18, 2013 (http://www.nytimes.com/2013/09/01/opinion/sunday/labor-then-and-now.html?_r=0).

29. Robison, Peter. "Top 1% Got 93% of Income Growth as Rich-Poor Gap Widened."

30. Ibid.

31. Norris, Floyd. 2013. "US Companies Thrive as Workers Fall Behind." *New York Times*, August 10, p. B3.

32. AFL-CIO. 2013., "CEO Pay and You." Retrieved January 7, 2014. (http://www.aflcio.org/Corporate-Watch/CEO-Pay-and-You).

33. Reich, Robert B. 1991. "Secession of the Successful." *New York Times Magazine*, January 20, pp. 16–17, 42–45.

34. Tocqueville, Alexis de. 1985 (originally published 1840). *Democracy in America*. Vol. II. New York: Knopf, pp. 137–138.

35. Durkheim, Émile, cited in Steven Lukes. 1973. *Émile Durkheim: His Life and Work, a Historical and Critical Study*. New York: Penguin.

36 Ibid.

37. Ibid.

38. Marx, Karl, cited in Robert C. Tucker. 1972. *The Marx-Engels Reader*. New York: W. W. Norton & Company.

39. Marx, Karl and Frederick Engels. 1932 (originally published 1848). *The Manifesto of the Communist Party*. New York: International Publishers.

40. See Derber, Charles and Yale Magrass. 2010. *Morality Wars*. Boulder, CO: Paradigm Publishers.

41. Derber, Charles. 2010. *Greed to Green: Solving Climate Change and Remaking the Economy*. Boulder, CO: Paradigm Publishers.

42. Smith, Adam. 2003 (originally published 1776). *The Wealth of Nations*. New York: Bantam Classics.

43. Marx, Karl. 1992 (originally published 1876). *Capital: A Critique of Political Economy*, Vol. 1. New York: Penguin Classics.

44. Baran, Paul and Paul Sweezy. 1966. *Monopoly Capital*. New York: Monthly Review.

45. Marx, Karl. 1992 (originally published 1876). *Capital*, Vol. 1, pp. 690–703.

46. Bellamy, John Foster and Fred Magdoff. 2009. *The Great Financial Crisis*. New York: Monthly Review Press.

47. Durkheim, Émile, cited in Steven Lukes. *Émile Durkheim*.

Chapter 2

1. CNN.com. 2004. "Peterson Guilty of Murder." CNN.com, November 12. Retrieved January 2006 (http://www.cnn.com/2004/LAW/11/12/peterson.verdict/).

2. Yan, Harriet. 2004. "Financial Analyst Gary Nienhuis Said Scott Peterson's Fertilizer Business Was Struggling to Survive at the End of 2002." Court TV, August 2. Retrieved January 2006 (http://www.courttv.com/trials/peterson/080204_ctv.html).

3. ABC 30. 2013. "Jury finds Kathryn Ellis guilty of murdering her husband, Robert, last September." ABC 13 Local News, August 21. Retrieved January 8, 2013 (http://abclocal.go.com/ktrk/story?section=news/local&id=9214486).

4. Ibid.

5. ABC 30. 2013. "Kathryn Ellis sentenced to life for killing her husband." ABC 30 Local News. Retrieved February 5, 2014 (http://abclocal.go.com/kfsn/story?id=9260619).

6. Kravets, David. 2008. "Hans Reiser Guilty of First Degree Murder." Wired.com, April 28. Retrieved February 5, 2014 (http://www.wired.com/threatlevel/2008/04/reiser-guilty-o/).

7. Phoronix Forum. 2008. "The Hans Reiser Murder Trial: Timeline and Tapes." Retrieved August 25, 2009 (http://www.phoronix.com/forums/showthread.php?t=7544).

8. Lee, Henry K. 2008. "Prosecutor Implies Hans Reiser Is Narcissistic." *San Francisco Chronicle*, February 22. Retrieved August 25, 2009 (www.sfgate.com/cgi-bin/article.cgi?f=/c/a/2008/02/22/BALHV6GDV.DTL).

9. Ibid.

10. Lee, Henry K., 2008. "Hans Reiser Trial, April 29, 2008." *San Francisco Chronicle*, April 29. Retrieved August 25, 2009 (http://www.sfgate.com/cgi-bin/blogs/localnews/category?blogid=37&cat=1428&o=10). See also Phoronix Forum. "The Hans Reiser Murder Trial."

11. CBS News, 2008. "Black Widows Guilty in Homeless Murders." CBS News, April 17. Retrieved August 25, 2009 (http://www.cbsnews.com/stories/2008/04/16/national/main4021508.shtml). See also Coogan, Mark. "Grannies Convicted of Murder," *CNET TV Video*, CBS/AP. Retrieved August 25, 2009 (http://cnettv.cnet.com/grannies-convicted-murder/9742-1_53-50031210.htm).

12. CBS News. "Black Widows Guilty in Homeless Murders."

13. McGinniss, Joe. 1989. *Blind Faith*. New York: Signet, p. 420.

14. Ibid., p. 62.

15. Ibid., p. 86.

16. Ibid., p. 414.

17. Ibid., p. 297.

18. Ibid., p. 436.

19. Bass, Alison. 1990. "Cold-Blooded Killers Rarely Stand Out from the Crowd." *Boston Globe*, January 15, p. 34.

20. Ibid.

21. Fox, James Alan and Jack Levin. 1990. "Inside the Mind of Charles Stuart." *Boston Magazine*, April, pp. 66*ff*.

22. Bass. "Cold-Blooded Killers." p. 34.

23. Fox and Levin. "Inside the Mind of Charles Stuart."

24. Derber, Charles. 2013. *Sociopathic Society*. Boulder, CO: Paradigm Publishers.

25. Hussman, Lawrence. 1983. *Dreiser and His Fiction*. Philadelphia: University of Pennsylvania Press.

26. Sennott, Charles M. 1994. "Kin Have Misgivings about Death Penalty." *Boston Globe*, November 8, p. 10.

27. Adler, Jerry. 1994. "Innocents Lost." *Newsweek*, November 14, pp. 27*ff*. Also, "Night That Turned Mom into a Killer." *National Enquirer*, November 14, pp. 28*ff*.

28. Sennott, Charles M. 1994. "Bid to Climb Social Ladder Seen in Smith's Fall to Despair." *Boston Globe*, November 8, pp. 1, 10.

Chapter 3

1. Pascale, Anthony. 2009. "Man Wielding Bat'leth Robs 2 Colorado 7-11s [UPDATE: Surveillance Cam Image]." February 4. Retrieved August 25, 2009 (http://trekmovie.com/2009/02/04/man-weilding-batleth-robs-2-colorado-7-11s/).

2. Kansas Progress. 2009. "Lenexa Police E-Watch." February 2. Retrieved August 25, 2009(http://www.kansasprogress.com/wordpress/index.php/2009/02/04/lenexa-police-e-watch/).

3. Barstow, David and Sarah Kershaw. 2000. "Teenagers Accused of Killing for a Free Meal." *New York Times*, September 7, p. 1.

4. Reeves, Jay. 2000. "Woman Given 13-Year Prison Term in 'Road Rage' Slaying." *Boston Globe*, December 5, p. A6.

5. Bach, Elizabeth, 2003. "Police Say 'Road Rage' Driver Struck Officer with Car." *Boston Globe*, June 25, p. B1.

6. Mathieu, Maccorley. 2009. "Survivor: Is It Still a Great Show?" Starpulse. com, February 2. Retrieved January 9, 2014 (http://www.starpulse.com/news/Maccorley_Mathieu/2009/02/19/survivor_is_it_still_a_great_show_).

7. AP. 2006. "Ex-'Survivor' Hatch Found Guilty of Tax Evasion." MSNBC, February 2. Retrieved August 25, 2009 (http://www.msnbc.msn.com/id/11023392/).

8. Belluck, Pam. 2006. "A New Reality for First 'Survivor' Winner: Tax Evasion Trial." *New York Times*, January 22, p. 14.

9. Sloan, Allan, 1996. "Jobs—The Hit Men." *Newsweek*, February 26, pp. 44–48.

10. Shales, Tom. 2009. "Shark Tank: ABC Is Out for Blood." *Washington Post*, August 8. Retrieved January 10, 2014 (http://archive.today/Z1yA9).

11. St. John, Warren. 2005. "What Men Want: Neanderthal TV." *New York Times*, December 11, section 9, pp. 1–2.

12. Ibid.

13. Ibid.

14. Ibid.

15. Ibid.

16. Ibid.

17. Segal, David. 2011. "The Dark Art of Breaking Bad." *New York Times*, July 6. Retrieved on March 15, 2014 (http://www.nytimes.com/2011/07/10/magazine/the-dark-art-of-breaking-bad.html?pagewanted=all).

18. Ginsberg, Merle. 2011. "'Breaking Bad' Star Bryan Cranston on Walter White: 'He's Well on His Way to Badass' (Q&A)." *The Hollywood Reporter*, July 16.

19. Meslow, Scott. 2013. "Breaking Bad Series Finale Recap." *The Week*, Sept. 30. Retrieved January 9, 2014 (http://theweek.com/article/index/250351/breaking-bad-series-finale-recap-felina).

20. ABC News. 2014. "Obama interview with George Stephanopoulos." ABC News, reprinted from *Huffington Post*, February 16.Retreived March 20, 2014 (http://www.huffingtonpost.com/2014/02/16/kevin-spacey-house-of-cards_n_4798751.html?view=print&comm_ref=false--).

21. Francis Underwood (Character). 2013. From "House of Cards." Retrieved March 20, 2014 (http://www.imdb.com/character/ch0369160/quotes).

22. Ibid.

23. Fiske, Edward B. 1990. "Fabric of Campus Life Is in Tatters, a Study Says." *New York Times*, April 30, p. A15.

24. Rogers, Abby and Gus Rubin. 2012. "The Most Dangerous Colleges in America." *Business Insider*, November 20.

25. Knox, Richard A. 1994. "Binge Drinking Linked to Campus Difficulties." *Boston Globe*, December 7, pp. 1, 15.

26. Bergstrom, Bill. 1995. "Plot to kill draws 4 years." *Lakeland Ledger*, October 4. Retrieved March 20, 2014 (http://news.google.com/newspapers?nid=1346&dat=19951004&id=DfEvAAAAIBAJ&sjid=-PwDAAAAIBAJ&pg=6473,3465035).

27. Biography.com. 2014. "Seung-Hui Cho." Retrieved March 17, 2014 (http://www.biography.com/people/seung-hui-cho-235991?page=2).

28 *Jeremiah Project*. 2009. "Survey of Teen Violence." Retrieved August 25, 2009 (http:// www.jeremiahproject.com/prophecy/school-violence.html). For a review of several deaths discussed in this paragraph, see also Powers, Elia. 2008. "Campus Violence, Viewed from Afar." *Inside Higher Ed*, March 20. Retrieved August 25, 2009 (http://www.insidehighered.com/news/2008/03/20/violence).

29. Lewis, Bob and Steve Szkotak. 2011. "Ross Truett Ashley, Virginia Tech Shooter, Described As 'Friendly.'" HuffingtonPost.com, December 10. Retrieved March 17, 2014 (http://www.huffingtonpost.com/2011/12/10/ross-truett-ashley-friendly_n_1141210.html).

30. Stevens, Matt. 2012. "'Multiple fatalities' in Oakland religious school shooting." *Los Angeles Times,* April 2. Retrieved March 17, 2014 (http://latimesblogs.latimes .com/lanow/2012/04/multiple-fatalities-in-oakland-religious-school-shooting. html).

31. Kang, Jay Caspian. 2013. "That Other School Shooting." *New York Times Magazine,* March 28. Retrieved March 17, 2014 (http://www.nytimes.com/2013/03/31/ magazine/should-it-matter-that-the-shooter-at-oikos-university-was-korean. html?pagewanted=all&_r=0).

32. Powers. "Campus Violence, Viewed from Afar."

33. Fiske. "Fabric of Campus Life," p. A15.

34. James, Lang. 2013. "How college classes encourage cheating." *Boston Globe*, August 4.

35. Butterfield, Fox, 1991. "Scandal over Cheating at M.I.T. Stirs Debate on Limits of Teamwork." *New York Times*, May 22, p. 12.

36. Landergan, Katherine. 2012. "Half of students in Harvard cheating scandal required to withdraw from the college." Boston.com. Retrieved February 2013 (http://www.boston.com/yourcampus/news/harvard/2013/02/half_of_students_in_harvard_cheating_scandal_required_to_withdraw_from_the_college.html).

37. Healy, Patrick. 2000. "College Admission Offices Targeting Fraudulent Essays." *Boston Globe*, November 27, pp. 1, B4.

38. Kim, Susann. 2013. "Penn State Leads List of Highest Paying Public Universities for President." ABC News, May 12.

39. Willie, Matt. 2012. "Taxing and Tuition: A Legislative Solution to Growing Endowments and the Rising Costs of a College Degree." *Brigham Young University Law Review* (5): 1665.

40. "Student Loans in Bankruptcy." Lawyers.com. 2011. See also "Student Loan Bankruptcy Options." money-zine.com. 2011.

41. Taibbi, Matt. 2013. "Ripping Off Young America: The College Loan Scandal." *Rolling Stone*, August 15.

42. Ibid.

43. Ibid.

44. Ibid.

45. Ibid.

46. Kirkham, Chris. 2013. "University of Phoenix Accreditation Hits Snag as Panel Recommends Probation." *Huffington Post*, February 25. Retrieved January 13, 2014 (http://www.huffingtonpost.com/2013/02/25/university-of-phoenix-accreditation_n_2762168.html).

47. Gormley, Michael. 2013. "New York AG Sues Trump, 'Trump University,' claims fraud." *USA Today*, August 26. Retrieved January 13, 2014 (http://www.usatoday.com/story/money/business/2013/08/24/trump-university-fraud-ny/2696367/).

48. Taibbi, Matt. "Ripping Off Young America."

49. Ibid.

50. Ibid.

51. Schmidt, Michael S. and Steve Eder. 2013. "Baseball Pays for Clinic Documents Tied to Doping Case." *New York Times*, April 11.

52. Lengel, David and Steve Busfield. 2013. "Alex Rodriguez and 12 other players suspended in Biogenesis PED Scandal." *Guardian*, August 5.

53. Nightengale, Bob. 2009. "Superstars Under Fire—Manny's Out; A-Rod's Back." *USA Today*, May 8–10, pp. 1–2.

54. SEC Sports Fan. "Patriots Belichick Spygate News." Retrieved from http://www.secsportsfan.com/patriots-belichick-spygate-news.html on August 25, 2009. (This site has ongoing, continuous updates and archived pieces on the Spygate scandal.)

55. Belson, Ken. 2014. "With NFL Concussion Deal, Two Tiers of Payouts." *New York Times*, January 11. Retrieved March 17, 2014 (http://www.nytimes.com/2014/01/12/sports/football/with-nfl-concussion-deal-two-tiers-of-payouts.html).

56. "Full Transcript: Lance Armstrong on Oprah." *Armchair Spectator*, January 23, 2013.

57. Ibid.

58. Ibid.

59. In what follows, I draw heavily on the Mitchell Report. Mitchell, George. 2007. "Report to the Commissioner of Baseball of an Independent Investigation into the Illegal Use of Steroids and Other Performance-Enhancing Substances by Players in Major League Baseball. December 13. Retrieved August 25, 2009 (mlb .mlb.com/mlb/news/mitchell/index.jsp).

60. Nightengale. "Superstars Under Fire," p. 2.

61. Mitchell. "Report to the Commissioner of Baseball." See also Nightengale, Bob. "Superstars Under Fire."

62. Nightengale. "Superstars Under Fire," p. 2.

63. Ibid.

64. Mitchell. "Report to the Commissioner of Baseball."

65. Ibid.

66. For a discussion of the role of the 1994 strike, and the relation between steroids use and performance, attendance, and revenues, see Levine, Zachary. 2007. "But Steroids Saved Baseball. Or Did They?" *Houston Chronicle* Blog, December 16. Retrieved August 25, 2009 (http://blogs.chron.com/unofficialscorer/2007/12/ but_steroids_saved_baseball_or.htm).

67. I want to express appreciation to Colleen Nugent, who provided me with many of the sources that I relied on to write this section on video games, and also helped me think through the importance of the games to the wilding phenomenon.

68. Bushman, Brad J. 2013. "Don't Buy Your Kids Grand Theft Auto V for Christmas." HuffingtonPost.com Blog, December 13. Retrieved March 17, 2014 (http://www.huffingtonpost.com/brad-j-bushman/dont-buy-your-kid-grand-theft-auto-v-for-christmas_b_4440477.html).

69. Ibid.

70. Shor, Susan B. 2004. "Violent Video Games Too Accessible to Kids, Say Watchdogs." Technewsworld.com, November 18. Retrieved January 2006 (http://www.linuxinsider.com/story/38455.html).

71. AskMen.com. 2009. "Top Ten Most Violent Video Games: No. 4: Mad-World." Retrieved August 25, 2009 (http://ca.askmen.com/top_10/videogame/top-10-most-violent-video-games_4.html).

72. AskMen.com. 2009. "Top Ten Most Violent Video Games: No. 7: Gears of War 2." Retrieved August 25, 2009 (http://ca.askmen.com/top_10/videogame/top-10-most-violent-video-games_7.html).

73. Anderson, C. A. and K. E. Dill. 2000. "Video Games and Aggressive Thoughts, Feelings, and Behavior in the Laboratory and in Life." *Journal of Personality and Social Psychology* 78:772–791; Schor, Susan B. "Violent Video Games Too Accessible."

74. Walsh, David, Douglas Gentile, Jeremy Gleske, Monica Walsh, and Emily Chasco. 2004. "Ninth Annual Media Wise Video Game Report Card." National Institute on Media and the Family, November 23. Retrieved January 2006 (http://www .mediafamily.org/research/report-vgrc-2004.shtml).

75. Both Gee quotes cited in Carlson, Scott. 2003. "Can Grand Theft Auto Inspire Professors?" *Information Technology* and *Chronicle of Higher Education*, August 15. Retrieved January 2006 (chronicle.com/free/v49/i49/49a03101.htm).

76. Ibid.

77. Bakan, Joel. 2005. *The Corporation*. New York: Free Press.

Chapter 4

1. Manik, Julfikar Ali and Jim Yardley. 2013. "Building Collapse in Bangladesh Leaves Scores Dead." *New York Times*, April 24. Retrieved February 5, 2014 (http://www.nytimes.com/2013/04/25/world/asia/bangladesh-building-collapse .html?pagewanted=all&_r=1&).

2. Ibid.

3. Ibid.

4. Ibid.

5. Williams, Holly. 2013. "CBS News goes undercover in a Bangladesh clothing factory." CBS News clip, May 22. Retrieved February 5, 2014 (http://www .cbsnews.com/news/cbs-news-goes-undercover-in-a-bangladesh-clothing-factory/).

6. Jamieson, Dave, Emran Hossain, and Kim Bhasin. 2013. "How Bangladesh Garment Industry Traded Workplace Safety For Jobs." *Huffington Post*, May 23. Retrieved January 14, 2014 (http://www.huffingtonpost.com/2013/05/23/ bangladesh-garment-industry_n_3288266.html).

7. Anderson, Sarah, John Cavanaugh, and Thea Lee. 2000. *Field Guide to the Global Economy*. New York: New Press.

8. Durkheim, Émile. 1997 (originally published 1897). *Suicide*. New York: Free Press.

9. Derber, Charles and Yale Magrass. 2012. *The Surplus American*. Boulder, CO: Paradigm Publishers.

10. For a concise, readable interpretation of globalization as a "race to the bottom," see Brecher, Jeremy and Tim Costello. 1998. *Global Village or Global Pillage?* 2nd ed. Boston: South End Press.

11. Institute for Global Labour and Human Rights. 2009. "High Tech Misery in China." Report, February 9. Retrieved February 9, 2014 (http://www .globallabourrights.org/reports/high-tech-misery-in-china).

12. Ibid.

13. Ibid.

14. Institute for Global Labour and Human Rights. 2006. "Blood and Exhaustion: Behind Bargain Toys Made in China for Wal-Mart and Dollar General." Report, August 10. Retrieved February 5, 2014 (http://www.globallabourrights.org/reports/blood-and-exhaustion).

15. Barnet, Richard and John Cavanaugh. 1994. *Global Dreams*. New York: Simon & Schuster, pp. 321*ff*. Also see Fuentes, Annette and Barbara Ehrenreich. 1992. *Women in the Global Factory*. Boston: South End Press, pp. 10*ff*.

16. Barry, Tom. 2008. "Maquila Industry Symptom of Mexico's Dependent Development," Border Lines, June 23. Retrieved August 25, 2009 (http://borderlinesblog.blogspot.com/2008/06/maquila-industry-symptom-of-mexicos.html).

17. University of Houston Students Against Sweatshops. 2009. "February 18—Free Film Screening with Talk by Main Cast Member Carmen Duran." January 29. Retrieved August 25, 2009 (http://uhstudentsagainstsweatshops.wordpress.com/2009/01/29/february-18-film-screening-with-talk-by-main-cast-member-carmen-duran/).

18. Ibid.

19. Barry. "Maquila Industry Symptom of Mexico's Dependent Development."

20. Ibid.

21. La Botz, Dan. 1992. *Mask of Democracy: Labor Suppression in Mexico Today*. Boston: South End Press, p. 162.

22. Ibid., p. 164.

23. Ibid., pp. 164–68.

24. Thompson, Ginger. 2001. "Chasing Mexico's Dream into Squalor." *New York Times*, February 11, pp. A1, A8.

25. For a discussion of the new movements and their vision of a just global economy, see Derber, Charles. 2003. *People before Profit*. New York: Picador.

26. Barnet and Cavanaugh, *Global Dreams*. See also Phillips, Kevin. 1994. *Arrogant Capital*. Boston: Little, Brown, chap. 1.

27. Brecher and Costello. *Global Village or Global Pillage?*

28. Derber, Charles. 2000. *Corporation Nation*. New York: St. Martin's Press, chap. 14; Brecher, Jeremy, Tim Costello, and Brendan Smith. 2000. *Globalization from Below*. Boston: South End Press.

29. Brecher and Costello. *Global Village or Global Pillage?*

Chapter 5

1. Zambito, Thomas, José Martinez, and Corky Siemaszko. 2009. "Bernie Madoff Pleads Guilty in Manhattan Court to Ponzi Scheme Charges; Remanded Immediately to Jail." *New York Daily News*, March 17. Retrieved January 14, 2014 (http://www.nydailynews.com/money/2009/03/12/2009-03-12_bernie_madoff_pleads_guilty_in_manhattan.html).

2. Ibid.

3. Seal, Mark. 2009. "Madoff's World." *Vanity Fair*, April, p. 121*ff*.

4. Ibid.

5. Berenson, Alex and Matthew Saltmarsh. 2009. "Madoff Investor's Suicide Leaves Questions." *New York Times*, January 1, p. 1. Retrieved August 29, 2009 (http://www.nytimes.com/2009/01/02/business/02madoff.html).

6. Krugman, Paul. 2009. "America the Tarnished." *New York Times*, March 30, p. A27.

7. Johnson, Simon. 2009. "The Quiet Coup." *Atlantic*, May. Retrieved February 5, 2014 (http://www.theatlantic.com/magazine/archive/2009/05/the-quiet-coup/307364).

8. Ibid. Cited also in Krugman. "America the Tarnished."

9. Derber, Charles. 2010. *Greed to Green: Solving Climate Change and Remaking the Economy*. Boulder, CO: Paradigm Publishers, Chapter 9. See also John Bellamy Foster and Fred Magdoff. *The Great Financial Crisis*. 2009. New York: Monthly Review Press.

10. Phillips, Kevin. 2008. *Bad Money*. New York: Viking.

11. Johnson. "The Quiet Coup."

12. Derber. *Greed to Green*, chap. 9, 11. See also Bellamy and Magdoff. *The Great Financial Crisis*.

13. Office of Illinois Attorney General. 2008. "Illinois Attorney General Madigan Leads $8.7 Billion Groundbreaking Settlement of Lawsuit Against Mortgage Giant Countrywide." Press Release, October 6. Retrieved February 5, 2014 (http://www.ag.state.il.us/pressroom/2008_10/20081006.html).

14. Morgenson, Gretchen and Geraldine Fabrikant. 2007. "Countrywide's Chief Salesman and Defender." *New York Times*, November 11. Retrieved February 5, 2014 (www.nytimes.com/2007/11/11/business/11angelo.html?).

15. Ibid.

16. Ibid.

17. Ibid.

18. Goodman, Peter S. and Gretchen Morgenson. 2008. "Saying Yes, WaMu Built Empire on Shaky Loans." *New York Times*, December 28. Retrieved February 5, 2014 (www.nytimes.com/2008/12/28/business/28wamu.html).

19. Morgenson and Fabrikant. "Countrywide's Chief Salesman and Defender."

20. Parloff, Roger. 2009. "Wall Street: It's Payback Time." *CNN Money*, January 6. Retrieved February 5, 2014 (http://money.cnn.com/2009/01/05/news/newsmakers/parloff_payback.fortune/index.htm).

21. Ellis, Blake. 2010. "Countrywide's Mozilo to pay $67.5 million settlement." *CNN Money*, October 15. Retrieved February 5, 2014 (http://money.cnn.com/2010/10/15/news/companies/mozilo_SEC/). Also see Morgenson, Gretchen. 2010. "Angelo Mozilo of Countrywide Settles Fraud Case for $67.5 Million." *New York Times*, October 16. Retrieved February 5, 2014 (http://www.nytimes.com/2010/10/16/business/16countrywide.html?pagewanted=all).

22. Morgenson, Gretchen. 2008. "How the Thundering Herd Faltered and Fell." *New York Times*, November 9. Retrieved February 5, 2014 (www.nytimes.com/2008/11/09/business/09magic.html).

23. McKim, Jennifer B. 2009. "State Gets Subprime Loan Cuts for 700." *Boston Globe*, May 12, pp. 1, 10.

24. Henning, Peter J. 2013. "Justice Department Again Signals Interest to Pursue Financial Crisis Cases." *New York Times Dealbook*, August 26. Retrieved February 5, 2014 (http://dealbook.nytimes.com/2013/08/26/justice-dept-again-signals-interest-to-pursue-financial-crisis-cases/?_r=0).

25. O'Toole, James and Evan Perez. 2013. "JP Morgan Agrees to $13 billion mortgage settlement." *CNN Money*, November 13. Retrieved February 5, 2014 (http://money.cnn.com/2013/11/19/investing/jpmorgan-mortgage-settlement/index.html).

26. Protess, Ben and Jessica Silver-Greenberg. 2013. "JP Morgan faces possible penalty in Madoff case." *New York Times DealBook*, October 23. Retrieved February 5, 2014 (http://dealbook.nytimes.com/2013/10/23/madoff-action-seen-as-possible-for-jpmorgan/?src=dlbksb&_r=0).

27. Eisinger, Jesse. 2013. "A Moot Effort to burnish the reputation of Goldman Sachs." *New York Times DealBook*, October 23. Retrieved February 5, 2014 (http://dealbook.nytimes.com/2013/10/23/a-moot-effort-to-burnish-the-reputation-of-goldman-sachs/).

28. Taibbi, Matt. 2011. "The People Against Goldman Sachs." *Rolling Stone*, May 11. Retrieved February 5, 2014 (http://www.rollingstone.com/politics/news/the-people-vs-goldman-sachs-20110511).

29. Ibid., p. 3.

30. Ibid.

31. Ibid., p. 6.

32. Ibid., p. 6.

33. Ibid.

34. Delaney, Arthur. 2009. "White House Advisor: AIG Deserves 'Nobel Prize for Evil.'" *Huffington Post*, April 16. Retrieved February 5, 2014 (http://www.huffingtonpost.com/2009/03/16/white-house-advisor-aig-d_n_175408.html).

35. Andrews, Edmund L. and Peter Baker. 2008. "After 170 Billion Bailout, AIG to Pay $165 Million in Bonuses." *Boston Globe*, March 15, p. A8.

36. *New York Times* Editorial. 2009. "Following the AIG Money." *New York Times*, March 15, p. 11.

37. Morgenson, Gretchen. 2009. "At AIG, Good Luck Following the Money." *New York Times*, March 15, p. B1. Retrieved February 5, 2014 (www.nytimes. com/2009/03/15/business/15gret.html).

38. CNN Money. 2009. "Follow AIG money, not bonuses—Spitzer." *CNN Money*, March 19.Retrieved February 6, 2014 (http://money.cnn.com/2009/03/19/ news/companies/aig_spitzer/index.htm?utm_source=feedburner&utm_ medium=feed&utm_campaign=Feed%3A+rss%2Fmoney_news_ companies+(Companies+News).

39. Fons, Jerome S. and Frank Portnoy. 2009. "Rated F for Failure." *New York Times*, March 16, p. A2.

40. Ibid.

41. Segal, David. "Buffet Is Unusually Silent on Ratings Agencies." *New York Times*, March 18, 2009.

42. Ibid.

43. Fons and Portnoy. "Rated F for Failure."

44. Brady, Diane. 2009. "Jon Stewart Thrashes Jim Cramer." *Business Week*, March 12.

45. Ibid.

46. Kennedy, Simon. 2009. "Stiglitz Criticizes 'Bad Bank' Plan as Swapping 'Cash for Trash.'" Bloomberg.com, February 1. Retrieved February 6, 2014 (www .bloomberg.com/apps/news?pid=20601087&sid=a.GJvNfWtCX0&refer=home).

47. Both the *New York Times* and Paul Krugman, the Nobel Prize–winning economist, have called for nationalization, arguing that the public has put in so much money to the banks that it is a de facto owner and deserves the control accorded any dominant shareholder. See *New York Times* Editorial. 2009. "The Never-Ending Bailout." *New York Times*, March 3, p. A26. See also Krugman, Paul. 2009. "Money for Nothing." *New York Times*, April 27, p. A21.

48. Story, Louise. 2009. "A Rich Education for Summers (After Harvard)." *New York Times*, April 5. Retrieved February 6, 2014 (http://www.nytimes .com/2009/04/06/business/06summers.html?_r=1&hp).

49. Derber. *Greed to Green*, chap. 10.

50. Ferguson, Thomas. 1995. *Golden Rule: The Investment Theory of Party Competition and the Logic of Money-Driven Political Systems*. Chicago: University of Chicago Press.

51. Derber, Charles. 2005. *Hidden Power*. San Francisco: Berrett-Koehler.

52. Labaton, Stephen. 2003. "Wall Street Settlement: The Overview; 10 Wall Street Firms Reach Settlement in Analyst Inquiry." *New York Times*, April 29, p. A1.

53. Derber. *Hidden Power*.

54. Greenwald, Glenn. 2013. "The Untouchables: How the Obama administration protected Wall Street from prosecutions." *Guardian*, January 23. Retrieved February 6, 2014 (http://www.theguardian.com/commentisfree/2013/jan/23/untouchables-wall-street-prosecutions-obama).

55. Krugman, Paul. 2013. "Rich Man's Recovery." *New York Times*, September 13, p. A19.

56. Derber. *Hidden Power*.

Chapter 6

1. Reich, Robert. 2013. "Detroit and the Bankruptcy of America's Social Contract." *Nation of Change*, September 7. Retrieved February 7, 2014 (http://www.nationofchange.org/detroit-and-bankruptcy-america-s-social-contract-1374412531).

2. Davey, Monica and Mary Williams Walsh. 2013. "Billions in Debt, Detroit Tumbles Into Insolvency." *New York Times*, July 18. Retrieved February 19, 2014 (http://www.nytimes.com/2013/07/19/us/detroit-files-for-bankruptcy.html?pagewanted=all).

3. Reich. "Detroit and the Bankruptcy of America's Social Contract."

4. Durbin, Dee-Ann and Tom Krishner. 2013. "Detroit's bankruptcy follows decades of decay." *Associated Press*, July 18. Retrieved March 20, 2014 (http://bigstory.ap.org/article/detroits-bankruptcy-follows-decades-decay).

5. Ibid.

6. Derber, Charles. 2013. *Sociopathic Society*; Reich, Robert. 2012. *Beyond Outrage*. New York: Vintage Books.

7. Derber, Charles and Yale Magrass. 2012. *The Surplus American*. Boulder, CO: Paradigm.

8. Ibid.

9. Yen, Hope. 2012. "80% of U.S. Adults Face Near-Poverty, Unemployment: Survey." *Associated Press*, July 28. Retrieved March 20, 2014 (http://www.huffingtonpost.com/2013/07/28/poverty-unemployment-rates_n_3666594.html).

10. Ibid.

11. Derber and Magrass. *The Surplus American*; Derber. *Marx's Ghost*; Krugman. *End This Depression Now*.

12. *New York Times* Editorial. 2013. "Fast Food Fight." *New York Times*, August 7. Retrieved February 19, 2014 (http://www.nytimes.com/2013/08/08/opinion/fast-food-fight.html).

13. Ibid.

14. Bannon, Brad. 2013. "The Strike Against Corporate Greed." *US News & World Report*, August 29. Retrieved February 19, 2014 (http://www.usnews.com/opinion/blogs/brad-bannon/2013/08/29/fast-food-workers-strike-for-a-liveable-wage).

15. Fastenberg, Dan. 2013. "100 WalMart protestors reportedly arrested in 15 city strike." *AOL Jobs*, September 6. Retrieved February 19, 2014 (http://jobs.aol.com/articles/2013/09/05/walmart-protest-petition-arrests/).

16. Bannon. "The Strike Against Corporate Greed."

17. Derber. *Marx's Ghost*; Derber. *Sociopathic Society*; Collins, *99 to 1*; Reich. *Beyond Outrage*.

18. Collins. *99 to 1*.

19. Norris, Floyd. 2013. "US companies Thrive as Workers Fall Behind." *New York Times*, August 10, p. B3.

20. Derber. *Marx's Ghost*.

21. Derber. *Sociopathic Society*; Derber. 2004. *Regime Change Begins at Home*: San Francisco: Berrett-Koehler.

22. Ibid. See also Derber, Charles. 2000. *Corporation Nation*. New York: St. Martin's Press.

23. Derber. *Sociopathic Society*; Derber. *Corporation Nation*.

24. Derber. *Marx's Ghost*.

25. Ibid.

26. Derber. *Sociopathic Society*.

27. Reich, Robert. 2013. "Detroit and the Bankruptcy of America's Social Contract." *Nation of Change*, September 7. Retrieved February 19, 2014 (http://www.nationofchange.org/detroit-and-bankruptcy-america-s-social-contract-1374412531).

28. Ibid.

29. Ibid.

30. Ibid.

31. Derber. *Sociopathic Society*.

32. Derber. *Sociopathic Society*; Derber. *Regime Change Begins at Home*.

33. Matthews, Dylan. 2013. "The Sequester: Absolutely everything you could possibly need to know in one FAQ." *Washington Post*, February 20. Retrieved February 19, 2014 (http://www.washingtonpost.com/blogs/wonkblog/wp/2013/02/20/the-sequester-absolutely-everything-you-could-possibly-need-to-know-in-one-faq/).

34. Scheller, Alissa. 2013. "Infographic: Social Programs Cut By the Sequester." Center for American Progress, March 1. Retrieved February 19, 2014 (http://www.americanprogress.org/issues/budget/news/2013/03/01/55201/infographic-social-programs-cut-by-the-sequester/).

35. Matthews. "The Sequester."

36. Krugman, Paul. *End This Depression Now*; Derber and Magrass. 2014. *Capitalism: Should You Buy It?* Paradigm, January.

37. Ibid.

38. Matthews. "The Sequester."

39. Derber. *Sociopathic Society*.

40. Davey and Walsh. "Billion in Debt, Detroit Tumbles Into Insolvency."

41. Office of the Governor. 2013. "Snyder confirms financial emergency in Detroit, turnaround expert Kevyn Orr appointed EFM." Michigan.gov, Office of the Governor, Press Release, March 14. Retrieved February 19, 2014 (http://www .michigan.gov/detroitcantwait/0,4839,7-293—297136—,00.html).

42. Derber. *Sociopathic Society*. Also, SCOTUS blog. "McCutcheon v. Federal Election Commission." Retrieved April 15, 2014 (http://www.scotusblog.com/case-files/ cases/mccutcheon-v-federal-election-commission/).

43. Derber, Charles. 2012. "Kochamamie Democracy." Tikkun Daily, October 23. Retrieved February 19, 2014 (http://www.tikkun.org/tikkundaily/2012/10/23/ kochamamie-democracy/). See also Derber. *Sociopathic Society*.

44. Ibid.

45. Ibid. See also Derber. *Corporation Nation*; Derber. 2005. *Hidden Power*. San Francisco: Berrett-Koehler.

46. Derber. *Marx's Ghost*.

47. Mears, Bill and Greg Botelho. 2013. "'Outrageous' or Overdue?: Court strikes down part of historical voting rights law." CNN, June 26. Retrieved February 19, 2014 (http://www.cnn.com/2013/06/25/politics/scotus-voting-rights/index .html).

48. Berman, Ari. 2013. "North Carolina passes the Country's worst voter Suppression Law." Billmoyers.com, July 30. Retrieved February 19, 2014 (http://billmoyers .com/2013/07/30/north-carolina-passes-the-countrys-worst-voter-suppression- law/).

49. Ibid.

50. Derber. *Marx's Ghost*.

Chapter 7

1. Tampa Bay Times. 2012. "A review of the evidence released in the Trayvon Martin case." *Tampa Bay Times,* May 17. Retrieved June 30, 2012 (http://www .tampabay.com/news/a-review-of-the-evidence-released-in-the-trayvon-martin- case/1230750).

2. Simon, Mallory. 2012. "Zimmerman charged with second degree murder." CNN, April 11. Retrieved February 19, 2014 (http://news.blogs.cnn.com/2012/04/11/ prosecutor-to-announce-decision-on-zimmerman/).

3. Tienabesco, Seni and Christina Ng. 2013. "Zimmerman Charged With Aggravated Assault of Girlfriend." ABC News, November 18. Retrieved February 19, 2014 (http://abcnews.go.com/US/george-zimmerman-charged-aggravated-assault/story?id=20926767).

4. Tienabeso, Seni and Matt Gutman. 2013. "George Zimmerman Jury Sees Photos of Slain Trayvon Martin Lying in Grass." ABC News, June 25. Retrieved March 24, 2014 (http://abcnews.go.com/US/george-zimmerman-jury-sees-photos-slain-trayvon-martin/story?id=19479056).

5. Tienabesco and Ng. "Zimmerman Charged With Aggravated Assault of Girlfriend."

6. Brown, Tom. 2013. "Florida lawmakers want overhaul of 'Stand Your Ground' Law," Reuters, July 18. Retrieved February 19, 2014 (http://www.reuters.com/article/2013/07/18/us-usa-florida-shooting-lawmakers-idUSBRE96H1HP20130718).

7. Jealous, Benjamin Todd. 2013. "The Law of the Wild West." US News & World Report, August 9. Retrieved February 19, 2014 (http://www.usnews.com/opinion/articles/2013/08/09/stand-your-ground-laws-lead-to-unjustified-killings-like-trayvon-martin).

8. Ibid.

9. New York Times Editorial. 2013. "The Arms Race at Home." New York Times, July 17. Retrieved February 19, 2014 (http://www.nytimes.com/2013/07/18/opinion/the-arms-race-at-home.html).

10. Ibid.

11. Ibid.

12. Ibid.

13. Candiotti, Susan, Greg Botelho, and Tom Watkins. 2013. "Newtown Shooting Details Revealed in Newly Released Documents." CNN, March 29. Retrieved February 19, 2014 (http://www.cnn.com/2013/03/28/us/connecticut-shooting-documents).

14. Castillo, Mariano and Chelsea J. Carter. 2012. " Background of Colorado shooting suspect full of contrasts." CNN, July 21. Retrieved February 19, 2014 (http://www.cnn.com/2012/07/20/us/colorado-theater-suspect-profile/). See also Williams, Pete, Bill Dedman, and NBC News staff. 2012. "Aurora suspect James Holmes was buying guns, dropping out of graduate school." NBC News, July 22. Retrieved February 19, 2014 (http://usnews.nbcnews.com/_news/2012/07/20/12854157-aurora-suspect-james-holmes-was-buying-guns-dropping-out-of-graduate-school?lite).

15. The Arizona Republic. 2011. "Arizona Congresswoman Giffords shot; doctors 'optimistic" about recovery chances." Arizona Republic, January 8. Retrieved February 19, 2014 (http://www.azcentral.com/news/articles/2011/01/08/20110108arizona-giffords-brk.html?nclick_check=1).

16. Dolak, Kevin. 2013. "Guns for Kids Marketing Debate Ignited by Latest Child Death." ABC News, May 2. Retrieved March 24, 2014 (http://abcnews.go.com/ US/youth-gun-marketing-debate-ignited-latest-child-death/story?id=19086960).

17. Ibid.

18. Hemenway, David. 2006. *Private Guns, Public Health.* Ann Arbor: University of Michigan Press; see also Frum, David. 2013. "Obama Needs a Plan B on Guns." CNN, February 8. Retrieved February 19, 2014 (http://www.cnn .com/2013/02/18/opinion/frum-obama-plan-b-on-guns/index.html?hpt=hp_c2).

19. Ibid.

20. United Nations Office on Drugs and Crime. 2011. "2011 Global Study on Homicide." December 12. Retrieved February 19, 2014 (http://www.unodc .org/documents/data-and-analysis/statistics/Homicide/Globa_study_on_ homicide_2011_web.pdf).

21. Hemenway, D. and M. Miller. 2000. "Firearm availability and homicide rates across 26 high-income countries." *Journal of Trauma* 49(6):985–988. Also, Hepburn, L. M. and D. Hemenway. 2004. "Firearm availability and homicide: A review of the literature." *Aggression and Violent Behavior* 9(4):417.

22. United Nations Office on Drugs and Crime. "2011 Global Study on Homicide."

23. Pew Research Center. 2013. "Who Owns a Gun? Gun Ownership Trends and Demographics." Report from *General Social Survey*, Section 3, March 12. Retrieved February 19, 2014 (http://www.people-press.org/2013/03/12/section-3-gun-ownership-trends-and-demographics/).

24. Ibid.

25. Joffe, Joe. "US State Violence Statistics." State of Enlightenment, March 25, 2013. (http://stateofenlightenment.com/2013/03/25/us-state-gun-violence-statistics).

26. James, Sarah, Henry Austin, and Alastair Jamieson. 2013. "US gun culture is 'corrupting the world,' Australia ex-deputy PM says after Okla. Slaying." NBC News, August 23. (http://www.nbcnews.com/news/us-news/us-gun-culture-corrupting-world-australia-ex-deputy-pm-says-v20131976)

27. Joffe. "US State Violence Statistics."

28. Hemenway. *Private Guns, Public Health,* p. 70.

29. Derber. *Sociopathic Society.*

30. Webb, Susan. 2012. "Profits are driving force behind gun epidemic." *People's World,* December 19. Retrieved February 19, 2014 (http://peoplesworld.org/profits-are-driving-force-behind-gun-epidemic-2/).

31. Sorkin, Andrew Ross. 2012. "Gun Reform Not a Cause On Wall St." *New York Times,* December 18, p. B1.

32. Derber, Charles and Yale Magrass. 2012. "History's Magic Mirror: America's Economic Crisis and the Weimar Republic of Pre-Nazi Germany." *Truthout,* November 2. Retrieved March 25, 2014 (http://truth-out.org/opinion/ item/12477-historys-magic-mirror-americas-economic-crisis-and-the-weimar-

republic-of-pre-nazi-germany). Also, McIntire, Mike. 2013. "Selling A New Generation on Guns." *New York Times*, January 27, p. 1.

33. RT. 2013. "At least 18 murdered in Chicago in the first 10 days of the year." *RT*, January 11. Retrieved March 25, 2014 (http://rt.com/usa/18-chicago-year-murder-812/).

34. Ibid.

35. Ibid.

36. Hacker, Jacob, et al. 2012. "Economic Insecurity Across States." Economic Security Index, June. Retrieved February 19, 2014 (http://economicsecurityindex.org/assets/state_reports/ESI_cross_state.pdf).

37. Ibid.

38. Ibid.

39. Derber, Charles and Yale Magrass. 2011. *Morality Wars*. Boulder: Paradigm Publishers.

40. Derber and Magrass. "History's Magic Mirror."

41. Derber and Magrass. *Morality Wars*.

42. Miller, Todd. 2013. "War On the Border." *New York Times*, August 18. p. 1 (section E).

43. Hemenway. *Private Guns, Public Health*.

44. Drash, Wayne and Toby Lylee. "States Tighten, Loosen Gun Laws after Newtown." CNN, June. Retrieved March 25, 2014 (http://www.cnn.com/2013/06/08/us/gun-laws-states).

45. Ibid.

46. Phillips, Rich. 2013. "Dream Defenders end sit-in protest of Florida's stand your ground law." CNN, August 15. Retrieved March 25, 2014 (http://www.cnn.com/2013/08/15/us/florida-stand-your-ground-protest).

Chapter 8

1. Hansen, James. 2008. "Global Warming Twenty Years Later: Tipping Points Near." Testimony to Congress, June 23. Retrieved August 25, 2009 (http://www.columbia.edu/~jeh1/2008/TwentyYearsLater_20080623.pdf).

2. McKibben, Bill. 2008. "Civilization's Last Chance." *Los Angeles Times*, May 11. Retrieved February 18, 2014 (http://www.latimes.com/la-op-mckibben11-2008may11,0,4213543.story#axzz2ti9WH5sY); see also Bill McKibben's Web site, www.350.org.

3. Ibid.

4. Miller, Peter. 2012. "Weather Gone Wild." *National Geographic*, September. Retrieved February 18, 2014 (http://ngm.nationalgeographic.com/2012/09/extreme-weather/miller-text).

5. Ibid.

6. Ibid.

7. Ibid.

8. Derber, Charles. 2013. *Sociopathic Society*. Boulder, CO: Paradigm Publishers.

9. Ibid.

10. American Meteorological Society. 2013. "2012 State of the Climate." Climate.gov, August 2. Retrieved February 18, 2014 (http://www.climate.gov/news-features/understanding-climate/state-climate-2012-highlights).

11. Ibid.

12. Miller. "Weather Gone Wild."

13. American Meteorological Society. "2012 State of the Climate."

14. Hansen. "Global Warming Twenty Years Later."

15. Ibid.

16. Derber, Charles. 2008. *Greed to Green*. Boulder, CO: Paradigm Publishers, chap. 7.

17. Ibid.

18. Ken Cohen of Exxon, cited in Wynn, Greg. 2007. "Exxon Says It Never Doubted Climate Change." *Reuters*, June 14.

19. For an extended discussion of Stage 2 denial, see Derber. *Greed to Green*, chap. 7.

20. Friends of the Earth. 2002. "Greenwash Oscars." August 23. Retrieved August 25, 2009 (http://www.foe.co.uk/campaigns/economy/news/earth_summit_23_august.html).

21. Browne, John.1997. "Climate Change Speech." Stanford University, May 19. Retrieved August 25, 2009 (www.dieoff.org/page106.htm).

22. Derber. *Greed to Green*, chap. 7.

23. Derber. *Greed to Green*, chap. 9. See also Foster, John Bellamy. 2002. *Ecology Against Capitalism*. New York: Monthly Review Press.

24. For elaboration, see Derber, *Greed to Green*, especially chap. 9; see also Foster, John Bellamy. *The Great Financial Crisis*.

25. Derber. *Green to Greed*.

26. Ibid.

27. Wolfe, Tom. 1988. *The Bonfire of the Vanities*. New York: Bantam Books.

28. Derber. *Green to Green*, chap. 13 and 14.

29. Veblen, Thorstein. 1924 (originally published 1899). *The Theory of the Leisure Class*. New York: Dover Books.

30. For elaboration about the idea of coerced consumption, see Derber, *Greed to Green*, chap. 11.

31. Leonard, Annie. 2008. "The Story of Stuff." YouTube, July 12. Retrieved August 25, 2009 (http://www.youtube.com/watch?v=gLBE5QAYXp8).

32. McKibben, Bill. 2007. *Deep Economy*. New York: Times Books.

33. Obama, Barack. 2006. "Energy Independence and the Safety of Our Planet." Speech, April 3. Retrieved August 25, 2009 (http://obamaspeeches.com/060-Energy-Independence-and-the-Safety-of-Our-Planet-Obama-Speech.htm).

34. Derber. *Sociopathic Society*.

35. Tar Sands Action. 2013. "48 Environmental, civil rights, and community leaders engage in historic act of civil disobedience to stop Keystone XL pipeline." February 13. Retrieved February 19, 2014 (http://www.tarsandsaction.org/48-environmental-civil-rights-community-leaders-engage-historic-act-civil-disobedience-stop-keystone-xl-pipeline/#more-2286).

36. Ibid.

37. EcoWatch. 2013. "Influence of Grassroots Anti-Fracking Movement Spreads Like Wildfire." June 20. Retrieved February 19, 2014 (http://ecowatch.com/2013/influence-grassroots-anti-fracking-movement-like-wildfire).

38. Jones, Van. 2009. *The Green Collar Economy*. New York: HarperOne.

39. Schor, Juliet. 2012. *True Wealth*. New York: Simon and Schuster. See also Siegel, Charles. 2008. *The Politics of Simple Living*. Berkeley, CA: Preservation Institute.

40. Hansen, James. 2008. "Twenty Years Later: Tipping Points Near on Global Warming." *Huffington Post*, June 23. Retrieved February 19, 2014 (http://www.huffingtonpost.com/dr-james-hansen/twenty-years-later-tippin_b_108766.html).

Chapter 9

1. In Fiscal Year 2013, the U.S. allocated $525 billion to the Department of Defense, and $613 billion when you add in emergency and supplemental measures, which still leaves out many other military expenditures. United States Department of Defense. 2012. "Fiscal Year 2013 Budget Request." Retrieved April 15, 2014 (http://dcmo.defense.gov/publications/documents/FY2013_Budget_Request_Overview_Book.pdf).

2. Wallerstein, Immanuel. 2000. *The Essential Wallerstein*. New York: New Press.

3. Arrighi, Giovanni. 1994. *The Long Twentieth Century*. London: Verso.

4. MacFarquhar, Neil. 2002. "Humiliation and Rage Stalk the Arab World." *New York Times*, April 13, section 4, p. 1.

5. Sachs, Susan. 2003. "Egyptian Intellectual Speaks of the Arab World's Despair." *New York Times*, April 8, pp. B1–2.

6. Shadid, Anthony. 2003. "Hospitals Overwhelmed by Living and the Dead." *Washington Post*, April 8, p. A29; Thanassis, Cambanis. 2003. "Iraqis in Basra Weigh Freedom's Cost." *Boston Globe*, April 8, p. B1.

7. Galston, William. 2002. "Perils of Preemptive War." *The American Prospect,* 13, no. 17, September 3. Retrieved March 22, 2006 (http://prospect.org/article/perils-preemptive-war).

8. Falk, Richard. 2002. "The New Bush Doctrine." *Nation*, July 15. Retrieved January 31, 2006 (http://www.thenation.com/article/new-bush-doctrine).

9. Chen, Edwin. 2003. "Bush: No Signs Yet of Illegal Weapons." *Los Angeles Times*, April 25, p. A17. Retrieved March 26, 2014 (http://articles.latimes.com/2003/apr/25/news/war-weapons25).

10. CNN.com. 2004. "Report: No WMD Stockpiles in Iraq." CNN.com, October 7. Retrieved January 31, 2006 (www.cnn.com/2004/WORLD/meast/10/06/iraq.wmd.report/). The Duelfer final report is posted at https://www.cia.gov/library/reports/general-reports-1/iraq_wmd_2004/.

11. Savage, Charlie. 2013. "Obama Tests Limits of Power in Syria Conflict." *New York Times*, September 9, p.1.

12. Lemann, Nicholas. 2002. "The Next World Order." *New Yorker*, April 1; Bacevich, Andrew J. 2002. *American Empire: The Realities and Consequences of U.S. Diplomacy.* Cambridge, MA: Harvard University Press, pp. 44–45.

13. Ibid. Also, Project for the New American Century. 2000. *Rebuilding America's Defense.* Washington, DC. Retrieved March 26, 2014 (http://www.webcitation.org/5e3est5lT).

14. Henriques, Diana B. 2003. "Who Will Put Iraq Back Together?" *New York Times*, March 23, section 3, p. 1.

15. Bumiller, Elisabeth and Alison Mitchell. 2002. "Bush Aides See Political Pluses in Security Plan." *New York Times*, June 15, p. A1.

16. Kifner, John. 2003. "Britain Tried First, Iraq Was No Picnic." *New York Times*, July 20.

17. Escobar, Pepe. 2004. "From Guernica to Fallujah." *Asia Times Online*, December 2. Retrieved January 31, 2006 (www.atimes.com/atimes/Middle_East/FL02Ak02.html).

18. BBC News. 2005. "US Used White Phosphorus in Iraq." BBC News, November 16. Retrieved January 2006 (www.news.bbc.co.uk/2/hi/middle_east/4440664.stm).

19. For a recent mainstream discussion of the economic foundations of U.S. military interventions, see Bacevich, *American Empire*. For a more radical view emphasizing many of the same themes, see Chomsky, Noam. 1993. *What Uncle Sam Really Wants.* Tucson, AZ: Odonian Press.

20. Obama, Barack. 2008. "Acceptance Speech to the Democratic Convention." August 28. Retrieved August 25, 2009 (http://www.demconvention.com/barack-obama).

21. Pessin, Al. 2009. "More US Troops May Be Needed in Afghanistan, Says Pentagon Advisor." *Voice of America*, July 29. Retrieved August 25, 2009 (http://www.voanews.com/content/a-13-2009-07-29-voa61-68819747/413381.html).

22. Stewart, Rory. 2009. "The Irresistible Illusion." *London Review of Books*, July 9, pp. 1–12.

23. Cited in Benjamin, Medea. 2012. *Drone Warfare*. San Francisco: Or Books, pp. 11-12.

24. Ibid.

25. Ibid.

26. Ibid.

27. BBC News. 2013. "Pakistan PM Nawaz Sharif urges end to US drone strikes." BBC News, June 5. Retrieved June 8, 2013 (http://www.bbc.co.uk/news/world-asia-22779669); Saud Mehsud. 2013. "Angry Pakistan summons envoy after U.S. drone strike kills nine." *Reuters*, June 8. Retrieved June 8, 2013 (http://www.reuters.com/article/2013/06/08/us-pakistan-drone-idUSBRE95707520130608).

28. Meilke, James. 2012. "Jimmy Carter savages US foreign policy over drone strikes." *Guardian*, June 25. Retrieved February 13, 2014 (http://www.theguardian.com/world/2012/jun/25/jimmy-carter-drone-strikes).

29. Hakim, Yalda. 2013. "Why Drone attacks in Yemen are like 'trying to hit a ghost.'" BBC News, Aug 17. Retrieved February 13, 2014 (http://www.bbc.co.uk/news/world-middle-east-23595388).

30. Woods, Chris and Christina Lamb. 2012. "Covert Drone Warfare: CIA attacks in Pakistan involve targeting rescuers and funerals." Bureau of investigative Journalism, February 4. Retrieved February 13, 2014 (http://www.thebureauinvestigates.com/2012/02/04/obama-terror-drones-cia-tactics-in-pakistan-include-targeting-rescuers-and-funerals/).

31. Benjamin. *Drone Warfare*, p. 136.

32. Ibid., pp. 135, 137.

33. Ibid., p. 130.

34. Howerton, Jason. 2013. "Confidential Justice Dept Memo: Drone Strikes on American citizens ok if . . ." *The Blaze*, February 4. Retrieved February 13, 2014 (http://www.theblaze.com/stories/2013/02/04/confidential-justice-department-memo-killing-american-citizens-with-suspected-terror-ties-ok/).

35. Saenz, Arlene. 2013. "How Obama Can bypass Congress on Syria Strike." ABC News, August 29. Retrieved February 13, 2014 (http://abcnews.go.com/blogs/politics/2013/08/how-obama-can-bypass-congress-on-syria-strike/).

36. Jones, Brian. 2013. This Drone Test Changes Everything About Unmanned Aerial Warfare" *Business Insider*, July 10. Retrieved February 13, 2014 (http://www.businessinsider.com/x-47b-drone-lands-on-aircraft-carrier-2013-7#ixzz2dHwzRjkS).

37. Baldor, Lolita C. 2005. "21 Detainees Killed in US Custody, ACLU Says." *Boston Globe*, October 25, p. A19.

38. The exchange between Gonzales and Kennedy at the hearings is posted at Center for Cooperative Research, "Profile: Edward Kennedy," in a subsection titled "January 6, 2005, Torture in Iraq, Afghanistan and Elsewhere." Retrieved January 2006 (www.cooperativeresearch.org/entity.jsp?id_1521846767-2387).

39. Steele, Jonathan. 2005. "A global gulag to hide the war on terror's dirty secrets." *Guardian*, January 15. Retrieved February 13, 2014 (http://www.theguardian .com/world/2005/jan/14/usa.guantanamo).

40. Priest, Dana. 2005. "CIA Holds Terror Suspects in Secret Prisons." *Washington Post*, November 2, p. A01. Retrieved February 13, 2014 (http://www.washingtonpost .com/wp-dyn/content/article/2005/11/01/AR2005110101644.html).

41. International Committee of the Red Cross. 2007. "ICRC Report on the Treatment of Fourteen 'High Value Detainees' in CIA Custody." February. Cited in Danner, Mark. 2009. "US Torture: Voices from the Black Sites." *New York Review of Books*, April 9, Vol. 56, No. 6. Retrieved February 14, 2014 (http:// www.nybooks.com/articles/archives/2009/apr/09/us-torture-voices-from-the-black-sites/).

42. Ibid.

43. Ibid.

44. Ibid.

45. Ibid.

46. Ibid.

47. Graham, Bradley. 2005. "US Seeks to Soften Reaction to Report of Burned Taliban." *Boston Globe*, October 21, p. A9. Also, *New York Times* Editorial. 2005. "Legalized Torture, Reloaded." *New York Times*, October 26, p. A26.

48. Human Rights First. 2009. "Obama Vows No Torture While Cheney Defends Its Use." January 9. Retrieved February 13, 2014 (http://www.humanrightsfirst .org/2009/01/09/obama-vows-no-torture-while-cheney-defends-its-use).

49. Ibid.

50. Lewis, Anthony. 2005. "License to Torture." *New York Times*, October 15, p. 14.

51. Sensenbrenner, James. 2013. "How Obama Has Abused the Patriot Act." *Los Angeles Times*, August 19. Retrieved February 13, 2014 (http://www.latimes .com/opinion/commentary/la-oe-sensenbrenner-data-patriot-act-obama-20130819,0,1387481.story?track=rss&utm_source=feedburner&utm_medium= feed&utm_campaign=Feed%3A+latimes%2Fnews%2Fopinion%2Fcommentary+ %28L.A.+Times+-+Commentary%29).

52. Lichtblau, Erich and James Risen. 2005. "Spy Agency Mined Vast Data T rove, Officials Report." *New York Times*, December 24, p. 1. Retrieved February 13, 2014 (http://www.nytimes.com/2005/12/24/politics/24spy .html?pagewanted=all&_r=).

53. Bajaj, Vikas. 2006. "Gore Is Sharply Critical of Bush Policy on Surveillance." *New York Times*, January 16. Retrieved February 13, 2014 (www.nytimes .com/2006/01/16/politics/16cnd-gore.html).

54. Baker, Peter and Charles Babington. 2005. "Bush Addresses Uproar over Spying." *Washington Post*, December 20. Retrieved February 13, 2014 (www .washingtonpost.com/wp-dyn/content/article/2005/12/19/AR2005121900211. html).

55. Jones, Susan. 2008. "Has Bush Committed an Impeachable Offense?" CNSnews .com, July 7. Retrieved February 13, 2014 (http://cnsnews.com/news/article/has-bush-committed-impeachable-offense-senator-asks).

56. Turley, cited in Greenwald, Glenn. 2009. "An Emerging Progressive Consensus on Obama's Executive Power and Secrecy Abuses." Salon.com, April 13. Retrieved February 13, 2014.

57. Lichtblau, Eric. 2013. "In Secret, Court Vastly Broadens Power of NSA." *New York Times*, July 6. Retrieved February 13, 2014 (http://www.nytimes .com/2013/07/07/us/in-secret-court-vastly-broadens-powers-of-nsa. html?pagewanted=all).

58. Terkel, Amanda. 2013. "Rand Paul: NSA Spying 'Unconstitutional,' Can't be Saved by More Oversight." *Huffington Post*, August 18. Retrieved February 14, 2013 (http://www.huffingtonpost.com/2013/08/18/rand-paul-nsa_n_3775821.html).

59. Ibid.

60. Choney, Suzanne. 2013. "Loophole Lets NSA search US emails, phone calls without warrant, says Guardian." NBC News, August 9. Retrieved February 14, 2014 (http://www.nbcnews.com/technology/loophole-lets-nsa-search-us-emails-phone-calls-without-warrant-6C10885858).

61. Greenwald, Glenn. 2013. "Obama DOJ formally accuses journalist in leak case of committing crimes." *Guardian*, May 20. Retrieved February 14, 2014 (http:// www.theguardian.com/commentisfree/2013/may/20/obama-doj-james-rosen-criminality).

62. Ibid.

63. Eley, Tom. 2009. "Obama Seeks to Institutionalize Indefinite Detention." World Socialist Web Site, August 6. Retrieved August 35, 2009 (http://www.wsws.org/ articles/2009/aug2009/pers-a05.shtml).

64. Fein, cited in Greenwald. "An Emerging Progressive Consensus on Obama's Executive Power and Secrecy Abuses."

Chapter 10

1. Tocqueville, Alexis de. 1985 (originally published 1840). *Democracy in America*. Vol. II. New York: Knopf, pp. 119–20, 121, 123.

2. Ibid., p. 128.

3. Ibid., p. 129.

4. Bradshow, Larry and Lorrie Beth Slonsky. 2005. "The Real Heroes and Sheroes of New Orleans." September 9. Retrieved January 2006 (www.socialist worker .org/2005-2/556/556_04_RealHeroes.shtml).

5. Solomont, Alan and Steve Goldsmith. 2009. "With Volunteerism on the Rise, a Chance to Save the Day." *Boston Globe*, August 22, p. A9.

6. Blake, John. 2009. "Shaky economy forces Americans to rediscover community." CNN, March 26. Retrieved March 26, 2014 (http://www.cnn.com/2009/ LIVING/03/26/community2/).

7. Obama, Barack. 2008. "Acceptance Speech to the Democratic Convention." August 28. Retrieved August 25, 2009 (http://elections.nytimes.com/2008/ president/conventions/videos/20080828_OBAMA_SPEECH.html). For an extended discussion of Obama's theme of "my brother's keeper, my sister's keeper" as a guiding new moral philosophy, see Derber, Charles and Yale Magrass. 2010. *Morality Wars*. Boulder, CO: Paradigm Publishers, chapter 10.

8. Phillips, Kevin. 1990. *Politics of Rich and Poor*. New York: Random House, chap. 1.

9. Radin, Charles. 1990. "Consensus Fuels Ascent of Europe." *Boston Globe*, May 13, p. 19.

10. Alperovitz, Gar. 2013. *What Then Must We Do: Straight Talk about the Next American Revolution*. White River Junction, VT: Chelsea Green Publishing.

11. Obama. 2008. "Acceptance Speech to the Democratic Convention."

12. Derber. 2010. *Greed to Green*, chap. 15.

13. Ibid.

14. Ibid., chap. 10–11, 15.

15. For relevant survey data, see Adam, Katherine and Charles Derber. 2008. *The New Feminized Majority: How Democrats Can Change America with Women's Values*. Boulder, CO: Paradigm Publishers.

16. Henkin, Louis, cited in Savoy, Paul. 1991. "Time for a Second Bill of Rights." *Nation*, June 17, 252, no. 23, p. 797.

17. Savoy, Paul. 1991. "Time for a Second Bill of Rights." *Nation*, June 17, pp. 815– 16.

18. Ibid.

19. Tocqueville. 1985. *Democracy in America*.

20. Greenhouse, Steven. 2013. "AFL-CIO has plan to add millions of non-union members." *New York Times*, September 6. Retrieved February 19, 2014 (http:// www.nytimes.com/2013/09/07/business/afl-cio-has-plan-to-add-millions-of- nonunion-members.html?nl=todaysheadlines&emc=edit_th_20130907&_r=0).

21. Ibid.

22. Ibid.

Index